MAHLANGENI

'An excellent read.'
Eastern Province Herald

'... there is a measured sensuality in the prose that compels one's being into the heart of bushland paradise and drama... it's a can't-put-it-down book, and an immediate reread is called for to ensure that you haven't missed a single word!'
Natal Witness

'In a remote part of the Kruger National Park, Kobie Krüger relates her story with great humour, a unique style of storytelling, and a warmth that is evident throughout.'
The Citizen

'Written with humour and warmth, this captivating tale will delight both young and old.'
Custos

'A fascinating and absorbing read, written with pace and humour.'
Fish Eagle

'Lovers of nature will be delighted.'
Cape Times

'It's a feel-good book ... packed with delightful anecdotes, recounting a time and space where pleasures are simple and experiences are rich.'
Weekly Mail & Guardian

D1059481

MAHLANGENI

Stories of a Game Ranger's Family

Kobie Krüger

with illustrations by Julie Davidson

PENGUIN BOOKS

PENGUIN BOOKS

Published by the Penguin Group
27 Wrights Lane, London W8 5TZ, England
Viking Penguin, a division of Penguin Books USA Inc,
375 Hudson Street, New York, New York 10014, USA
Penguin Books Australia Ltd, Ringwood, Victoria, Australia
Penguin Books Canada Ltd, 10 Alcorn Avenue, Toronto, Ontario, Canada
M4V 3B2
Penguin Books (NZ) Ltd, 182-190 Wairau Road, Auckland 10, New Zealand
Penguin Books (South Africa) (Pty) Ltd, 1A Eton Road, Parktown,
South Africa 2193

Penguin Books (South Africa) (Pty) Ltd, Registered Offices:
1A Eton Road, Parktown, South Africa 2193

First published by Penguin Books 1994
Reprinted 1996
Reprinted 1997

Copyright © Text: Kobie Krüger 1994
        © Illustrations: Julie Davidson 1994

All rights reserved
The moral right of the author has been asserted

ISBN 0 140 24293 7

Typeset by Iskova Image Setting
Printed and bound by Interpak, Natal
Cover design by Hadaway Illustration & Design

Except in the United States of America, this book is sold subject to the condition
that it shall not, by way of trade or otherwise, be lent, resold, hired out or
otherwise circulated without the publisher's prior consent in any form of binding
or cover other than that in which it is published and without a similar condition
including this condition being imposed on the subsequent purchaser.

For
Kobus
Hettie, Sandra and Karin

Contents

Mahlangeni

F ar from everywhere, in a remote corner of a vast expanse of lonely wilderness, two rivers meet: the Little Letaba and the Greater Letaba. On the northern bank of the confluence, you will find our house.

It's not an easy place to find.

If you approach it from the south, you may not be able to get across the river — the road ends there. If you approach it from the north, you will probably get lost. The road forks into branches that scatter and fade away in the savannah. You can't reach it from the west either: there's another river. It's best to approach it from the east: there's a road there. Actually, it's a dirt track and it's not on the map. You'll need a compass and a four-wheel-drive vehicle.

The area is called Mahlangeni, which is the Tsonga word for 'meeting place'. It must refer either to the meeting of the two rivers, or to the meeting of wild animals. Nothing else meets here that I know of.

In the hour just before day-break, when the frogs and the crickets fall silent, you can hear the solitude. It's a hush that extends from the soundless universe to the woodlands and savannahs of Mahlangeni. Occasionally the howl of a lone hyena or the cry of a jackal may drift through the darkness, and the echo will linger a while in the silence. The African bush seems tranquil in the pre-dawn hush.

But it's only an illusion.

At the first, faint hint of dawn, a pair of wild geese swoop to a landing on a rock outside our bedroom and startle the world

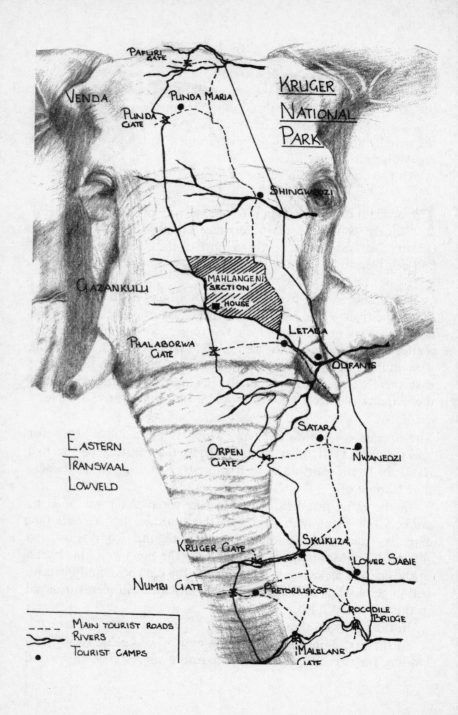

KRUGER
NATIONAL
PARK

VENDA

PAFURI GATE

PUNDA MARIA

PUNDA GATE

SHINGWEDZI

GAZANKULU

MAHLANGENI
SECTION

HOUSE

LETABA

PHALABORWA GATE

OLIFANTS

EASTERN
TRANSVAAL
LOWVELD

SATARA

NWANEDZI

ORPEN GATE

KRUGER GATE

SKUKUZA

LOWER SABIE

NUMBI GATE

PRETORIUSKOP

CROCODILE BRIDGE

MALELANE GATE

--- MAIN TOURIST ROADS
    RIVERS
•   TOURIST CAMPS

awake with raucous trumpeting. The baboons in the jackalberry trees across the river start muttering and chattering or quarrelling and screaming, depending on the mood in which they awaken. As the silvery dawn touches the water, the hippos come to life and call out to one another in booming voices. By this time, a thousand and one birds are performing fortissimo from a vast repertoire of musical ideas.

And so the daily bush concert begins.

Mahlangeni is one of the most remote ranger stations in the Kruger National Park.

One would think that life in such a remote place would be quiet and peaceful. But it's not.

It's hardly ever quiet here. And it isn't too peaceful either. Alarming things often happen — like the night we moved into our new home...

A Dramatic
Welcome

I t had been a long day and by nightfall we were exhausted. The
house was in chaos, with boxes, crates and bits of furniture all
over the place. We did manage, at least, to have our beds in
position and had found bedding for everyone in the midst of the
confusion. So, it was early to bed.

About an hour after retiring, I was woken by a strange sound.

'What's that?' I asked my slumbering husband. He slept on,
unhearing. I lay awake for a while, listening and thinking about
the strange, dark house. I began to wonder whether I had really
heard something, or whether it had merely been my imagination.
Just as I was dozing off, I heard the sound again. This time I woke
my husband up.

'What's that?' I asked him.

He said, 'Hmm?'

'A strange noise,' I said. 'Didn't you hear it?'

'Hmm?' he said.

All was quiet. I lay quietly, waiting for the sound to repeat
itself, but it didn't. My husband Kobus drifted back to sleep and
after a while I was about to do the same when suddenly I heard it
again.

I woke Kobus once more, saying urgently, 'Kobus! Did you
hear that?'

He said, 'Huh?'

'That noise . . .' I said.

An owl screeched outside and Kobus mumbled, 'Owl.'

'No, not that! It was . . . a sort of . . . huffing noise . . .'

'Probably a leopard,' he muttered sleepily.

'Leopard?' I asked, alarmed. 'But it sounded as though it was right here in the bedroom!'

We remained silent for a while, listening. Down by the river a million frogs were croaking to high heaven. A hippo snorted. Far away, a jackal wailed. Other strange sounds drifted through the night. But inside the house all seemed quiet.

Finally, Kobus said, 'You're probably imagining things. Try to relax ... get some sleep ...'

'Yes, OK,' I said. It most probably was my imagination, I decided.

The strange, dark house was unnerving me.

I fell into a deep sleep.

Later in the night I was woken by one of the children who needed the bathroom and couldn't find her way in the dark.

It really is dark here at night. We can't switch on a light because the electric generator runs only during the daytime. I reached for my torch on my bedside cabinet and got up.

After helping my daughter, I returned to our bedroom. And then suddenly I remembered the strange sounds that had alarmed me earlier in the night. I played the beam of the torch around the bed and something — perhaps a movement or a shadow — caught my attention. I raised the torch slightly, and recoiled in horror: part of a huge, glossy, dark blotched reptilian body loomed in the light of the torch. Wheeling the torch crazily, I illuminated the rest of the scene: the 'thing' had its tail section inside the half-open drawer of my bedside cabinet, its middle part was coiled on top of the cabinet, and the rest was woven into the slats of the bed's headboard. It was such a bizarre sight that it took me a while to register what I was looking at.

'Kobus!' I gasped. 'Wake up!'

Prompted by the urgent tone of my voice, he woke immediately and asked, 'What's wrong?'

'A snake ... moving on to the bed!' I stammered.

Kobus leapt from the bed like a bolt of lightning entangled in a bedsheet. 'Stand back!' he ordered me.

I didn't need to be told that. I had already reversed into the opposite wall.

Disengaging himself from the sheet, Kobus groped his way towards me in the darkness. I handed him my torch and he shone it on the snake.

'It's a python,' he told me.

The commotion in the room had frightened it, and it was recoiling and moving back into the safety of the drawer. As we stood watching it with morbid fascination, the sight of the half-open drawer sparked a memory. Earlier in the day, while furniture had been standing outside waiting to be carried in, I had walked past the bedside cabinet and, noticing the drawer half open, I had pushed it closed. I had been in a hurry and was carrying a big box, so I had pushed it shut with my foot and hadn't been able to see what was inside it. In all likelihood, the python had been in the drawer already, and someone had later unknowingly carried the cabinet into the house with the snake inside it.

The noises I had heard earlier in the night must have come from the snake — huffing and puffing in its battle to push the drawer open and find its way out.

My torch had been standing upright on the cabinet — probably right in the middle of the coiled-up body — and it was pure luck that my aim in the darkness had been true.

It was a young python, only some two metres long — which is not very long for a python but horribly long for a snake. Using his rifle cleaning rod, Kobus 'helped' the snake manoeuvre itself back into the drawer. Once the whole snake was finally inside, he pushed the drawer shut and carried the cabinet outside into the garden. I accompanied him with my torch. He put the cabinet down some distance away from the house and carefully reopened the drawer. The snake remained shyly inside. We left the cabinet there and went back to bed, leaving it to the snake to choose its time of exit.

Though it seemed a rather dramatic welcome to our first night at Mahlangeni, this was in fact an appropriate prelude to our new lifestyle in the wilderness, where nature's creatures roam free, and humans must take care not to bother them.

A Leopard for a Neighbour

A few nights later Kobus woke me, saying, 'Listen: a leopard!'

'Outside?' I asked, alarmed. 'Or next to the bed?'

But then I heard the leopard too. And he was outside, of course. He sounds somewhat like a saw dragging on wood, or like someone snoring in his sleep in a rhythmic, staccato way.

We often hear the leopard in the night. He lives in the thickets on the bank of the Shibyeni creek and enjoys a nocturnal stroll along our fence. Or perhaps he patrols the fence in the hope of finding a way through it into our garden.

Our garden is large — some 120 metres east to west and 80 metres north to south — and surrounded by a sturdy three metre high fence. I often worry that the leopard might some night think of a way to get into our garden. I know that a leopard can't scale a fence that high. But still...

We have other nocturnal visitors such as civets, honey badgers and porcupines. I'm not sure how the civets get into the garden, but the porcupines and honey badgers get in by digging holes under our gates. I know that leopards don't do that. But still...

Kobus says it's romantic to have a leopard for a neighbour, and I agree, but the idea worries me when I have to go out at night to switch off the generator. Usually, Kobus does this, but when he's away from home, it is my responsibility.

The generator room is about fifty metres from the house, against the northern fence line. If you know how pitch-dark the nights in the bush can be, you'll understand how scared one can feel walking a distance of fifty metres from one's house at night.

7

Lions once killed a waterbuck right against that northern fence. And I've often heard hyenas howling and giggling near the wire.

One night, about a month after we had moved in, I had such a shocking experience on my way to the generator room that I almost died of fright. Kobus was away and I had to go out to switch the machine off. Armed with my torch, and mindful of the puffadder I had found right in front of the generator room the previous evening, I lit the ground carefully as I walked. A puffadder is a very poisonous snake. It's also a mean and lazy snake. It doesn't try to get out of your way, as other snakes do. It waits for you to step on it so that it has an excuse to bite you.

I picked my way cautiously as I played the slender beam of the torch over the ground and into the shadows of suspicious-looking vegetation. The beam startled a frog, and it leapt up and collided with my leg. Ugh. Somewhere in the darkness a hyena howled ominously, reminding me unnecessarily that the night belongs to predators, and that primates should be safely up their trees (or in their houses).

In the last twenty-metre stretch the roar of the machine drowns out other sounds and dulls one's senses, making it difficult to concentrate on one's surroundings. The closer one gets to the noise, the more vulnerable one feels. I was only a few paces from the machine room, feeling very vulnerable and checking the ground carefully for signs of the puffadder, when something huge leapt on me from behind. Its paws pushed down hard on my shoulders, almost knocking me to the ground. The torch flew from my hand, rolling some distance into the darkness, and my senses screamed: 'Leopard!'

Struggling to regain my balance, I turned to try to get my arms between myself and my attacker. It pounced on me again, knocking me off balance once more — and started licking my face. It took me a very long second to register that it was our new ridgeback. Another ranger had given us the dog a few days before: a fully grown ridgeback bitch who had the habit of knocking people over in boisterous greeting.

I tried to say hello to the dog, but my voice was obliterated by the chattering of my teeth.

We often hear the leopard, but we never see him. I know that leopards are secretive nocturnal animals and are seldom seen, but it feels strange to have a neighbour whose voice you know so well but whose face you never see. I guess I wouldn't really want to meet him face to face. But it would be nice to get a glimpse of him some day — at a distance of, say, fifty metres. In broad daylight. With the fence between us.

Sandra, the second of our three daughters, almost saw him one day. She was eleven years old at the time. We have two horses, and Sandra had gone riding that day. Unless Kobus accompanies them, the girls may ride only within the grounds or on the surrounding firebreaks. During the dry season, when the grass is short and the trees are bare, they may also ride on the nearby patrol tracks, but only within close range of the house.

It was on a summer's day in the rainy season when the vegetation is dense, that Sandra got a bit adventurous, forgot the rules and, following a narrow winding path, made her way northward along the bank of the Little Letaba River.

At one point the path meanders through a dense thicket. As she entered the thicket, she heard a sudden movement above her in the trees. Before she could even look up into the branches above her, the horse had spun around and, whinnying with fright, started galloping homewards at an alarming speed. Luckily, Sandra rides well and although she had no control over the horse, she managed to stay aboard. The horse, in his panic, didn't consider his rider at all and miscalculated the clearance into the gates.

Hearing the thunder of hooves, I rushed outside and saw them approaching at breakneck speed. I realised with shock that the horse would barely make it into the gates and that the gatepost would connect with Sandra's leg, or at best her stirrup, and dash her from the horse's back. But Sandra was wide awake and holding her own: she jerked her feet from the stirrups and threw herself clear of the horse just in time to miss the gatepost. She fell hard and rolled some distance in the dirt. I ran to her, but before I could reach her, she was on her feet and, hobbling painfully, had started making her way towards the stable.

'Are you OK?' I called in a shaky voice.

She had no time to answer my question. She needed to go and talk to her horse first.

'Shame on you!' I heard her admonishing the animal. 'Even if you get a big fright, think of me too! You could have killed me!'

She inspected the side of his rib-cage where the gatepost had grazed him, and said angrily: 'See? My leg would've been crushed!'

Evidently the horse understood most of the conversation. As Sandra limped away, his head hung low in disgrace.

My poor daughter looked a mess. Her clothes were torn and stained with dirt and blood. I suggested that we go and treat her injuries right away. But she told me that she had to attend to the horse first. 'I'll need some disinfectant,' she said. 'And some sugar.'

'What's the sugar for?' I asked.

'For the horse, of course,' she replied. 'He's suffering from shock. He's seen the leopard.'

We have all been frightened by the leopard, or by the idea of him, on several occasions but, not counting the horse, none of us has actually seen him in person yet, even though we've been neighbours for almost ten years now.

The Mean Hippo

T he ranger section under Kobus's control is almost one thousand square kilometres in extent, and stretches northward from the Greater Letaba River. Our house stands on the northern bank of the river, just inside Kobus's area of responsibility. Our nearest town, Phalaborwa, lies some fifty kilometres to the south of the river. To get to town, therefore, we have first to cross the river.

Nowadays we have a causeway across the river, which makes life a lot easier — except when the river is in spate and the causeway under water. But in earlier years, before the causeway was built, we had to row across the water to where we parked our 'town car' on the far side of the river in a lean-to under the jackalberry trees.

The resident hippos didn't like our intrusions into their territorial waters. As soon as the boat was launched, they would start grunting, bellowing and swearing at us. And they would plunge and splash about, dive and surface, and raise their gaping jaws in our direction, displaying their huge tusks in a bid to intimidate us.

Hippos are aggressively territorial, and most hippo attacks in the water are the result of bulls defending their territories. Being rather dim-witted and habitually paranoid, a bull hippo perceives a boat as an intruder with dubious designs on the resident lady hippos.

Although many cases have been recorded of hippo attacks in the water, most attacks in fact take place on land. Hippos are herbivores and have to leave the water to graze. Being even more paranoid on land, they will attack anyone or anything that comes between them and their safety zone — the water.

At first, our local hippos intimidated us with their dramatic, big-mouthed threats. But since they never actually carried out any of the threats, we eventually became so used to their sabre-rattling that we stopped bothering to worry about them. The hippos, in turn, seemed satisfied that their displays adequately cowed the boat and therefore didn't deem it necessary to obliterate it. And so, as time went by, we learnt to ignore their threats and became almost nonchalant about them — until the day one of the bulls decided that sabre-rattling wasn't enough.

The girls and I were making the crossing when he came right up to our boat and bumped it so hard that we spun around almost full circle. We hadn't even seen him coming. He must have sneaked up on us from behind.

That evening, when I told Kobus about the incident, he insisted that, from that day on, I should always carry a firearm when making the crossing. I wasn't too happy with the idea. I don't feel comfortable with a gun. In fact, I'm terrified of guns. And in any case I didn't think the hippo really meant us any harm. He'd probably only wanted to give us a good fright, and perhaps he wouldn't do it again. Perhaps he had bumped into the boat accidentally.

But Kobus reminded me that hippos can be very dangerous animals and that we shouldn't take their threats too lightly. If that bull hippo became too resentful of our intrusions into his territory, he might attack the boat, or he might capsize it and then attack us in the water.

Kobus's lecture really scared me, and I decided that a gun was something I was going to have to get used to. The trouble with a gun, as Kobus often reminds me, is that most of the time you don't really need it, but when you *do* need it, you don't need it just a little — you need it desperately.

Kobus also insisted that, whenever he was away, I should recruit Filemoni as our oarsman so that I could be free to concentrate on the behaviour of the hippos and to fire the gun if necessary. Filemoni is the caretaker of Mahlangeni's vegetable garden and water pumps — an elderly but amazingly strong Shangaan man who, I discovered, could row us across the water in almost half the

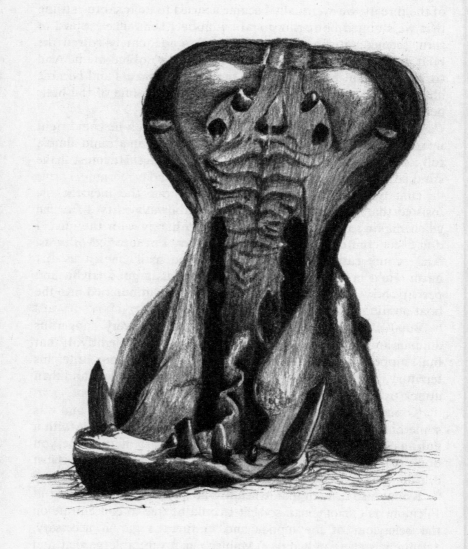

time it usually took me to do it. Actually, that's not as helpful as it may sound. He is a strong rower, but not a good one. He jerks the oars through the water with short, irregular strokes, causing the boat to leap, plunge, bounce and bump over the water, instead of gliding through it, as a boat should. And we get sprayed with water every time he brings the oars up. We're usually soaked by the time we reach the far bank. But I won't criticise Filemoni for that. He's been here at Mahlangeni for ever, I think, and is the most bush-wise person I know.

Our daughters attend school in Phalaborwa and stay in the Park's private school hostel during the week. The hostel is situated inside the Park, near the Phalaborwa gate. Early each Monday morning, I drive the girls to the hostel, and collect them again on Friday afternoons.

After the hippo bull had bumped our boat that first time, the girls and I acquired the habit of scanning the water attentively every time we rowed across. And whenever we spotted a V-shaped ripple coming towards us across the water, we knew it was that mean hippo — on his way to bump our boat again. That was my cue to cock the gun and fire a shot into the water between the boat and the approaching hippo. Luckily, the hippo always backed off and swam back to the herd when I fired.

Even so, there were a couple of occasions when we didn't sight the approaching ripple and were badly shaken when the hippo bumped the boat. Another unnerving trick of his was to sneak unnoticed right up to the boat, and then suddenly explode from the water right alongside us.

After a period of repeated encounters with the mean hippo, during which I'd fired into the water close to him on several occasions, the hippo backed off for a while, leading me to believe that he'd finally admitted defeat.

But one day, a couple of weeks later, he proved me wrong.

Our whole family was in the boat, chatting away and not taking much notice of the hippos. They had been very tranquil for a while, and the mean hippo had been ignoring us for quite some time.

Karin, our youngest, who was about four or five at the time, was trailing a thin reed in the water alongside the boat as we rowed. Suddenly, with a deafening roar, the mean hippo exploded from the water right next to the boat, his mouth open so wide that I had a momentary vision of him swallowing us all. What's more, he surfaced in almost exactly the spot where Karin had been trailing her reed. She got such a fright that she tumbled backwards off her seat, falling — luckily — into the bottom of the boat. But apparently the hippo's dramatic arrival had shocked me more than it had her: when she climbed back on to her seat, looking indignant, all she said was, 'Heavens, why can't that silly hippo behave?'

Meanwhile, the hippo had submerged himself again and we were still wondering where he had gone when a sudden, hard thump from underneath the boat made us all jump. The boat heaved and keeled dangerously, but luckily didn't capsize. By this time we had all acquired the habit of clinging on to the boat whenever an encounter with the hippo seemed imminent, and so we had all been holding on at the moment of impact, and fortunately no one was thrown overboard.

But Kobus decided angrily that the hippo had sealed his own fate and that deportation papers were in order. He was on his way to Skukuza for the annual aerial census and couldn't arrange the deportation of the hippo right away, but promised that he'd do so as soon as he returned.

The following day a pair of national servicemen from a nearby military base were sent to Mahlangeni by their commanding officer to deliver a message to Kobus. Kobus was still at Skukuza, of course, and I was busy inside the house and didn't notice their vehicle arriving on the far bank. Filemoni, however, did and promptly rowed over to collect the young men.

I was not aware of their arrival until they appeared at the front door. I invited them in and, over coffee, found out that they were city boys, quite out of their depth in the wild. As they were preparing to leave, I suddenly remembered the mean hippo and suggested that they make their way down to the shore while I fetched a firearm. Neither of them was armed and, besides, wouldn't know what to do if the hippo attacked.

It took me a while to find the keys to the gun-safe, and to open it and select a gun. Remembering the dramatic events of the previous day, I decided to take one of the bigger rifles. Having checked that it was loaded, I went outside — and saw to my dismay that the soldiers were already in the boat and on the water, with Filemoni at the oars. Either they or Filemoni hadn't understood that I'd intended to accompany them in the boat. I hurried through the garden, out the front gate, down the stone stairway and across the shore, scanning the water as I did so. By the time I reached the waterside, the boat was already almost half-way across the river. And then I saw it: that telltale V-shaped ripple on the water, coming downstream and heading directly towards the boat.

I raised the rifle and took aim at a point between the ripple and the boat, but felt too scared to pull the trigger. I had never fired over such a distance — about eighty metres — and was terrified of hitting one of the occupants of the boat. To move my aim would mean to risk hitting the hippo, and one never knows what havoc a wounded hippo might cause.

And then, to my unbelievable horror, the hippo suddenly surfaced and started homing in on the boat with furious speed and determination — a thing he had never done before. Alarm signals flashed in my mind as it dawned on me that this was it: the hippo's obsession with the boat had finally driven him to distraction. He couldn't stand it any longer — he was going to annihilate the boat once and for all.

I raised the rifle again and aimed carefully. The bead of the foresight settled into the vee of the express leaf just to the left of the hippo's nose, but before I could squeeze the trigger, the hippo's head appeared in the sight. I started trembling and couldn't steady the aim.

Filemoni rowed as fast as he could, but the hippo moved faster. The bead of the foresight quivered crazily as I moved the aim to keep it ahead of the hippo's nose. I wondered how it was possible to steady an aim if you had to keep moving it. My hands became slippery with perspiration. The hippo lifted his head to check the distance before hurling himself on to the boat. I held my breath in an effort to stop trembling. The bead settled into the vee of the express leaf — right in front of the hippo's face, and much too close to the boat. I wished there was time to yell at Filemoni and the soldiers to duck before I squeezed the trigger. The recoil slammed me so hard in the shoulder that I almost sat down on the ground, and my senses reeled from the echoing thunderclap of the blast. But, even so, I managed to note that a fountain of water had exploded right in front of the hippo's open mouth, soaking the occupants of the boat. The hippo reared his massive head, slammed his mouth shut and submerged. I quickly reloaded and scanned the water, trying to find some clue as to where the hippo had gone. A few seconds later I finally spotted the V-shaped ripple a good distance away from the boat, heading back upstream towards the rest of the herd.

I sat down on the sand, pretending to be enjoying a few minutes of relaxation while admiring the view. But the truth is, I was shaking like a leaf and my legs would no longer support me.

I guess the two soldiers were relieved when they reached the opposite bank safely. I can imagine how uncomfortable it must be for a city person to find himself in a small boat on a wide river, right in the path of a warmongering hippo — and this while a woman on the shore is aiming a rifle in your direction.

The soldiers waved to me from the far bank as they disembarked, and I returned the greeting. But I sat in the sand, admiring the view, until their truck had disappeared over the bank.

Then I waited until Filemoni was safely back. We walked across the stretch of sand together and climbed up the stone stairs. We didn't talk. Filemoni isn't much of a talker. He grunts. So, he grunted. And I groaned in reply. And we both knew it had been a pretty close shave that day.

A few days later Kobus returned from Skukuza and immediately put the deportation orders into action. He rowed out towards the mean hippo — who was easily recognised by a notch in one of his ears — and while the hippo was still wondering to what he owed the visit, Kobus stood up in the boat and fired several shots with his .375 Magnum into the water close to the hippo. As the thunderclaps echoed across the landscape, fountains erupted from the surface of the water on all sides of the hippo.

The mean hippo got the message and lost no time in deciding to emigrate. He made his way north up the Little Letaba River and must have found himself a more peaceful home elsewhere because we never saw him again. The rest of the herd also took note and behaved themselves for quite a while afterwards.

Beware of Elephants

W hen you have lived in the Kruger Park for some years, you lose your fear of wild animals. That's because you realise that they don't lie in wait for you behind every bush, ready to pounce on you and eat you up.

Or so they say.

I'm not so sure.

I don't trust lions, for instance, and I've lived here for almost ten years. In fact, lions still scare the living daylights out of me every time we come across them, even though Kobus always carries a rifle when we walk in the bush, and even though the lions are always the first to back away.

But actually lions aren't the worst of my fears.

Elephants are.

It was an incident some years back that instilled in me an everlasting fear of elephants.

A lone elephant bull always used to graze on the riverbed in front of our house. On two or three occasions when we wanted to row across the river, we had to wait patiently while he grazed his way past the spot where the boat was moored. One Saturday morning, when Kobus and the girls were on their way to a school athletics meeting, the elephant was grazing right next to the boat, and it was obvious that he was in no hurry to leave.

Kobus and the girls had no choice but to wait it out. They made themselves comfortable at the top of the stone stairway which leads down the steep bank to the riverbed. It looked as though it was going to be a long wait — it didn't bother the elephant that the girls might be late for their athletics meeting.

I decided to capture the scene on film and went inside to fetch my movie camera.

After some time the elephant finally decided to take his leave and ambled off, moving along the waterside in a westerly direction. Kobus and the girls made their way down to the boat while I waited at the top of the stairs to wave them goodbye.

From the bottom of the stairway to the boat's mooring-place is a walk of about eighty metres. As Kobus and the girls moved across the sand, the elephant continued peacefully on his way, and the scene was utterly tranquil. A family of Egyptian geese grazed on the shore and, in the background, the hippos floated lazily in the water. I raised my camera, determined to record the moment. By this time the elephant was about sixty or seventy metres from my family, and he seemed totally unperturbed even when they appeared on the riverbed. In fact, I wasn't sure he had even noticed them.

They had almost reached the boat when, in a flash, the peaceful scene was transformed into chaos. Without any apparent reason, the elephant spun around and, trumpeting and screaming with fury, came thundering across the riverbed like a runaway train — heading straight for Kobus and the girls.

Kobus unslung his rifle and, releasing the safety catch, took aim. The two older girls, Hettie and Sandra, started to run but almost instantly and simultaneously remembered a rule of the wilderness: when there is danger, stay with the person who is armed. They skidded to a halt, turned, and stood courageously, facing the charging elephant.

But Karin panicked — she was barely five years old — and though she knew the rules as well as her sisters did, the sight of the screaming, infuriated giant must have filled her with such terror that her instincts commanded her to take flight. And so she fled.

I looked on helplessly as she sprinted across the eighty-metre stretch of open sand towards the stairway. And I could do nothing but stand there, watching. I dared not run to her. It might

have attracted the elephant's attention and drawn him to her and, at that moment, she was more vulnerable than the others.

Kobus, Hettie and Sandra stood dead still, waiting. The earth trembled as the six-ton beast bore down on them. Kobus had his finger on the trigger and, having waited until the last possible moment before firing, was about to squeeze the trigger when, suddenly and surprisingly, the elephant came to a dramatic stop, a fountain of sand and pebbles flying up from the ground at his feet as he slammed on the brakes. He stood for a moment, staring at them disdainfully with myopic eyes. Then he tossed his massive head and, with one last ear-splitting trumpet, turned and walked away.

By this time Karin had reached the stairway and came sprinting up the stairs towards me. I met her half-way down and hugged her to me. There was a lump in my throat when all she said — stammering and panting for breath — was: 'He... he almost gave me a fright!'

We walked over the sand to meet Kobus and the other two girls. We stood together and watched the elephant strolling away into the distance, wondering what on earth could have been the reason for his sudden demented behaviour. Perhaps he didn't like people sneaking to their boat behind his back. Or perhaps he was, as Hettie suggested, a deranged elephant.

Unfortunately, this was not to be our last encounter with the deranged elephant.

In the late afternoon of the following day, we noticed the elephant grazing to the west of our house on the bank of the Little Letaba River.

Unlike the Greater Letaba, which is a perennial river, the Little Letaba is essentially a seasonal river in which only a few pools remain when the water disappears from it during the dry season. We often see buffalo, elephant and other game cross the Little Letaba in the dry season to graze on the far bank. And sometimes, when they get the idea that the grass is greener on the other side of the boundary fence, they will break through it to go grazing in Gazankulu.

Whenever elephant or buffalo are seen crossing the Little Letaba, Kobus goes after them to stop them from breaking through the fence and to herd them back to our side of the river. One of the reasons why game rangers discourage animals from crossing the Park's boundary fences is to prevent the spread of foot-and-mouth disease, which is endemic to the Park. Another reason is to avert the possibility of our animals becoming trophies for hunters in the unprotected areas on the other side of the fence.

The elephant continued to graze on the bank of the Little Letaba for a while and then walked across the dry riverbed to the opposite bank. Kobus kept a watchful eye on him, and when it became apparent that the elephant was on his way to the boundary fence, Kobus went after him. This was really nothing out of the ordinary. Kobus had, on numerous previous occasions, stopped elephants and other big game from breaking through the fence.

What *was* out of the ordinary, however, was the behaviour of this particular elephant.

When a game ranger sets out to persuade an elephant to turn away from a boundary fence, he approaches the elephant and claps his hands and shouts at him until he gets the message. In the case of an obstinate animal, the ranger may fire a number of shots into the air to make the message yet more clear.

But when Kobus walked up to the deranged elephant on that day, the elephant was in no mood for discussion and promptly charged. Kobus ran and hid behind a tree, but the elephant came looking for him. As the massive grey beast came crashing through the bush towards him, Kobus abandoned his cover and sprinted towards the bank of the Little Letaba. The elephant followed at an unbelievable speed, ears flat against his skull, trunk tucked under his chest, silent and deadly serious. The only sound following Kobus was that of great clumps of earth and bush debris exploding from under the elephant's smashing feet.

Kobus reached the bank of the Little Letaba and rushed headlong through the riverine bush, reasoning that the elephant wouldn't follow him down the steep bank. But to his surprise, the elephant came crashing down the bank after him. When Kobus's feet hit the thick sand of the riverbed, he realised that he could never outpace the elephant in the soft sand. Having no other choice, he turned and fired a warning shot into the sand right in front of the elephant's feet. A fountain of sand and pebbles exploded from the riverbed as the deafening thunderclap reverberated through the air, but the elephant didn't miss a step. He was less than fifteen metres away when Kobus aimed for a frontal brain shot (a small spot high up on the trunk between the eyes) and fired, but the massive head tossed, the bullet missed the brain and didn't even break the elephant's stride.

Kobus had only one bullet left — and very little time. His reflexes took over and he fired again, not hearing the whiplash of the shot nor feeling the slamming recoil, his eyes riveted on the huge forehead of the animal now less than ten metres away. The elephant stopped suddenly, his hind legs buckled and he went down in slow motion. His massive bulk struck the earth with a hollow sound.

Kobus stood motionless and silent for a while, having no bullet left to use in the event that the elephant was only stunned. But then, somehow, he knew the animal was dead and he walked up to it. Nine paces separated them. Nine human paces equal about two and a half elephant paces.

Hettie, who had been sitting in the garden reading at the time had jumped up at the echoing crack of the first shot and had run to the fence. She saw her father standing on the riverbed of the Little Letaba with the elephant bearing down on him, and she saw him fire the second shot, and then the third and fatal shot. When she saw the elephant go down only a few paces from her father she fled indoors.

I was busy inside the house when I heard the three express calibre shots. I ran outside and met Hettie on her way in. I stopped to ask her what had happened, but she was too shocked to talk and could only point towards the western fence of the garden.

When I reached the fence I looked down and saw the elephant lying in the sand of the Little Letaba, and Kobus standing quietly next to him. I knew Kobus was sad that he'd had to shoot the elephant. And I felt sorry that Hettie had had to witness her father's close shave with death, as well as the violent destruction of the majestic old giant.

Fortunately that has been the only occasion in the ten years we've lived here that Kobus has had to shoot an animal in self-defence.

But I guess I will probably never lose my fear of elephants now.

It's a pity, because elephants are beautiful animals. They are intelligent, sociable and generally good-natured. The calves are tenderly nursed, protected, instructed and reared to maturity by the breeding herd. The elephant herd is a complex family group characterised by a highly developed social structure and the deep bond that links its members. There are many documented cases of herds physically assisting injured or sick animals, propping them up as they walk along. Another clue to their level of intelligence is their sophisticated communication system, which consists of a variety of sounds produced in many different keys (some of them high above the register of the human ear), and of postures of the ears and trunk. On top of all that, elephants can be playful, imaginative and amusing.

Although elephants are generally known to be easygoing and tolerant, there are of course exceptions to the rule, and a grumpy elephant is certainly something one should avoid — that is, if you can get away fast enough to avoid him. If he's determined to get you, you're really in trouble.

Elephant cows are notorious for their temper tantrums when they suspect that their calves are being threatened. If ever you go elephant-watching, take care not to park your car near a cow and her calf — especially not between them. The mother's reaction might frighten you to death.

Some elephants don't like cars. I have often, on rounding a bend, found myself nose to nose with an elephant in the road, and even though I am always very quick at backing away humbly, the elephant will almost invariably follow and bully me into reversing at least several hundred metres back down the road before he is satisfied that my car and I have acknowledged his superiority.

Most game rangers (including my husband) will tell you that elephants are merely amusing themselves when they scare tourists with their mock charges and posturing and that, when an elephant stops a vehicle by blocking its path and forcing it to reverse, he's only looking for company and someone to play with.

I'm not so sure about that.
But even if it's true, I don't want to play with them.
I'm too small.

The Affectionate Honey Badger

O ne day Kobus brought home a honey badger cub that he had picked up in the bush. It was obvious that he had been attacked by another predator, and apparently his mother had been killed while defending him. Honey badgers are incredibly brave animals, and a mother will literally give her life in defence of her cubs.

The little animal was only a few weeks old. He was weak from hunger and deprivation and had a bad wound on his neck. We doctored his wound and made up a milk and honey solution which we fed him through a baby's feeding bottle. The gluttonous little fellow then demanded his feed every three hours, day and night. It became my responsibility to feed him and I soon suffered from lack of sleep, but the sight of the cuddly little fellow lying snugly in my arms, his forepaws hugging the bottle and his face a study in total contentment, never ceased to delight me.

His neck wound responded well to treatment but he remained lame in his hind legs. We were worried that he might have suffered damage to his nervous system and might never be able to walk. We didn't realise then that it was only through lack of nourishment that he was lame, and that the milk and honey solution would soon prove to be the perfect remedy. We were elated when, after a few days, he started stumbling about, then walking and finally running around.

We named him Buksie which, in Afrikaans, means 'little tough guy'.

Karin, then five years old and not yet at school, became Buksie's foster mother and before long Buksie was a very spoilt little honey badger. He expected Karin to play with him from morning till night, and he refused to go to sleep unless he had a finger — not a baby's dummy, but a human finger — to suck. Karin had to sit patiently, finger in his mouth, until he nodded off.

I've often wondered whether zoologists haven't overlooked the fact that the honey badger might be related to the bear. He moves with a bear-like gait, his paws look like those of a bear, and he's as clumsy as a bear. When he turns his head suddenly, for instance, the movement throws him off balance and he topples over.

I once read that a bear cub is probably the most affectionate and playful animal around. Perhaps that author hadn't yet met a baby honey badger.

A honey badger cub never tires of playing, and there is no way to escape from a honey badger who wants to play. You can pick him up (although he's a bit heavy), throw him as far away from you as you can and run like crazy in the opposite direction, but he'll catch up with you. He can run faster. You can hide from him, but he won't stop looking for you until he finds you — even if he has to turn the world upside-down doing so. You can lock yourself in a room and refuse to come out, but he'll bang and scratch on the door and beg you with his sweet, cooing noises to come out please and play some more, and eventually you relent.

Even our dogs fell under Buksie's spell and submissively permitted him to hug, cuddle and bully them. Buksie wanted to play with the horses too. But it's beneath a horse's dignity to play with a honey badger. They studiously ignored him. This didn't worry Buksie though — he went ahead and had his fun with the horses anyway. He'd charge at a horse, grab one of its hind legs, and try to clamber up it. In an attempt to ignore the honey badger and at the same time get rid of it, the horse would lift its leg, bending it at the knee and raising the lower leg to a horizontal position. But Buksie hung on. So the horse would stand with one leg in the air, pretending to be oblivious of the honey badger dangling from it.

At first Buksie slept inside the house, but as time went by his mischievous antics created havoc and we were forced to teach him to sleep outdoors.

When Buksie was about five months old it dawned upon him that he was a honey badger and not a human being, and he switched to being a nocturnal animal (as, indeed, all honey badgers are). He slept during the daylight hours and wanted to play at night.

We played with him in the evenings but refused to turn into nocturnal animals for his sake, even though he tried very hard to convert us. It was a difficult time for all of us: difficult for Buksie because he found it heartbreakingly boring to try to play with humans who wanted to sleep, and difficult for us because it's not easy to sleep while a honey badger is begging you to come out and play.

But, luckily, soon after Buksie realised that he was a honey badger, he also realised that he was a predator. He started roaming the riverine bush at night and discovered a host of delicious dishes — such as lizards, frogs and snakes. He became a serious hunter. He once turned up proudly carrying a dead cobra in his jaws. We shuddered at the sight, but to Buksie it was a feast.

As Buksie grew up, more and more of his inborn honey badger traits became evident. One of these was to change his sleeping place virtually every night. A honey badger has a very distinctive scent and I suspect the reason he changes his sleeping place so frequently is that other predators might detect his bed by the scent he leaves behind and set up an ambush for him. Buksie dug himself a variety of sleeping holes — first in our garden and later in the surrounding bush and in the steep bank of the river. Even so, he still turned up every evening at sunset to play with us before setting off on his nocturnal hunting trips.

In the bushveld, sunset is the magic hour. At Mahlangeni the sun sets right in the Greater Letaba River. From our front garden one can see the Greater Letaba snaking its way through the bush for three or four kilometres before it disappears on the western horizon. When the sun starts sinking into the water on the horizon, the whole river turns sparkling carmine, then magenta, and finally becomes silver in the smoky-blue dusk. Even the hippos look strangely beautiful as they laze in the magically coloured water. Their movements spread concentric ripples of shimmering colour about them, and the fading sunlight catches the spray which they blow skyward, turning it into glittering fountains.

Buksie always chose the magic hour to make his appearance.

From somewhere in the bush he would come running along and clamber his way up the high fence. He knew there was a gate he could use, but honey badgers don't need gates. Once he reached the top of the fence, he would simply let go and plummet to the ground on the inside of the fence. Then he would charge over to where we sat, purring and crooning with happiness, and start hugging, cuddling and bullying us.

While a honey badger might be the most affectionate animal I have ever known, he is also the naughtiest.

Buksie knew full well that he was no longer allowed in the house, but he never stopped looking for a way to sneak inside. He'd scamper around looking for an open door or window, and woe betide us if he found one. Once inside, he needed only a few moments to turn the whole house into a battle zone. With a few fast sweeps of his paws, he'd clear the bookshelves, up-end the pot plants, and then open cupboards and drawers and send their contents flying. (Honey badgers have an amazing technical aptitude which enables them to open anything that is openable, and also some things that aren't.) Even as we chased Buksie frantically from room to room he would, without missing a step, strip the beds and bat the cushions off the chairs. And anything on a shelf or table would also end up on the floor. He really enjoyed himself.

We quickly learnt our lesson. As dusk approached, every door and window was properly secured and would only be opened again after Buksie had finished his visit and departed on his nocturnal hunting expedition.

One night when Kobus wasn't at home Buksie decided to cut short his hunting trip and pay me a surprise visit. It was shortly before midnight and the sliding glass doors to our bedroom were open, with only a screen door blocking Buksie's access to the house. The glass doors have a clip mechanism which secures them, but the mesh doors are mounted on rollers and pose no problem for a honey badger. Lying on his side, Buksie would hook his long, curved talons into the mesh, and with one heave the screen door would slide wide open.

On this particular night, he opened the door and scrambled on to the bed. It's quite a shock to have a heavy animal land on you in the deep of the night. Luckily, I realised almost immediately who the culprit was. Perhaps in my sleep I had heard and recognised his affectionate crooning and purring as he approached. After giving me a bear hug, he started bullying me and messing up the bed. By the time I finally managed to wrestle him off the bed, drag him across the floor, shove him outside and secure the glass doors, I was exhausted and drenched in perspiration. It was a sweltering night and the inside of the house was like an oven. As the glass doors were now closed, the cooler air from the river couldn't be felt in the room. I lay glowing on the sticky sheets and felt sorry for myself for having to choose between melting in a hot, airless room, or being mauled by a honey badger.

Buksie was a year old by then, and he measured some thirty centimetres in height, ninety centimetres in length, and weighed in at about twelve kilograms (twenty-six pounds).

At about this time our chief ranger, Dirk Ackerman, paid us a most welcome visit. We have a guest cottage in the garden and, once Dirk had unloaded his suitcase and briefcase, as well as a large, rolled-up, geomorphological map of the Kruger Park, I made certain that all the windows of the cottage were firmly closed. We went out to the barbecue area in the front garden and made ourselves comfortable.

We were enjoying our drinks and catching up on the news of the other ranger families in the Park when Buksie turned up for his evening visit. In no time at all, he completely dominated the conversation. He started off by hugging, cuddling and bullying everyone in turn (the chief ranger included), and then he up-ended

the unoccupied chairs, knocked the table over, and dashed off with a six-pack of beer.

Actually, it's fascinating to watch a honey badger run off with a six-pack of beer. He grips the package with his teeth and holds his head high so that the beers don't drag on the ground. But then he can't see over the top of the pack, so he crashes into trees and shrubs. This doesn't bother him though, and it doesn't slow him down much either.

Kobus bolted after the honey badger to rescue the beers (which Dirk had brought along). Buksie sped through the garden, out the front gate and along the river bank, with Kobus hot on his heels. He finally caught Buksie and tried to wrestle the beers away from him, but Buksie had the pack in a powerful grip with both teeth and paws. In the ensuing battle, Buksie and the beers rolled down the steep river bank and disappeared into the deep darkness of the riverine bush. That was the last we saw of the beers that night.

But not the last we saw of Buksie.

Before long, he rejoined our company. This time, he latched on to Dirk's tobacco pouch and, again, Kobus had to give chase. But Kobus won this round: when he caught Buksie, he used all his weight to pin him down firmly and managed to retrieve the pouch.

Buksie charged right back to us and, behaving like a malicious little monster, continued to disrupt our evening. We decided that enough was enough, and that his embarrassingly bad behaviour − in the presence of our chief ranger, moreover − would not be tolerated. And so poor Buksie got his first (and only) hiding from us. Indignantly, he made his way off into the darkness . . . or so we thought.

We enjoyed a relaxed meal and good conversation before Dirk retired to the guest cottage. No sooner had he put his foot inside than we heard his yell of consternation. We dashed over. It appeared that the cottage door had not been properly closed, and Buksie had managed to push it open. The interior was a scene of utter devastation. Dirk's suitcase had been opened and his clothing lay scattered around the room. The bedding was a heap on the floor. And, worst of all, the geomorphological map − which Dirk was to present to a meeting at Skukuza the following day − was in tatters.

Feeling acutely embarrassed by the dreadful behaviour of our naughty honey badger (who was now nowhere to be seen), we apologised profusely to Dirk and tried to explain that Buksie wasn't usually so malicious and destructive. (Perhaps he'd only wanted to show the chief ranger who was really boss at Mahlangeni?)

A few months later, Buksie found himself a girlfriend. We started noticing two sets of honey badger spoor in the surrounding veld. And during his nightly visits Buksie often seemed preoccupied, as though he was waiting for someone to join him. The dogs would be barking somewhere near the fence, and we believed that another honey badger was hiding nearby, too scared to join Buksie inside the fence.

As time went by, Buksie's visits became less frequent, and we accepted that the call of his honey badger nature was becoming overpowering. After several months of erratic behaviour, he finally stopped visiting altogether and we never saw him again.

Although we miss Buksie a lot, we take comfort in the knowledge that he has managed to return to the wild and adapt to the natural life-style of a honey badger. We trust that he is happily married, and that by now has a large honey badger family of his own.

Troubles on a Lonely Track

T he Phalaborwa Gate to the Kruger National Park is some forty-five kilometres to the south of our home. The town of Phalaborwa (a mining settlement just outside the Park's western boundary) is a few kilometres further on. Distance-wise we don't live too far away from town, but it's getting there that isn't so easy.

First, we have to cross the river, and in the summer months when the river is often in spate, this can be a difficult and sometimes impossible task.

Once across the river, the road itself is a narrow, winding track, leading through steep dongas and dense mopani thickets. No other vehicles use the road, because it leads nowhere else — it's our own private road, exclusively linking Phalaborwa and Mahlangeni. A lot of things can happen along the way. And if your vehicle breaks down en route, you have two choices: fix it yourself, or walk the rest of the way.

On Monday mornings when I take the girls to the school hostel, we have to leave early. A private bus collects the Park children from the hostel and takes them to their schools in town. The hostel is just inside the boundary of the Park, near the gate. If we're delayed on the road and arrive too late for the bus, I have to drive the girls into town and to school myself, and explain to the school principal why we're late.

During the summer months, the sun rises early, before we set off. In winter, however, the stars are still bright when we leave and we're some distance from home before we see the sun rise.

During the winter months, when the road is in fairly good condition, our journey takes just over an hour. Unless, of course, there are delays — which there often are — such as herds of buffalo or elephants taking their own sweet time to cross the road, or sometimes just standing in the road with no intention of going anywhere. Or when a certain bull elephant — usually waiting for us in the area of the Shimangu creek — blocks the road and forces us to reverse several hundred metres back down the track, proclaiming his ownership of the road. Or when elephants have felled a tree across the track and you have to chop the tree up with an axe to clear a way through. Or when the dopey impalas insist on running along in front of the car.

One would think that, since we have travelled the road regularly on Monday mornings for years now, the impalas would have grown used to the sight of my car. But they haven't. In defence of their stupidity, I might mention that animals in this part of the Park very seldom see vehicles of any description as we are so far from the tourist roads. Yet, one would still expect that the sight of my Suzuki jeep would have become familiar to them by now.

But impalas on the road freeze at the very sight of us and remain immobile until we're only metres away from them. Then they take off, straight down the road in front of the car. After a while, the more intelligent among them veer off into the bush, but the simple-minded ones stick to the road. They jump and dash from side to side but remain stubbornly on the track.

Driving then becomes a stop-start exercise. When we stop, they stop. When we move on, so do they — straight down the track again. The idea of moving off into the bush just doesn't occur to them. There's no way we can squeeze past them. The track is too narrow and the bush is too dense. And since they don't run in a straight line in front of the car, but jump and dash from one side of the road to the other, there is a definite possibility of a collision should we try to get past them.

The only thing to do is to stop, switch off the engine, and wait patiently until even the impalas become bored and eventually stroll off into the bush.

It doesn't always work, though. We once had an impala in front of the car who flatly refused to move from the road, no matter how long we waited. And the moment we started the car, he'd start fleeing down the road again, right in front of us. We tried squeezing past him several times but were worried that he would jump right into the car the moment we tried to overtake him.

Eventually Sandra's frustration reached breaking point. We were already late for school and, besides, she was starting to feel sorry for the impala which had been running in front of us for such a long distance. She asked me to stop so that she could get out and personally chase it off the road.

Sandra is a good athlete, and once she started off after the impala a dramatic scene ensued. The impala fled down the road, bouncing from side to side, his leaps getting higher and higher. Sandra, running in a straight line and thus making better progress distance-wise, chased him in a flurry of dust, up hill and down dale, and finally off into the bush. I was really proud of her.

Sometimes we get a flat tyre on the road, but with the girls' assistance it usually doesn't take long to change a wheel.

Our real troubles come with the wet season. Washaways erode the surface of the road, and even with my jeep's four-wheel-drive engaged, it can take a long time to reach town. Sometimes the track becomes so muddy and slick that we literally slip-slide our way along. This is tricky and must be done at very low speed, or you will lose control and skid right off into the bush, or spin around and travel some distance in the wrong direction.

Once when I lost control, the jeep started skidding and almost completed a figure-eight before ending up in a muddy ditch at the side of the track. I was alone, having already dropped the children off at school, and getting out of that ditch without help wasn't easy. I had to drag logs, branches and other bush debris into the ditch and pack it all under and in front of the car's wheels until I had more or less built a track leading out of the ditch. The 'track' collapsed several times, until I was on the point of giving up in tears and abandoning the car. But contemplation of the fifteen-kilometre walk home added a lot of determination to my efforts.

A typical feature of the African bushveld landscape is the innumerable watercourses (referred to as creeks, gullies and dongas) that remain dry most of the year, but suddenly fill up with fast-moving torrents of water after a downpour.

When the watercourses are in spate, we have to stop at each one and wade barefoot through it to gauge the depth of the water and to check for washaways under the surface. If we find that we can't drive through, we have to turn back for home and wait for the flow to subside — it usually takes a day or two.

In the summer months when the bush is dense and verdant, you have to drive carefully as you can't see into the thickets on either side of the narrow track. Animals often come dashing out of the bush, right in front of the car. Bends must also be negotiated slowly. If you speed round a curve and find that something huge and grey is suddenly obscuring your view, watch out: that's an elephant, and you're in big trouble.

During a recent school vacation, as Hettie and I were on our way home from Phalaborwa after a day's shopping, a kudu suddenly leapt out of the bush right in front of the car. It happened at the Tsugama creek where the road winds downhill around a bend. As I swerved to avoid the kudu, the jeep rolled and landed on its roof. Neither of us was injured and we climbed out through the shattered windscreen. I was so relieved that we were intact that I decided not even to think about the jeep lying on its roof in the creek until we were safely home and drinking a cup of sweet, strong tea.

The Tsugama creek is only about five kilometres from home — a distance that takes no more than forty to fifty minutes to walk — but I had forgotten to take my gun along that day and it was a little daunting walking through the bush, unarmed and without dogs. Actually, Hettie wasn't scared. My children won't agree that the bush can be dangerous. So I had to be scared for both of us. Luckily, the only animals we encountered on our way home were a herd of impala and a trio of giraffes who stood in a clump of trees near the road and peered down at us with puzzled expressions. At the river bank we were greeted by monkeys, warthogs and some bushbuck, but fortunately nothing that looked either hungry or angry.

Whenever Kobus is free, he'll drive the girls to and from the hostel, but since he's not often free, I do it most of the time. If you take into account the fact that I make the ninety-kilometre round trip to the hostel and back almost every Monday and Friday, you'd expect that I'd be quite adept at doing it on my own by now.

But you'd be wrong.

My confidence doesn't grow.

It diminishes.

The more I travel on that lonely track, the more I become aware of all the possible disasters that could occur on it, and the more apprehensive I become.

Yet I must admit that, in ten years of travelling on that track, we have always managed to get home unscathed, even though we've experienced a wide variety of incidents and accidents.

One such incident (which has contributed a good deal to my uneasiness) occurred some years back on a Friday afternoon when the girls and I were on our way home.

We were about half-way home when, without warning, the jeep's engine died on us, and no amount of trying would get it going again. Eventually, I peered under the bonnet and tried to remember the things Kobus had taught me about a car's engine. But nothing came to mind. Then I remembered my sister's philosophy: 'If all else fails, read the instructions.' I found the instruction manual and started reading. (Actually, I think her philosophy applies only to household appliances.) Anyway, I read the instruction manual from cover to cover but, according to it, there was nothing wrong with my car. I gave up. We were well and truly stranded.

Since we know almost by heart the landscape along the route we've travelled so often, we knew that we were just over twenty kilometres from home.

We put our heads together and discussed our options. Had Kobus been home, he would have come looking for us once he realised we were overdue, but he was busy in the eastern border area and wasn't expected home for at least another week. No one else would realise that we weren't home, and thus no search parties would be sent out. We had no choice: we would have to walk.

A walk of twenty-odd kilometres would take about three and a half hours. I looked at my watch. It was almost four o'clock — we wouldn't be able to make it home before dark. At dusk the predators start their nocturnal activities, and all good primates return to the safety of their trees. I didn't want to spend the night up a tree, and so I suggested that we stay where we were, spend the night in the jeep, and tackle the walk first thing in the morning. Hettie and Sandra (then aged thirteen and eleven) reckoned that we should be able to get home before dark if we jogged all the way. I pointed out to them that Karin was only six years old and couldn't be expected to jog twenty kilometres. (For that matter, neither could I.)

It was settled. We would spend the night in the car and walk home the next morning.

It was hot in the car, so we made ourselves comfortable under a mopani tree next to the road and drew pictures in the sand to while away the long afternoon.

Luckily, after collecting the girls at the hostel that day, I had popped into town to do some shopping and, amongst other things, had bought some fresh bread and oranges. Our two-litre water bottle was already half drained, but the oranges would help to quench our thirst. The girls told me that we could also chew mopani leaves if the thirst got too bad.

We drew pictures and played pebble games in the sand, and I tried not to worry too much about the long walk facing us the next day. But I did worry. One can expect to encounter quite a number of animals over a distance of twenty kilometres. I thought of the lone rhino bull that we often saw grazing in the Nhlarweni marsh, and of the leopard we had spotted near the Tsugama creek the previous week. I thought of the lions that frequent the Shimangu area, and of the elephant herds that can be anywhere, any time. Luckily, I had my pistol with me. It's a powerful 9 mm parabellum. But one doesn't shoot at a rhino or an elephant with a pistol. Actually, I don't think you shoot at a buffalo or a lion with a pistol either. Probably the best thing to do is make sure they don't notice you. If they do, you take care not to bother them. If they think you're bothering them anyway, well, then I guess you run away. But I'm not sure.

We were still drawing and playing games in the sand when a faint sound caught our attention. We looked up, straining our ears to identify and locate it.

It was a low, distant rumble. After a while we realised that we were listening to the steady drone of a heavy vehicle approaching from the north. But it wasn't on our road; it was outside the boundary fence in Gazankulu. Then it struck me that we were not far from the boundary, and that there was a road running parallel to the boundary fence. In fact, it's not really a road, but rather a firebreak which was made to prevent bush fires in Gazankulu from spreading to the Park. Occasionally military vehicles use the firebreak as a road.

I told Karin to sound the jeep's hooter, and the two older girls and I took off, sprinting towards the fence as fast as we could. It was some four hundred metres away and there was no time to find an easy way through the dense tangles of mopani scrub. By the time we reached the fence, we were out of breath, badly scratched and, worst of all, too late. The occupants of the truck had neither seen nor heard us and were well past us.

Despite my disappointment, I told myself that if one vehicle had come along the firebreak, it was possible that another would be on its way. I sent Hettie and Sandra back to Karin and sat down near the fence, listening and waiting. Some red-billed hoopoes in a nearby tree startled me with a sudden outburst of hysterical cackling. But when they finally shut up the bush was silent. After some time I detected the distinctive smell of buffalo and heard movement in the woodland to the north. It sounded like a fairly big herd. Although lone bulls can be very dangerous, buffalo in a herd don't usually pose any threat, being generally mild-mannered and easygoing. What worried me, though, was that you often find lions in close attendance on buffalo herds. I jogged back to the jeep and, fetching my pistol, warned the girls not to stray far from the car and to be on the look-out for lions.

Back at the fence I smelled the buffalo again, but after a while both the smell and the sounds faded as they moved off in a north-easterly direction.

Time dragged on, and apart from the repetitious, monotonous calling of a bush shrike, no other sounds came from the quiet landscape. After about half an hour — which seemed like an eternity — I was as bored as the lonely bush shrike and longed for the company of my daughters. I no longer felt so sure that another vehicle would put in an appearance, and decided to go back to the jeep. But as I got to my feet, a brilliant idea suddenly came to me: I would build an obstacle across the road. If a vehicle should happen to come along it would have to stop, and the occupants would have to get out to remove the barrier. This would give us time enough to dash to the fence and attract their attention.

I climbed through the high fence, ripping my blouse and slacks in the process. I stood still for a few seconds to absorb the fact that this was the first time in my life that I had set foot in Gazankulu — homeland to the Tsonga-Shangana people. Then I started hauling logs and branches out of the Gazankulu bush and piling them on the road. It's surprising how many logs and branches are needed to construct a barricade large enough to stop a big truck, even on a narrow track. My exertions left me saturated with perspiration and covered in a fine red dust, and my shadow on the ground showed that my hair was in total disarray.

Finally, after much effort, I felt satisfied that the obstruction was imposing enough to do its job. Taking a stick, I scraped the word HELP on either side of the barrier with big arrows pointing towards the fence. I stood back to admire my handiwork before making my way back into the Park and my daughters. And then, to my surprise, I heard a distant hum approaching from the north. I waited and listened, hardly daring to breathe in case I missed some important clue. It was definitely another vehicle, and it was coming our way. But, strangely, it didn't sound like an army truck. The pitch of the engine's drone wasn't deep enough. That baffled me a bit, because no other vehicles ever travel on the firebreak along the boundary. Although the firebreak is outside the fence, it is in fact inside the cadastral boundary of the Park, and only army vehicles have permission to travel on it.

The volume of the drone increased steadily and, after some time, an old, dilapidated pick-up truck appeared in the distance. I stood wondering what on earth a vehicle like that was doing out there, when suddenly the driver caught sight of me and slammed on his brakes. It seemed that he was going to turn around and drive away. I frantically waved my arms, called out and beckoned him to please come back. Apparently the sight of me had scared him out of his wits. I guess you couldn't blame him. One doesn't expect to find a woman out alone in the bush, miles from anywhere. Add to that my appearance — tousle-haired with dirty, torn clothes, wearing a pistol — and, of course, the road block behind me. I quickly drew my pistol and laid it in a patch of grass beside the road. All the while I waved and smiled at the driver, trying to indicate in as friendly a manner possible that I only wanted to talk to him.

Hesitantly, he drove to where I was standing. The driver was a youngish man, apparently of Portuguese origin. His passenger, a Shangaan man, looked just as alarmed as the driver. The driver didn't speak Afrikaans, and very little English. I resorted to a mixture of English and Tsonga and, along with much gesturing, explained that my car had broken down inside the Park. Luckily the driver understood a fair amount of Tsonga, but he indicated that he couldn't help me, not being able to fix cars. I asked if he would take a message to Phalaborwa gate; after all, he was heading in that direction and would pass close to the gate before joining the main road. He looked strangely worried and preoccupied, and was definitely annoyed with me. I wondered why he was so reluctant to help me. I quickly went on to explain that I had my children in the car, and that we were thirsty and far from home.

Eventually he agreed to help, so I asked if I might trouble him for a pencil and a piece of paper. He found a blunt pencil and a scrap of dirty paper in the truck. I wrote a short message to the gate official, Desmond Wilcox:

Please help. Stranded approximately 25 kilometres
north of gate on Mahlangeni road.
Kobie and kids.

I handed the note to the driver. He stuffed it into his shirt pocket and stared suspiciously at the barricade on the road in front of him. I walked over and began dismantling the structure, heaving logs and branches out of the way, expecting the men to lend a hand. But they didn't budge. I felt cross and irritated that I had to do all the work while they sat and watched.

Once I'd cleared sufficient space for them to get through, they drove past me without a single word or gesture. And it was only then, as the pick-up moved past me, that I noticed the large tarpaulin stretched across the back of the vehicle, and the blood stains on one corner of the tarpaulin. And I knew then that the two men were poachers and that they had been hunting illegally in Gazankulu. No wonder they had seemed so wary of me — and my pistol and my road block.

I went through the fence again and back to my daughters. When I told them about the episode with the two poachers, they doubted as much as I did that my note would be delivered. If the Park officials at the gate spotted the blood-stained tarpaulin on the back of the pick-up, they would investigate further, and if there was an antelope beneath the tarpaulin, as I believed there was, the poachers would be apprehended and reported right away.

It was by then late afternoon and the shadows were lengthening across the bush. The water bottle was empty, so we ate some oranges to quench our thirst. The girls suggested that we build a small fire in the road as soon as dusk settled in — just for the fun of it. A fire always looks cosy in the bush. I agreed that it was a great idea. We also started planning our dinner, taking stock of our supplies in the jeep: a loaf of fresh bread, a number of oranges, one bag each of flour, mealie meal, powdered milk, oats and sugar, some baker's yeast, and three packets of coffee beans.

If we had had water we could have cooked the oats and eaten them with milk and sugar — if we had had a cooking utensil. I always keep a pocket knife, box of matches, axe and first aid kit in my car, and of course a bottle of water, but not cooking utensils.

And then suddenly we remembered the tin of sweetened condensed milk. Sandra had asked me to buy it to make a batch of fudge during the weekend. The girls found the tin underneath the bag of flour and were elated. They decided that fresh bread dipped in condensed milk would make a superb meal. And in the morning, as soon as it was light enough, we could use the empty tin to fetch some water from the muddy pool in the gully behind us and boil the water to sterilise it. We would sterilise enough water to fill the water bottle and take it with us on the long walk home.

The sun was moving rapidly towards the western horizon, and we decided to sit outside under our mopani tree a while longer to enjoy the onset of the magic hour.

A family of warthogs and a herd of impala crossed the road nearby. We sat very still, hoping that our presence wouldn't alarm them. They remained unaware of us, and it was delightful to watch them ambling by so peacefully — less than thirty metres away. Later on, we heard the eerie, hooting calls of wild dogs far off to the east. A pair of red-eyed doves in a nearby tree gurgled a sweet song, and occasionally zebras barked from the southern bank of the gully behind us.

But for the most part the bush was silent. A soft, golden glow settled on the grass and trees as the sky turned a deeper, darker blue. A lone elephant bull startled us when he silently appeared from the mopani bush some forty or fifty metres away. We rose quickly, moved quietly back to the car and got inside. We watched him as he tore a branch off a mopani tree, loaded some foliage into his mouth and stood chewing and thinking for a while before moving on.

When we got out of the car again, we decided that it was a good time to start gathering twigs and wood for our camp-fire.

I had just started breaking some small dead branches from a fallen tree when a distant, barely audible sound attracted my attention, and I looked up. I noticed that the girls had also halted their activities and were looking up with alert expressions, straining to identify and locate the sound.

It was a faint hum, far away to the south. We stood very still as we listened. Was it only the wind? Or could it be a vehicle, on our road, coming from the direction of the gate?

The hum became a soft, persistent droning — still far away — but gradually gaining volume. It wasn't the wind. We waited, and we listened and listened — worried that the sound might go away if we stopped listening. Occasionally the volume of the sound diminished and even disappeared for short periods of time. But we knew it was only the dips in the landscape coupled with the direction of the wind that caused the changes. Finally, we heard a distinct change in the pitch of the drone, and we knew that the vehicle had turned into the nearby gully. A few seconds later the pitch changed again as it climbed out of the gully, and then we saw it: a Parks Board Land Rover, coming towards us on the winding track. It was a wonderful sight, and we ran forward to meet it.

The driver was Robert van Lente, a Parks Board engineer. He lives in the personnel village in the Park near the gate. We were really happy to see one another. Robert had been very anxious about us, as the message sent to his house by the gate official read:

Kobie and kids in trouble, 25 kilometres on
Mahlangeni road. Need help! URGENT!

Poor Robert. He had actually been worried that he might not find us alive.

We untied the girls' hostel luggage from the jeep's roof-carrier and loaded it into Robert's Land Rover together with the groceries. And then we were, at last, on our way home.

When we arrived at the southern river bank dusk had already settled, but the magenta sky above the western horizon still shimmered on the water, enabling us to keep an eye on the hippos as we rowed over the river. When we reached the northern bank, we looked across the water and saw Robert's silhouette on the far bank where he had waited to see us safely over. We waved before he disappeared into his car and drove off.

Later, while enjoying a delicious supper of home-grown vegetables and home-caught fish (not bread and condensed milk), we decided that it was really good to be home and that we owed a debt of gratitude to the poachers who had, after all, been good enough to deliver my note to the gate official.

This was not the last of our troubles and adventures on the lonely track, but I believe I have recounted enough of them to explain why I always feel apprehensive at the start of a journey.

I should mention, though, that I have a recurring dream in which my car breaks down and I have to walk home. I encounter a pride of lions on the way, and since in my dream I have always forgotten my gun at home, I have to try to sneak past the lions without being noticed.

It really is a nightmare.

Sweet Solitude

K obus and I met at the University of Pretoria. We got married after we graduated. We then moved to Windhoek, the capital of Namibia, where Kobus worked as news editor for the Broadcasting Corporation, and I as translator for the Language Bureau. After three years we moved to Johannesburg, where Kobus continued working as a news editor and later as a film editor.

Kobus has a Bachelor of Arts degree in African languages, as well as a National Diploma in Nature Conservation. Towards the end of 1979, his lifelong dream of becoming a game ranger became a promising possibility when he received a letter from the Warden of the Kruger National Park, inviting him to Skukuza for an interview.

Skukuza is the largest of the tourist camps in the Kruger Park. It is also the headquarters of the offices of. Nature Conservation, Tourism and Maintenance Services. The letter from the Warden stipulated that 'the applicant's wife must be present at the interview'. I wondered why, but lost no time in making arrangements for my mother to look after my three young children for a couple of days so that I could accompany 'the applicant'.

The interview was conducted by the chief ranger, Dirk Ackerman, and the Park Warden, Dr Tol Pienaar. They asked Kobus a couple of questions, such as: why had he applied for the job, and why did he want to leave a good job in the city to work in the bush? Kobus answered simply that he had wanted to be a game ranger for as long as he could remember. They seemed satisfied.

They then turned their attention to me and attempted to intimidate me. They described the hardships and privations that a game ranger's wife can expect to endure; they warned me of the almost unbearable heat of the summer months; the ever-present danger of malaria, and the general hazards of the bush. They stressed the inconvenience of living far from doctors, schools, shopping centres and all the other amenities that city people take for granted. They reminded me that not even basic commodities, such as telephones and a regular mail service, were available. Then they held forth on the horrors of solitude, describing the extreme loneliness that one might experience at a remote ranger station. They warned me that a game ranger's work often took him away from home for long periods of time, leaving his wife home alone — with no neighbours, no telephone, no one to talk to. How would I cope with that, they wanted to know.

Eager to give them as good an answer as Kobus had, I told them that I had wanted to be a 'remote' person for as long as I could remember.

But they said: 'Go home and think carefully about this. Give it at least a month. And if you both decide, without reservation, that you're still interested, let us know.'

I understood then why they had insisted that the 'applicant's wife be present at the interview'.

They don't want rangers whose wives can't take it.

I scare easily, but I don't like being patronised into admitting defeat. Their tales of gloom and doom evoked a resolve in me to prove that I had more spunk than they thought. If other game rangers' wives could take it, so could I. And, anyway, I didn't want to see my husband's lifelong dream evaporate. Actually, I was a little scared. It wasn't the solitude that scared me. I like solitude. It was the heat, the malaria, the general hardships, and the dangers of the bush that bothered me.

Two months later, at the beginning of 1980, we had sold our house in the city, packed our belongings and our children, and were on our way to a new life in one of the largest and most beautiful conservation areas in the world.

Getting used to the seclusion and isolation in the initial years at Mahlangeni was really nothing compared to adapting to the heat, the innumerable bugs and mosquitoes, malaria, tick fever, dramatic encounters with wild animals, the whims of the electric generator, the unpredictable river, the paranoid hippos, and the perils of the lonely track. The solitude simply didn't get much of a chance to feature as a problem. In fact, by the time we actually got down to thinking about it, we realised that we could no longer imagine a life amongst crowds of people.

Perhaps, initially, solitude takes some getting used to. But once you feel comfortable with it, it grows on you, and you become addicted to it. You even become possessive of it. And when you feel possessive of your solitude, and of your vast, uncluttered living space, you may at times experience an acute reluctance to share it with other people. That happens to me sometimes: I get something close to an anxiety attack when I hear that we are expecting visitors. Luckily, it doesn't happen to me all the time and, luckily, we don't get visitors very often. If the visitors are good friends, or dear family, it can be really wonderful to share Mahlangeni with them for a couple of days. But not too often, and not for too long.

Shopping trips to Phalaborwa are my main source of distress. I become so upset and agitated when people crowd me that I often end up going home with only half the items I set out to buy.

Although I miss Kobus when he spends days or weeks away from home in the course of his duties, I am never really lonely. Our two dogs keep me company, and so do our horses and bantams, as well as the family of squirrels and the many wild birds who live in our garden — and whom I now know personally and would call by their first names, if they had them. A number of bushbuck that graze on the river bank in front of the house every day also provide company. They're so tame that if I talk to them, they look me straight in the eye.

Naturally, I'm also well acquainted with the resident hippos. I sometimes walk down to the river to say hello to them. They always swim closer as I approach and regard me with curiosity, but when I talk to them they become mute and just stare at me. They only come to life when I turn away and walk back home.

MAHLANGENI

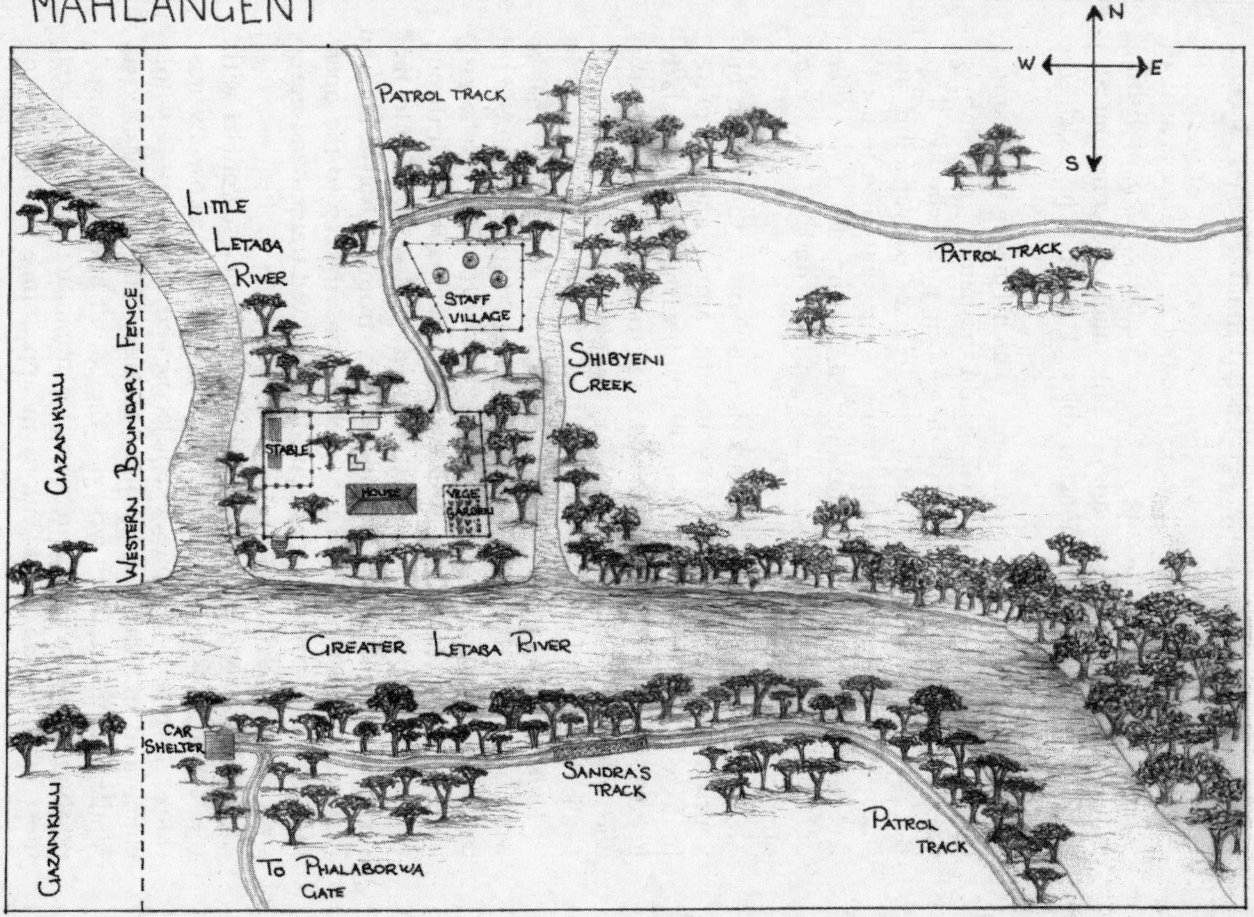

N
W — E
S

Patrol track

Lime Letaba River

Patrol track

Shibyeni Creek

Staff Village

Western Boundary Fence

GAZANKULU

House

Stable

Greater Letaba River

Sandra's Track

Patrol track

To Phalaborwa Gate

Car Shelter

GAZANKULU

Then they start communicating noisily behind my back. I know they talk about me.

And then there's old Filemoni to talk to. He's always around somewhere, either pottering in the vegetable garden or fishing down by the river. But he doesn't talk much. He communicates mostly in grunts and monosyllables. I respect his wish for solitude.

If I were desperate for company (which I never really am), I could walk over to the staff village on the bank of the Shibyeni creek and chat to the families of the game guards who live there. But my Tsonga isn't quite up to easy, relaxed conversation, and since their ways and traditions remain somewhat alien to me I'd feel hesitant and shy about intruding on their privacy. I visit them only when either they or I have a problem and we need each other's help.

The best thing about solitude is that you have no one but yourself to consider, no one but yourself to amuse, and you're free to do whatever you choose, whenever you wish. I am particularly good at amusing myself. I read and listen to music, I garden, bake and sew and — like all good solitary people — I keep a diary and I talk to myself.

I also love walking. Although our garden is large and has a wide and wonderful view over the two rivers, I sometimes need to escape the confines of the fence. Whenever my wanderlust overcomes my fear of the bush (which is fairly often), I call our two dogs, sling a gun over my shoulder, and walk off into the surrounding bush. I don't wander too far from the house, and in the summer months when the bush is dense I keep to the open firebreaks and patrol tracks. Our dogs are well trained and never stray from my side.

Our excursions into the bush bring us into close contact with the 'small folk' of the wilderness: the lizards, geckos, agamas, skinks, tortoises, terrapins, chameleons, and leguaans — a whole community of bizarre and exotic creatures. (They are classified as reptile fauna. But, don't worry — they don't bite and they aren't poisonous.) Some of them resemble miniature dinosaurs, and most of them are so ridiculous in appearance in one way or another that they must surely be the quaintest, the oddest and the most weird members of the animal kingdom.

The most exotic must be the tree agama with his amazing technicolor dreamcoat, and the oddest, I think, is the chameleon who changes the colour of his coat for every occasion, but spends most of his life hesitating about whether to go anywhere at all. The most weird must be the river leguaan. He looks like a cross between a giant lizard and a miniature brontosaurus. The quaintest would be the thicktoed gecko with his large eyes and sweet, angelic face.

The dogs are usually as fascinated by these wild creatures as I am. But they know that they are allowed only to sniff and look, and not to taste.

There is no time to be lonely when such a wealth and variety of creatures abounds in the neighbourhood.

It's only at night that the vastness of the wilderness sometimes strikes home. But it's not a thought that bothers me. The dogs sleep on the patio right outside the sliding doors to the bedroom and I need only call their names softly to hear the swishing of their wagging tails as they acknowledge my call.

Much as I enjoy solitude, I always look forward to Fridays when I can fetch my children from their schools in Phalaborwa, and to the days when Kobus will be home again. And I must admit that there are times, though few and far between, when solitude tends to scramble one's sense of perspective a little. When that happens to me, I become obsessive about small problems, such as the shape of my nose, or the fact that I have a husband who loses coffee mugs — *my* coffee mugs. And as time goes by the problems grow in my mind until I feel overwhelmed by them. But, strangely, as soon as I come into contact with people again, the problems diminish and shrink, and are soon forgotten.

Some years ago, when I was alone at home, I spent a morning gardening and listening to music. The record player inside the house was turned to full volume so that the beautiful strains of a Mozart symphony filled the whole of the garden. And then, unexpectedly, a vehicle turned into our back gates and a strange young man got out. As I approached him he looked at me briefly, confusion written all over his face. Then he stared at the house behind me, and looked even more confused. It was easy to tell that he was a lost person.

Occasionally — about once or twice a year — someone gets lost and turns up at Mahlangeni. Lost people are always surprised to find a house here. You can't blame them. If you travel on the long and sometimes lonely road between Letaba and Shingwedzi, and take the turn-off to the west at the Tsendze stream near Shipandani, you will find yourself on a totally desolate track, leading through solitary wilderness for more than sixty kilometres. And when you're finally convinced that you will never find signs of human life again, the road dips through a steep, dry water-course (the Shibyeni creek) and arrives at a T-junction from which, if you look to the south, a high fence with gates is visible. (In the daytime, the gates are open.) As a desperately lost person, you will perceive the fence and gates as a poignant reminder of civilisation, and as reassurance that your own species still exists on this planet. Naturally, you will choose the south road then, drive up to the gates, and through them. And, behold! There, amidst tall, shady trees in a lush garden stands a house.

The stranger stood gaping at the house behind me and, even before greeting me, asked in an unbelieving voice, 'Is there really a house out here?'

In the spirit of the moment I turned, took a good look at the house, and replied with a smile: 'Why, yes, I believe there is!'

Looking sheepish, the stranger introduced himself and explained that he was researching a project for a thesis on ecological engineering, and that he'd been granted a permit to travel to the Shimuwini dam on the Letaba River. He frowned, adding, 'But I guess I got lost.'

I said, 'Yes, indeed you have. Come into my husband's office. He keeps a large map of the area there. I'll show you how to get to Shimuwini.'

But he remained rooted to the spot, apparently hypnotised by the beautiful music.

'That's Mozart's Fortieth Symphony,' he informed me.

I told him that I knew that.

He stood listening attentively to the last haunting strains of the symphony's finale, and when the music had ended he asked: 'What other Mozart recordings do you have?'

At that stage we didn't have a very large Mozart collection, but we did have a nice selection of other composers — Beethoven, Vivaldi, Grieg, Chopin, Paganini, Haydn, Mendelssohn, Schubert, and others — and I invited him inside and showed him. He became totally absorbed in the record and tape collection, so I left him and went into the kitchen to make some coffee.

He chose Mozart's Coronation Concerto, put it on the turntable and absent-mindedly disappeared into the front garden. (Lost people tend to be rather strange and eccentric. I guess that's why they get lost in the first place.)

When I carried the coffee out, I found him sitting on our swing (a half-cut tyre, suspended on a beam between two mopani trees). Swaying gently to the rhythm of the music, he was watching the hippos play in the river down below. He was so lost in his reverie that he didn't hear me approaching. I put the tray down on the grass and sat down next to it to pour the coffee. When he noticed me, he got off the swing and joined me on the grass.

We drank our coffee and listened to the concerto. The warm and rich melody filled the garden and soared out over the river where even the hippos seemed entranced by its beauty. A fish eagle dived from the sky, and as it glided gracefully over the water, its echoing calls resounded in the music-filled landscape.

We didn't talk as we sipped our coffee and listened to the music. Half-way through the solo part of the larghetto movement, my guest poured himself a second cup of coffee and stirred it absent-mindedly, although he'd forgotten to put sugar in it.

When the last strains of the finale had faded away leaving their dulcet echoes in our heads, he peered into his empty coffee mug and informed me that, back home in Pretoria, the concerto didn't sound the same, and that he'd forgotten to put sugar in his coffee.

I told him I was sorry to hear that.

He got up and carried the tray back to the house for me. We went to Kobus's office where I showed him the map and explained to him how to get to Shimuwini. Just before he left he asked the question so often asked of me: 'Isn't it lonely for you out here?'

I told him no, that loneliness didn't bother me.

About a month later, a Mozart tape turned up in our mail. And ever since then, every other month or so, a new Mozart tape arrives with the mail. The postmark indicates that they come from Pretoria. It's not difficult to guess who the sender is.

But I wonder why he sends them. Perhaps he cherishes the memory of that day when he lost his way and unexpectedly came upon a Mozart symphony in a remote corner of the wilderness. And perhaps he sends the tapes so that he can rest in the knowledge that Mozart still plays at Mahlangeni.

Or perhaps he believes that it must, after all, sometimes be lonely for me here, and that Mozart will relieve the loneliness.

I'm never lonely here. But Mozart still plays at Mahlangeni.

Encounter on the Koppie

S ome ten kilometres from our house stands a lone, boulder-strewn koppie on a vast, flat stretch of mopani bushveld. A baobab tree which is more than a hundred years old graces the eastern slope of the koppie, its tapering branches reaching up towards the large boulders of the higher slopes. From the summit one can enjoy a wonderful view of the surrounding mopani plains and of a large pan some distance to the south. There is no nicer place to spend a lazy Sunday afternoon than on the flat boulders of the summit, armed with binoculars for spotting animals as they trek across the plains to drink at the pan.

A few years ago, good friends of ours from the city — Louis and Joan and their three children — came to visit for a weekend. We decided to take them on our favourite Sunday afternoon outing.

We drove in our pick-up to the foot of the koppie. Hettie (then aged 15), Sandra (13), Karin (8) and our friends' daughter Thelma (aged 6) all leapt from the back of the pick-up and scurried up the slope of the koppie, each wanting to be the first to enjoy the view from the top. I was about to caution the girls to wait for us, but my voice couldn't compete with their energetic enthusiasm, so I let them be.

Together with Louis and Joan and their two younger boys, Kobus and I followed at a more sedate pace. Our progress was slow, as Louis was leading both small boys by the hand, their young legs struggling with the climb.

Kobus had not brought his rifle along that day. This didn't really worry me as we had climbed the koppie on numerous previous occasions and had never seen anything other than dassies (hyrax) on the slopes.

We were still a long way below the girls when they reached the top of the koppie. Joan and I were deep in conversation when Kobus suddenly held up his hand. I know that signal. It means: Shut up and pay attention — the bush is transmitting danger signals.

Stopping in mid-sentence, I immediately shut up and paid attention.

And then we all heard it: a deep, low, rumbling sound coming from the slopes above. It sounded like a rock-slide to me. But when the rumbling stopped, Sandra's voice reached us from the summit. The single word she screamed was 'Leopard!'

Kobus, who had already started running up the slope towards the girls, yelled at them to come down.

I sprinted up the slope after Kobus, my only thought being to get to the girls before the leopard did.

The deep rumbling noise rose again, and even in the heat of the moment it dawned on me that the noise wasn't the rumbling of a rock-slide, nor the sound of a leopard, but the growl of an angry lion.

And then we saw her: a lioness bursting from the cover of boulders and shrubs. She stopped short of the children and crouched, gathering her hind legs beneath her flattened body. Her tail tuft jerked spasmodically as she uttered a deep warning growl that rose in volume until it rumbled like thunder over the landscape.

The girls fled headlong down the slope, crashing through shrubs and over rocks — all except little Thelma. She had stopped and turned, looked right into the face of the crouching lioness — less than ten metres away — and had immediately frozen with shock. She stood, rigid with fright, completely unable to do anything but stand and stare at the snarling animal.

Hettie, who had glanced over her shoulder and witnessed the scene, halted her descent, turned and clambered back up towards her friend. The lioness saw Hettie approaching and warned her with a crescendo growl not to come any closer, but Hettie rushed on, reached out and grabbed the paralysed little girl firmly in her arms, propelling her away from the scene and headlong down the slope, half dragging, half carrying her along. Meanwhile, Sandra had also glanced over her shoulder and, seeing Hettie scrambling away from the lioness with Thelma in tow, turned immediately and rushed back up the slope to help her sister flee with the shocked little girl.

Kobus and I were still sprinting up the slope towards them — oblivious of the shrubs and rocks that scratched and cut us as we ran, our eyes on the lioness and the children. Karin came tearing past us, her legs scratched and bleeding, but the only thing that mattered then was that she was safe — we were between her and the lioness. Then Hettie and Sandra, with the ashen-faced little girl between them, came running past us. And a few seconds later Kobus stood facing the lioness — unarmed.

With an angry warning snarl, she charged, drawing up very close to Kobus. Slowly, she lowered her body into a crouch and gathered her hind legs beneath her. She was coiled for attack.

Snatching up a rock about the size of a rugby ball, I rushed towards them, and took up a position some two or three metres behind Kobus.

Kobus stood his ground as the cat communicated her intentions to him in the thundering language of lions.

I was shaking like a leaf, my heart pounding in my ears as adrenalin pumped through my system. With my heightened senses, I experienced every moment and every tiny detail of what was happening in vivid slow motion.

Kobus was talking calmly to the crouching, snarling lioness: 'Easy now, old girl ... easy now ... calm down ...'

It's strange, but I always forget how big lions really are until I see one up close, and then the size of the animal strikes home with renewed shock. Perhaps it's the resurgent trauma that causes my recurring amnesia.

As I stood gaping at the huge cat, I tried to ignore the impact that her size was having on me. I decided to concentrate instead on some of her facial features. Her blazing yellow eyes didn't seem a good feature to concentrate on, so I chose instead the funny looking crinkles on her puckered nose. When a lion snarls, the nose always creases into these characteristic crinkles.

She roared again, making me jump, and the earth seemed to shudder. I held the rock steady, determined to throw it at her if she dared to move — she was so close to Kobus that she could have landed on top of him with one easy bound. But Kobus was still talking to her in his calm, soothing voice. 'Easy now, old girl, easy now... don't worry... we won't harm you...'

(We won't? Then why was I standing there clutching an enormous rock?)

Slowly, Kobus looked over his shoulder and signalled quietly but firmly that I should retreat. It dawned on me at last that his safety — as well as mine — depended on whether he succeeded in placating the lioness. If I left, she'd feel less threatened. Feeling slightly embarrassed, and being careful not to annoy her with any sudden movements, I put the rock down carefully, and turned quietly away.

As I made my way down the slope, I held my breath and listened. The lioness was still growling, but less aggressively now, and Kobus was still talking calmly, soothingly, pacifying her with his voice: 'Easy, old girl, easy now. Don't worry...'

Her growls became softer and softer...

Once I was safely away, Kobus followed.

The crisis was over.

When we reached the foot of the koppie and rejoined the others, we turned and, looking back, witnessed a magnificent sight. The lioness stood on a high rock, etched against the grey-blue sky, her coat golden in the late afternoon sunlight. A lone, dignified figure. She roared once more — a warning to us not to intrude again into her territory. And the ground seemed to vibrate with the volume of her voice.

Kobus told us that he'd noticed that she was in lactation, and he believed that she had chosen the koppie as a nursery for her cubs. That, of course, accounted for her aggressive behaviour. Her actions were those of a mother protecting her young.

The girls were still pale with fright and Karin, sobbing softly, said that her legs were hurting. On closer examination, we saw with relief that the wounds were superficial, and we realised that her tears were those of shock rather than pain. There was a lump in my throat as I hugged her. In her young life she had already fled from a charging elephant, and now from an angry lion. I hugged my other two girls too, but couldn't find the words to tell them how proud I was of them for not having hesitated to turn back to help their young friend.

Thelma, of course, had suffered the greatest shock of all of us. But her parents were hugging her tightly and doing a good job of comforting her.

I must tell Sandra's side of the story as well.

She had been the first to reach the summit, and as she turned to help Thelma over the last boulder, she heard a deep rumbling sound behind her. It was, of course, the lioness growling, but Sandra momentarily believed it to be the sound of moving rocks. She looked over her shoulder — right into the blazing yellow eyes of the big cat. Such was her fright and her anxiety to warn the others, that she did not register exactly what she saw, and heard herself screaming 'Leopard!' (In all fairness, one would expect to find a leopard rather than a lion on a koppie.)

While the other girls had sustained only superficial scratches and cuts, Sandra had a rather nasty gash on the top of her foot.

Back at the house we washed the blood and dirt from our arms and legs, and Kobus tended Sandra's injury. He cleaned, disinfected and bound the wound tightly.

Sandra was rather fed-up when, not being able to put a shoe on over the bandages, she had to attend school the next day with the dressing there for all to see. She is a girl who is not given to dramatics and she doesn't enjoy telling others of her adventures. Hettie, on the other hand, loves to relive interesting experiences and to share them with those who will listen.

Apparently, it didn't take long that Monday morning for the whole school to hear of the incident on the koppie. As a result, Sandra was extremely irritated because everyone who came across her that day wanted to know if the lioness had bitten her on the foot.

Bush Athlete

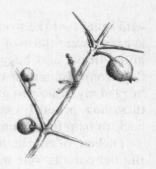

T hat Sunday on the koppie was not in fact the first time that Sandra and Karin had run away from lions.

About three years prior to that day, when Sandra was about ten years old and Karin about five, they accompanied their father on a field trip to repair a windmill in the area.

While Kobus and his game guard assistants were busy fixing the windmill, the girls spotted a herd of eland nearby. They were very excited, as the eland is one of the rarer species in the Kruger Park. But before they could have a good look at the large antelopes, the herd had disappeared into a nearby thicket. Sandra asked if they could follow the animals in order to have another look at them and Kobus, way up on top of the windmill, gave his permission — provided they didn't stray too far.

Our dog Janna, then but a few months old, was with the girls on that day. They started off after the eland, eyes on the ground as they followed the spoor. Sandra was in the lead, with Karin just behind her. Janna, being young and not yet fully trained, bounded around them, here one moment and there the next. After walking a fair distance, Sandra — concentrating on the spoor — heard Karin give a little yelp. Thinking that she probably had a thorn in her foot (the girls often walk barefoot), Sandra, without looking back, asked, 'What's the matter? A thorn?'

Receiving no reply, she looked over her shoulder and was greeted by the sight of her sister fleeing frantically back towards the windmill. Half turning her head in her flight, Karin yelled, 'Lions!'

Sandra spun around — and there, a short distance ahead, lay a pride of lions in a dry stream-bed. She turned instantly and sprinted after her sister. She is a good athlete and it wasn't long before she caught up with Karin. While overtaking her, she grabbed a fistful of her sister's T-shirt and virtually dragged her along. They ran so fast that Janna could barely keep up.

From their vantage point on the windmill, Kobus and the game guards saw the girls speeding back towards them, and one of the game guards remarked, 'Children who run like that are running from lions.'

Kobus climbed down and, reaching the girls, asked if they had come across lions. Breathlessly, they replied that they had, pointing back in the direction from which they had fled.

Kobus fetched his rifle and backtracked with the girls towards the stream-bed. The lions were still there when they arrived, but leapt up and ran off when they saw Kobus. From the tracks on the ground, Kobus could clearly see how close the girls had been to the lions — and also how suddenly first Karin, and then Sandra, had turned and fled.

Sandra is now sixteen years old and has in the past two years earned one bronze and two silver medals in the 200 and 400-metre sprints at the South African junior athletics championships.

People often tease her that she no doubt owes her speed to the fact that she lives in the Kruger Park and spends so much time running away from wild animals.

Sandra enjoys training over weekends and during the school holidays. To this end, Kobus has constructed a training track for her on the far bank of the Greater Letaba River. There's a patrol road there, but like the other roads in the region, it's really no more than a rough dirt track. It is, however, the only road in the area that runs fairly straight for a distance of some 250 metres, and Kobus has managed to flatten and compact the straight stretch with one of the Park's road graders.

It's not exactly a tartan track, but at least it's a lyrical track — with the river and riverine bush on one side and mopani woodland on the other. Sometimes elephant or buffalo use the track for their ablutions, and a clean-up exercise is necessary before Sandra can start training. And sometimes during training sessions, giraffe, kudu or other antelope appear shyly from the bush, usually some distance away, and stare curiously at Sandra as she does her warm-up exercises. But they only do so until Sandra launches herself from her starting blocks. Then they flee. They probably think that if Sandra has reason to take off so quickly, they had better do the same.

Kobus always accompanies Sandra on her training sessions — not only to coach her, but also to protect her.

On the weekends that Kobus is away from home I have to go with her. Although I don't know much about coaching, I can at least, with rifle and stopwatch in hand, read her time for her and keep a watchful eye on the surrounding bush. Before a training session we always patrol the whole stretch of road, making sure there are no elephant, buffalo or large predators in the immediate vicinity. On those occasions when we find fresh lion spoor, or hear lions grunting in the distance, or smell or hear buffalo or elephants in the area, we usually spend some time arguing whether or not to proceed with the training session. Sandra always reckons that the animals are far away, unaware of our presence and, in any case, totally uninterested in us. I always believe they're stalking us.

In all fairness, I must admit that although my judgement of the situation may not always be correct, Sandra is always the first to capitulate. But I suspect that she does this only because she feels sorry for me, knowing how easily I scare.

One day, when I accompanied Sandra on a training exercise, an awful accident almost happened.

After Sandra had completed her warm-up routine, she proceeded to practise her starts. When she bursts forth from her starting blocks, one is advised to stay well clear of her. Even though she is slightly built, the power and force she puts into her start would knock one flying.

At the very moment that Sandra shot out of the blocks on that particular day, a warthog sow suddenly burst from the scrub at the side of the road and dashed headlong on to the track — right in front of Sandra. I saw Sandra's whole body stiffen and envisaged her either crash-landing right on top of the sow, or else diving headlong over her into the hard surface of the track. But somehow, with magnificient effort and muscular control, Sandra managed to curb her impetus in mid-flight and force her catapulting body to an abrupt standstill, literally stopping in her tracks just in time to avoid the crash.

And then a baby warthog appeared from the scrub and dashed over the road after its mother, right in front of Sandra, its tail straight up in the air. And then another baby followed, and another, and another!

The mother warthog has reason to be grateful that Sandra managed to slam on her brakes so successfully, preventing a disastrous collision between athlete and warthog family.

Children of the Wild

All the schoolgoing children of the northern and central districts of the Park attend school in Phalaborwa and spend their weekdays in the Park's hostel. The hostel is inside the Park, about two kilometres from the gate, and is exclusively for Kruger Park children. There are usually about twenty residents in the hostel — both primary and high school pupils. Their schools are a number of kilometres away in town, and they have their own bus — supplied by the Parks Board — which ferries them to and fro each day.

Because they're all Kruger Park children, they feel at home with one another and regard themselves as part of one big family.

Our eldest daughter Hettie once wrote an essay about life in the hostel, and I quote a few paragraphs from it:

> Children who grow up in the wild don't really know what it's like to have friends until they start school. Growing up alone isn't that bad though, as long as you have a sister or brother or even a pet to play with. In any case, it doesn't occur to you that life could be different.
>
> When children who've grown up alone arrive at the hostel for the first time, they are astonished to find that they have such an abundance of playmates — and they become wild with joy. They chase each other around, shouting and laughing with excitement, and they play and wrestle, dance and shriek, and generally behave like clowning baboons — as if trying to make up for all the lost opportunities of their preschool years.
>
> But by nightfall they suddenly remember that they miss their mothers. And the nostalgia is profound, because in

their preschool years Mommy was always there. She never
went anywhere without them. The town is too far away, and
neighbours too distant. And baby-sitters don't exist out
here. Wherever Mom went, they went, and it never occurred
to them that there could come a time when Mommy would
be too far away for a comforting hug at bedtime.

When the tears start flowing here at night, the older
children step in and offer comfort where they can,
remembering only too well how they felt themselves, not
that long ago.

That, then, an excerpt from Hettie's essay on life in the hostel.

When we first came to live in the Kruger Park, Karin was barely
two years old. By the time she was five, she could name almost
every wild creature in the Park, including most of the birds. We
were very proud of our clever child. But we had overlooked the
fact that her world consisted only of the wilderness, and that she
had scant knowledge of the world outside.

One day, while driving to Johannesburg to visit my parents, we
saw a cow grazing in a field next to the road. Karin yelled for
Kobus to stop the car and, after having a good look at the cow,
asked: 'And what's that? A donkey or something?'

Later, at a filling station, we noticed a cat — an ordinary,
black domestic cat — in a tree nearby. Karin was fascinated.

'Oh wow!' she exclaimed. 'Look at that strange animal!'

I felt very guilty when I realised that she was totally unfamiliar
with domestic animals. I immediately bought her some picture
books about domestic animals so that she wouldn't appear too
ignorant when she started attending school.

She was fascinated by the pictures of the 'strange' animals.
But, thanks to the books, she was soon able to identify every
domestic animal that one might be expected to know. Even so,
when she started attending school, she was often out of her depth
in the world outside the Park.

One Friday afternoon when I arrived at the hostel to fetch the
girls, Karin announced that her school was holding an art

exhibition and that two of her drawings had been chosen. Feeling proud of my artistic child, I drove into town with the girls to attend the exhibition.

As we approached the stands on which the drawings of the grades one and two pupils were displayed, I couldn't help but recognise Karin's drawings, even at a distance.

There were two groups of pictures. One group depicted quiet rural landscapes, and it seemed that the teacher had briefed the children on what a landscape might consist of, because most of the pictures were remarkably similar: a pool of blue water surrounded by trees, flowers, birds and butterflies, and puffy white clouds in the background. But there was one drawing in which the pool of water dominated the whole scene, and the pool in its turn was dominated by a hippo (its huge mouth wide open) and a crocodile (also with wide open mouth and displaying a fearsome array of teeth). At the top of the drawing, behind the water-hole containing the two intimidating creatures, stood a lone tree and a few flowers, but there was no room left for clouds.

Karin was the only Kruger Park child in her class, and I guess when the teacher said 'water' my daughter heard her mother's voice: 'Don't go too close... watch out for crocodiles... keep an eye on the hippos...'

The second group of pictures dealt with road safety. There were figures on bicycles in busy streets, some with an arm outstretched to indicate that they were going to make a right or left turn, and others approaching traffic lights or a stop sign with the hand held upright to indicate that they were going to stop, and so on. But in one picture two men on bicycles rode along a winding track through the bush, rifles slung over their shoulders. Ahead of them the track wound its way over a rise upon which stood a marula tree, half leaning across the road.

I knew where my daughter's thoughts had been when she drew that picture. There is a place on the lonely track between Mahlangeni and the hostel where you will find a marula tree on a rise, half leaning across the road. The two cyclists were, of course, two of our game guards out on patrol. And the rifles slung over their shoulders portrayed my daughter's only understanding of road safety.

Their teachers have mentioned to me that my children tend to write peculiar essays. When asked to write an essay on the peace and harmony of nature, Hettie described a weekend we had spent camping on the banks of the Tsendze stream when a hyena had stolen one of our blankets and a cooking pot in the night, and baboons had ransacked our camp the next day, making off with a good portion of our food supplies while we were out fishing. She concluded that there is beauty and perhaps harmony in nature, but not much peace, and certainly no law and order.

Asked to describe an impending rain storm, Sandra wrote that the first sign of an impending storm was that the hippos got out of the water because they know, in some mysterious way, that it usually rains on the escarpment first and that consequently the rivers will soon be in spate. So they get out of the water because they don't want to drown in the floods.

In an essay describing a most cherished possession, Karin wrote that this would most certainly have been her new shoes, but they were eaten by a hyena one night when she'd forgotten them outside.

Hettie's teachers are often impressed by her lyrical prose and poetry. This is a constant source of irritation to Sandra who, being only eighteen months younger than Hettie, and only one year behind her in school, finds to her chagrin that teachers expect her to display the same talent for writing that her sister does.

According to Sandra, the expectant expressions on the teachers' faces always turn to dismay when they read her unwilling attempts. Some years ago, after Hettie had won yet another prize in a poetry competition, Sandra's new English language teacher (who had been Hettie's teacher the previous year) commissioned Sandra to write a poem on wildlife. Hating the task, and anticipating with dread the teacher's disappointed reaction, she nevertheless tried her best. Being a more scientifically orientated person rather than a romantic poet, she came up with the following:

71

THE BUFFALO AND THE EGRET

The buffalo giggles
because there's a bird on its back
that wriggles.
It's an egret who eats the ticks
and flies and things
found on buffalo skins.
The tail of the buffalo flicks
as the egret grabs the ticks
and the buffalo giggles
as the bird wriggles,
catching fleas and anything
that bites and even stings.

It may not be lyrical, but it is at least an interesting zoological observation that rhymes. And considering that English is our second language, I think Sandra deserves some credit for accomplishing the rhyme.

My daughters may be good at writing 'peculiar' essays, but they are unable to write essays of a dramatic nature. The reason for this, they claim, is lack of experience. Ask them to describe a dramatic encounter, or any kind of terrifying experience or incident, and they cannot think of even one. It is totally beyond them and unfair to expect it of them. Scary things happen only where lots of people live together and where you can expect to encounter hijacks, robberies, traffic accidents, muggings and murders.

I often lecture my children on the dangers of the bush. I remind them of the encounter with the lioness on the koppie, of the elephant who charged them in the riverbed, and of other similar frightening experiences. But, to my dismay, it seems that the only lesson they learnt from these incidents was that, no matter how scared they felt, nothing happened to them, and therefore the incidents are not to be taken seriously.

It is true, though, that my daughters are bush-wise. They are familiar with the behaviour of wild animals, they can read spoor, decipher the smells and sounds of the bush and recognise the alarm signals. Their senses are constantly attuned to their surroundings and they know how to avoid dangerous situations. They are also well versed in the rules to be observed in cases of confrontation.

Even so, it worries me that they have so little fear of the bush. I would feel a lot better if they took wild animals more seriously, especially lions.

The problem with lions is that they don't generally act like dangerous animals — at least not during the daytime. If we come across them in the daylight hours, they usually flee. But at night lions everywhere, even here at Mahlangeni, realise that they are the kings of the bush and revert to being supremely confident predators. And if you come across them at night, they don't flee.

I know, because I sometimes go camping with Kobus, and when there are lions around, they will inspect the camp and casually make themselves at home within metres of our tent. Even if you shine a torch at them, they will stare at you nonchalantly and then go about their business as if you didn't exist. On such nights, I sleep with a pistol under my pillow (in fact, I don't really sleep), even though I know that Kobus's rifle is right next to him on his side of the bed.

Actually, I love to go camping with Kobus, although not particularly if there are lions around. The girls always love to go camping, and especially if there are lions around.

On a winter's day during a school vacation some years ago, Kobus invited the girls and me to accompany him on a patrol trip to the Shipikana creek. There was a full moon that night and Kobus wanted to share with us the beauty of the veld by moonlight.

We arrived in the late afternoon and pitched our tent on the bank of the dry watercourse. There was about an hour and a half left before sunset, so we decided to take a walk along the creek.

Some two or three hundred metres from our camp, a pride of lions suddenly burst from the dry bed of the creek and streaked past us like lightning, fleeing as if they'd seen ghosts. It happened so suddenly and so close to us that I initially mistook them for a

herd of eland — they looked so huge from close up and have almost the same colouring as eland. And the ground seemed to reverberate as they fled, sounding more like eland hooves striking the earth than lion paws.

I had once again forgotten how big lions really are. They were some distance away before I realised that they were in fact lions, and by then it was luckily too late for me to register the full impact of the shock that always strikes me when we encounter lions. My idiotic family ran after the lions, following their spoor through the mopani scrub, in the hope of getting another look at them. I lagged behind, commanding one of our dogs to stay close to me.

I don't usually lag behind when my family behaves outrageously. I run after them, propelled by maternal instinct to keep a protective eye on my children. But on this particular day I was limping because of a torn ankle ligament — the result of a fall I'd had some weeks previously while climbing a koppie with my family. It's difficult to be a good mother when you have a limp.

The dog obediently stayed close to me. But being a conscientious dog who takes his responsibilities very seriously, he stopped at every clump of grass, sniffing each and every blade from the root upwards to assure himself that it wasn't concealing a lion. It seemed he had even more difficulty than I in remembering the actual size of a lion.

My family didn't find the lions again, and I found them waiting for me on a rise overlooking a plain on which a herd of elephant grazed. We settled ourselves comfortably to enjoy the magic hour of sunset. The savannah below us looked like a painting in soft autumn colours — a perfect backdrop for the dark shapes of the elephants. Their tusks glinted as the last rays of sunlight played on the ivory. We counted forty adult females and eighteen calves of whom four were infants. We might have missed a couple of infants, though, because baby elephants walk underneath their mothers' bellies between their legs most of the time and are not easy to spot.

The herd grazed quietly, and if they made any sounds at all, they would have been the low rumbling noises periodically emitted by the adult females in a herd to keep contact and communicate their positions to one another. But we were too far from them to pick this up.

The sky above the western horizon changed from carmine to magenta, and long shadows started to creep across the savannah. The vast silence of the landscape was interrupted occasionally by the plaintive piping of a plover and the off-key screeching of a francolin and, later, by the noisy swearing of a distant troop of quarrelsome baboons heading for the safety of their trees.

When the dusk began to settle too heavily on my shoulders and down my spine, I suggested to my family that we follow the example of the baboons and head for the safety of our camp. In Africa, twilight lingers, but when darkness finally comes it doesn't fall — it plummets. And you'd better be safely home before that happens or you might stumble over a lion or bumble into an elephant... or something.

We reached our camp just in time to avoid the plummeting of the black-out. But while we were preparing our supper at the fire, the full moon rose over the bush, bathing the trees and the veld in a bluish glow. The sweet, melodic call of a pearl-spotted owl started the evening serenade and was soon accompanied by the purring trill of a scop's owl. From somewhere, the haunting howls of a lone hyena soared out into the night and drifted across the landscape in rising and falling echoes. And then some lions started grunting and roaring to the west of our camp. Soon afterwards, another pride — probably the one we had come across earlier — started up to the east of us. This soon became a competition, with each pride endeavouring to outroar the other.

I was reminded of a dreadful incident that had once happened to Hugo van Niekerk, one of our Kruger Park pilots. He had to camp out in the bush one night with a group of visiting scientists and ecologists. Now, Hugo is a bush person who needs some solitude and personal space when resting, so he had pitched his tent some distance away from the other campers. As soon as he'd gone to bed, the local lion population commenced a roaring competition close by. It gradually gained in volume until it resembled an ongoing earthquake. Lying on his camp bed inside his tent, Hugo wished that the lions would shut up and go away so that he could get some sleep.

But, instead, the two contesting prides declared war and charged at each other, quite ignoring the fact that Hugo's tent occupied the space between them — the collision site, as it were. The cats let fly, attacking tooth and nail, raising vocal hell, and in the process breaking the guy ropes and more or less taking Hugo's tent with them. Hugo, wanting no part in the dispute, hastily abandoned his demolished quarters, leaving the frenzied animals to sort out their problems on their own. Luckily, the lions were too absorbed in their territorial quarrel to pay any attention to Hugo, and he escaped unharmed.

I tried not to think of Hugo's story while we enjoyed our supper around the camp-fire. The roaring competition was still raging, but I derived some comfort from the fact that the vocal exchange appeared to have an andante sort of quality about it. Perhaps the lions were only trading ideas and not actually threatening one another. They didn't let up, though, and we went to bed that night with the thundering stereophonic rumble in our ears.

Nowadays we have two tents, but back then we had only one. Kobus and I slept in the tent while the girls slept in the pick-up truck: Karin inside the cab and the two older girls in the back. Kobus had spread and tied a heavy tarpaulin across the rails over the open back so that they would be safe. But Hettie and Sandra decided that the tarpaulin would spoil the effect of the moonlight on the veld and folded it back at the rear of the pick-up so that they could enjoy the view (in their sleep!).

I hastily placed our wash-up basin on its three-legged stand right against the rear of the truck, comforting myself with the thought that any lion who intended to jump into the back of the truck would first walk into the wash-basin and stand, knock it over, and create enough noise to waken us.

Of course, we also slept with the flaps of our tent open. At least Kobus's rifle stood right next to his bed, and the dogs slept right outside. The continuing stereophonic roaring soon became too much for one of the dogs and he decided to go and sleep underneath the truck.

The lions continued their roaring all night, sometimes very close, sometimes further away.

Some time between three and four in the morning, the space in the back of the truck became too narrow for the two older girls, and a prolonged argument ensued. When Hettie complained for the umpteenth time that Sandra's knee and elbow were in her way, Sandra decided that she'd had enough. Grabbing her camping mattress and sleeping bag, she clambered out of the truck and went and made her bed on the ground next to the camp-fire — which by this time had died down to a few glowing embers. I called out to her and invited her to share the tent, but she declined.

The lions started up again.

Kobus repeated my invitation to Sandra, but she wasn't interested. When Sandra is upset with the world — or with her older sister — she needs to cool off on her own. (Perhaps, in defence of her obstinate nature, I should mention that she has fiery red hair.)

I was too tense to go back to sleep. The lions sounded too close to the camp for comfort. I called out to Sandra again, insisting that she come and sleep in the tent. But she answered that the dog had joined her by the fire and that she was perfectly safe.

Soon afterwards, a lion suddenly roared so close to us that we could hear the intake of his breath just before he sounded off. I flew out of my bed, but then saw that Kobus was already up and donning some warm clothes. He took his rifle and told me not to worry. He was going to sit by the fire and watch over Sandra.

I could finally relax and go back to sleep.

There was just over an hour to go before sunrise. Kobus stoked the fire, put the kettle on, and made himself some coffee. The lion roared on for a while, but Sandra slept peacefully through it all.

Shortly after sunrise, Kobus came into the tent and woke me with a cup of coffee. While we sat sipping our coffee, he told me that the dog had had a good night's rest next to Sandra. In his contentment, he had gradually encroached on to her mattress — first his head, then his paws, and finally the rest of his body had sidled on to her mattress. Sandra had meekly rolled over each time he'd nudged her, and had ended up sleeping on the hard ground next to the fire.

It crossed my mind that Sandra didn't really mind giving up her sleeping place, as long as it was to the dog and not to her sister. But that thought didn't really bother me. I know sisters. They may find it impossible to get along sometimes, but when it comes to the crunch they are the most loyal of friends. What *did* bother me was the realisation that a mammoth task awaited me: I would somehow have to get it into my red-haired daughter's head that lions are terribly dangerous in the night.

As much as I worry about my children's reluctance to share my fears of the bush, I sometimes find myself admiring their spunk.

One day recently, when Kobus was away from home, the girls noticed a large herd of buffalo crossing the dry bed of the Little Letaba and heading for the boundary fence. There were numerous calves amongst the herd. Hettie and Sandra saddled their horses, called the dogs, and set out after the buffalo. They drove them back across the river and herded them deep into the mopani bush to the north. (I should probably explain here that herding wild buffalo is — surprisingly — almost as easy as herding domestic cattle.) I stood watching the cloud of billowing red dust followed by two young girls on horseback, and I marvelled at the boldness of my bush-wise children. I knew that they weren't doing this out of bravado or a sense of adventure, but because of their love of wild animals. Only a few days previously, two of our elephants had been shot by hunters in Gazankulu. The girls hate the sound of gunshot coming from Gazankulu and they wanted the buffalo and their calves to be safe from the guns of hunters.

Perhaps I have given the impression that my daughters are totally fearless. They aren't. In the world outside the Park, their self-confidence can vanish very quickly.

My parents live in Johannesburg, and whenever we plan a trip to visit them the girls become very excited at the prospect of shopping in the luxurious centres of the city.

Grandma and Grandpa generously provide pocket-money as soon as we arrive, and the girls start compiling their shopping lists with excited anticipation.

It's the shopping itself that isn't so easy.

At first, the girls are overwhelmed by the abundance of new and wonderful things on display. But as the minutes pass, a subdued kind of anxiety seems to settle on them, and within less than an hour they complain of headaches and tummy-aches.

I recognise stress symptoms when I hear them.

Considering that their senses have been trained to register every sound and movement in their surroundings, and that they are tuned to react in some way or other to every signal received, I guess you can't blame them for being confused and intimidated by the constant noise and movement of city life.

The Game Rangers

V isitors to the Kruger Park are inclined to believe that anyone wearing the familiar khaki uniform with the green shoulder flashes is a game ranger.

Most of the people in uniform, however, are tourism officials, administrative staff and technical staff. Others in uniform are research staff, the veterinarians, the helicopter pilots, and the trail rangers who conduct walking tours in certain areas.

There are in fact only twenty-two game rangers, and a chief ranger who is based in Skukuza. Each game ranger is responsible for his own section of the Park, and the sections vary in size from six hundred to one thousand square kilometres.

The game rangers also wear the khaki uniform and green epaulettes, but if you look closer you will see a little gold-plated badge pinned to his shirt which reads: *Game Ranger*. That is, if you ever get the chance to look that closely at a game ranger. They are a rare species and are seldom seen, preferring the quiet solitude of the wilderness to the company of human beings. It's not that they are necessarily people-shy — it's because they love their work and are by nature solitary people.

Their daily and intimate involvement with the ways of the wilderness shapes them into a breed apart. They acquire a sixth sense which enables them to tune in to the mysterious frequencies of nature that transmit information about the whereabouts and state of mind of all wild creatures.

Or so I suspect.

A game ranger will look at a landscape, for instance, and remark: 'There were lion here.' Ask him how he knows that and he can't tell you because, apparently, no known vernacular provides the words to explain how such knowledge is obtained. Afterwards, you might find some fresh lion spoor that will verify his statement. But you will remember that he had made the remark prior to your finding the spoor. So it wasn't the spoor; it was something else that transmitted the information to him, something intangible — in the air, or in the ambience, or in the quietude of the landscape.

Once, while walking along the shore of the Letaba River in the company of a party consisting of Kobus, Ben (also a game ranger), his wife, and two visiting ecologists with their wives, the following happened.

Kobus and Ben, for no apparent reason, suddenly stopped abruptly and held up their hands for silence. We all shut up immediately and stood like statues, straining our senses for some clue of lurking danger. Kobus and Ben stood quietly for a while, their eyes following a hippo spoor in the sand (which looked no more suspicious to me than any of the other hippo spoors along the shore).

And then, as if guided by some secret signal, Kobus and Ben turned simultaneously to face a thicket of high reeds some ten metres to the left of us. We all turned to stare at the clump of reeds which suddenly looked dreadfully ominous — for no reason other than that Kobus and Ben were staring at it with such attentive expressions. As adrenalin sharpened my senses, I became aware that a cloud of flies and insects were circling a spot just above the reeds, and I realised that if there was a hippo in there, we were in trouble because we were right between the clump of reeds and the water. (Some years before, the wife of one of our game guards had been attacked and killed by a hippo bull which had been hiding in a clump of reeds near the water. She had been cutting reeds to make a mat when the tragedy occurred.)

Kobus and Ben signalled that we should turn quietly away and start backtracking. We had just started doing this, Kobus and Ben bringing up the rear, when I heard the metallic clicks of safety catches being released from rifles. Instinctively, I turned, and as I did so the reeds exploded and a bull hippo streaked across the sand like a runaway steamroller. Luckily, he wasn't in an

exterminating mood, and Ben and Kobus relaxed their aims as the hippo charged right past us into the water.

For a while nobody spoke, and then one of the ecologists' wives asked in a shaky voice: 'But how did you know he was there?'

Ben answered vaguely that something about the spoor and the reeds had bothered him, and Kobus nodded in equally vague agreement. Naturally, the lady looked confused, so I explained to her about the insects that had been circling the spot above the reeds where the hippo had been hiding. Hippo bulls often have festering sores as a result of their frequent territorial fighting, and while the wounds are healing they attract insects.

But I didn't remind her that Kobus and Ben had sensed the presence of the hippo even before they'd turned to stare at the reeds, because I really didn't know what clue it was that I'd missed about the spoor. I know, for example, that when a spoor is very fresh — only a few seconds old in fact — minuscule sand-slides can be seen along the edges of the imprints. But the sand, both inside and along the imprints had looked stable to me, so I don't know how the spoor could have alerted them to the presence of the hippo.

I guess they had been listening to those mysterious transmissions of nature again.

Another distinctive characteristic of game rangers is their impressive reflexes. They can dive out of the way of a charging buffalo bull with a speed that baffles even the buffalo. He will charge right past them and then slam on his brakes and stand still, wondering where everybody went. Although close encounters with fangs, claws and tusks feature in every game ranger's career, only a very few of them have ever had to use a firearm in self-defence — a testimony to their remarkable ability to get out of the way in time.

Another trait shared by game rangers is that they are generally non-materialistic people. Their khaki uniforms are about the only clothes they possess, and they seem quite happy about this state of affairs. They have a predilection for good, strong boots that will survive a lot of mileage but, apart from their boots and rifles, they have few other personal possessions. They are, however, sentimental collectors of bush debris and will jealously guard these personal valuables: pebbles, rocks, dead tree stumps, feathers, bones, horns, the odd lion tooth, or the skull of some long deceased animal.

One day, Kobus brought home a large dead tree stump which had apparently served as a rhino rubbing post for many years as the wood had been rubbed to a glossy sheen. Every game ranger who has visited here since has fallen madly in love with the stump and has tried to persuade Kobus to trade it for one or other of their personal valuables, but to no avail. That is, to no avail until the day ranger Tom Yssel dropped by. He took one look at the stump and knew he had to have it, no matter what the price. Intense and prolonged negotiations ensued. Finally, Tom offered a prized pair of boots which a friend had brought him all the way from the United States. And with that, a rhino rubbing post was exchanged for a pair of Yankee boots.

Ranger Paul Zway used to have a bantam cock which he claimed was of royal ancestry. (I'm not sure which royal family.) It had heavily feathered legs, tawny plumage, a cape of feathers around its neck and face, and a long upright crest. It looked as though it could have been a cross between an Egyptian vulture and a tawny eagle, although decidedly smaller in size, of course. Now Paul is a very tender-hearted and generous person, the type who will, in moments of passion, impulsively give away even the most treasured of his personal possessions. So, when one of Paul's best friends, the same Tom Yssel who had traded his boots for the rhino stump, finally got married after many years of lonely bachelorhood in the wilderness, Paul was so overwhelmed with happiness for his friend that he promptly gave away two of his most valued possessions. One was a strange-looking rock with a hole in it (which might or might not have had historical significance), and the other was his precious bantam cock. At their wedding, Tom received the enigmatic rock, and his wife Petro was presented with the bantam cock. Unfortunately, Petro's wedding present didn't last long as it soon got itself abducted by a martial eagle. Paul was crushed when he heard the news.

At the end of each year a function is held at Skukuza for all the game ranger families, and it is practically the only occasion that we get to dress up a little. The wives make their own pretty outfits for the occasion — nothing fancy or formal really, just something nice and different as a change from the somewhat drab, functional clothes that we normally wear in the bush.

The men, however, don't bother and would go in their khaki uniforms if their wives didn't remind them that the uniform is off-limits at a casual party where drinks may be enjoyed. So they wear whatever they have that doesn't date too far back into history. Now the dignified simplicity of their usually immaculate khaki uniforms suits them well, but in their casual, outdated party outfits they tend to look unassembled and displaced. If they are aware of this, it doesn't seem to bother them. Once you have attended a number of these functions, you will recognise each game ranger at a distance by the clothes he's wearing, because most of them will wear the same outfit year after year for a couple of decades.

But if this gives you the impression that game rangers are a bunch of backwoodsmen, you have it wrong. Surprisingly, they are essentially artistic-minded people: lovers of literature, music, art, and — of course — nature. A number of them are themselves gifted painters, sketchers or sculptors, and I know one who plays the violin.

Although the game rangers share a number of common traits, they are also individualists and I would do them an injustice if I continued to describe them in collective terms. So, I would rather tell you something about the work they do.

Actually, a game ranger's work consists of such a bewildering variety of duties and responsibilities that volumes could be written about it. But luckily, when all is said and done, it boils down to an easily defined mandate which consists of two parts:

(1) the game ranger must protect the conservation area from the destructive activities of man; and

(2) he must, to some extent, intervene in the ways of the wild in order to conserve it.

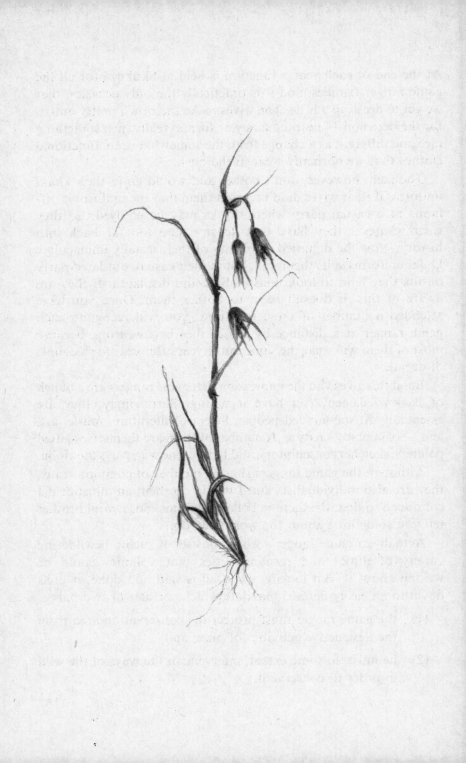

Now I know the second part of the mandate sounds wrong, because a conservation area is supposed to be a pristine area where nature is given some breathing space in which to run her own course, unhindered by human intervention. But the trouble with this premise is that nature needs a lot of space in which to run her course. And since we have already over-populated the planet, we just can't give her all that necessary space any more.

So we put tiny patches of the planet aside, proclaim them wilderness areas, and hand them over to mother nature. But even as we put these patches aside, we intervene by closing them off with unnatural borders and by dragging a certain amount of infrastructure into them in order to supply amenities which will make the patch of paradise accessible to man. And so disruption and intervention occur even though we didn't mean them to, and then we are surprised to find that nature is unable to solve her problems in her own way.

The first thing that goes wrong is that the game, now protected from man's destructive activities, starts increasing in numbers — which would be something to rejoice over if it weren't for the fact that they must eat. The pastures become overstocked and are eventually depleted by overgrazing. And the grazers can't migrate to new pastures because the conservation area is closed in. Bush fires, which are natural ecological phenomena, become hazards, not only because the human visitors must be protected, but also because the animals cannot escape the boundaries of the conservation area. If they don't perish in the fire, they might face starvation if the fires cause long-term damage to their pastures. Protracted droughts and disease outbreaks become catastrophes for the same reason — the animals cannot migrate. And since nature is not allowed to run her course, she is unable to solve her problems, and man is called upon to intervene.

Although the Kruger National Park is one of the largest conservation areas in the world — 19 485 square kilometres in extent (which is larger than the state of Israel) — it is situated in a region where any advantage due to sheer size is lost. The Park covers a narrow stretch of the eastern Transvaal lowveld, on average some sixty kilometres wide (east to west) and approximately four hundred kilometres from north to south. The northern and southern boundaries are rivers and thus are natural boundaries, but both the eastern and western boundaries are man-made. Furthermore, there are five major river systems that run through the Park from west to east, dividing the Park into individual ecological units that can exist independently of each other, but cannot support the needs of their natural inhabitants without putting undue strain on their resources. So, even in a conservation area as large as the Kruger Park, nature cannot find her own balance, and intelligent management of the natural resources is required to preserve the ecological balance.

But enclosing nature for her own protection raises a troublesome question. What do we hope to protect and preserve? In other words, what exactly is nature?

Every ecosystem is a complex, dynamic network made up of a vast array of interdependent organisms and physical factors. If one element shifts even slightly, the whole system can change. But contrary to the outworn metaphors which insist that nature should be left untouched — in other words, should not be changed — change happens anyway and has been happening from the beginning of time. What was natural three billion years ago — an empire of anaerobic bacteria — would strike most of us as decidedly unnatural today.

There is no 'original' state in nature, no steady-state nature in the sense that a fixed set of characteristics holds true, like that of the law of gravity, always and everywhere. Nature resembles less of a law and more of a story. And the story is not over.

So the question is: If there is no original state, how can we judge what should be conserved and restored? The answer, it seems, is that intelligent man may decide for himself what he wishes to conserve or restore.

In the Kruger Park, the aim is to conserve its diversity of life in optimum conditions without harming any of the vulnerable components.

This is where the scientists and the policy-shapers come in, to research, evaluate and formulate. Then the game rangers step in as the implementers of the policies — the frontline troops of conservation, and often co-researchers and policy-shapers themselves as a result of their intimate involvement with the conservation area and their continuous observation of the results of their work.

If nature had been left to run her course in the Kruger Park after its final boundaries were proclaimed in 1926, the Kruger Park today would be a barren wasteland (as happened in Tsavo National Park in Kenya in the late 1970s) because nature, unlike man, is not an intelligent being that can think, plan or act consciously. Nor is she a divine spirit with a masterplan for the protection of her creatures. Nature really doesn't care what happens to her creatures, because actually, you see, she doesn't exist. Nature is merely a term invented by man. And what happens to nature's creatures is an ongoing story that is not preordained by laws of nature, but by time, circumstance and contingency.

The survival-of-the-fittest theory is not a blueprint of nature devised to cull the sick, the lame and the lazy in order to make place for the strong and the healthy. It's a theory of circumstance, and should actually be called the survival-of-the-fittest-in-the-particular-circumstance theory. When a natural catastrophe occurs, those who survive it survive by chance — because they happen to carry the genes of whatever trait stands the best chance of surviving the particular catastrophe.

Nature herself doesn't care who survives and who doesn't.

For many centuries man didn't care either, until finally it dawned upon him that the activities of his own species were driving many other species into extinction. For some time it seemed impossible to stop the destruction, for even as conservation areas were being established man's ideas of conservation proved wanting and in many instances led to disaster. But dedicated conservationists persisted in their endeavours to save something of what was left of the natural wilderness of the planet, and in so doing finally came to realise that successful conservation policies would require scientific management of natural resources and would, to some extent, depend on man's abilities to intervene in nature.

We cannot make rain (yet). But we can drill holes into the earth and supply water. We may not be able to shift the boundaries of a conservation area when the pastures become depleted, but we can prevent the depletion through scientifically developed management techniques. We cannot always prevent fires, but we can fight them. We cannot prohibit diseases, but we can inhibit their progress.

And this is more or less what the game rangers do.

The most important facet of their work is the preservation of the vegetation, for without that there would be no herbivores to conserve, and without the herbivores there would be no carnivores.

In Africa, fire and water are the paramount factors in the conservation of pastures.

Fire, caused by lightning, is a natural ecological phenomenon which serves to promote new and nourishing growth of grass and discourage scrub encroachment. But in an enclosed conservation area like the Kruger National Park, a single blaze in unfavourable conditions can deprive the herbivore population of most of its food. Fires that occur in unfavourable conditions (such as when the air is hot and dry, and when a strong wind is blowing) are mainly accidental or man-made fires caused by poachers, refugees passing through the Park from Mozambique and, sometimes, careless tourists.

A wide network of firebreak roads is maintained by the game rangers in order to combat fires. While the roads in themselves are not likely to stop the advance of a large fire, they form comparatively safe lanes for back-burning (burning against the wind towards the advancing fire in order to obstruct its progress).

Since fire is necessary for the maintenance of the ecology, a sophisticated programme of controlled, rotational burning has been developed to simulate natural conditions. Controlled burning has two distinct advantages over haphazard fires: the first is that it can be done under selected conditions in order to maintain low fire temperatures, and the second is that maximum protection can be given to all levels of plant and animal life.

Water availability — the other paramount factor in pasture conservation — determines to a large extent the carrying capacity of a conservation area. Animal populations utilise only the pastures within the immediate vicinity of available water. In southern Africa, during the long dry months of winter, available water sources are often reduced to the perennial rivers. By supplementing the natural water sources with artificial ones overcrowding of the natural sources is prevented, thus preserving the surrounding bush which would otherwise be stripped bare and eroded by thousands of hooves.

The constant monitoring of pasture conditions and of water availability takes up most of a game ranger's time. Other duties related to pasture management include regular game counts and, when necessary, translocation of animals to other conservation areas. Disease control, assistance to the research department, anti-poaching patrols, and law enforcement also fall amongst the game ranger's duties.

And there are many others. Game rangers are on call twenty-four hours a day, and nature doesn't give her wardens much time off duty.

They patrol the far reaches of their sections, often on foot in the blazing African sun to track a sick or wounded animal, or to free it from a poacher's snare, sometimes at the risk of their own lives. They spend long nights hiding without shelter in the inhospitable Lebombo mountains, waiting for the armed poachers from Mozambique who hunt our elephants and rhino for their ivory. They fight raging bush fires driven by strong and unpredictable winds. They work in torrential downpours when rivers and watercourses are in flood and they are cut off from their homes. And in times of serious drought, they battle for long hours to rescue animals from mudholes and dried-up pans where they have been trapped in their desperate search for water.

Close encounters with death are part of their daily lives, and many of them bear the scars of such encounters.

Yet, if one should ask a game ranger if what he's doing is really worth all the trouble he would probably, like Jeremiah Johnson, ponder the question for a while and then ask: 'What trouble?'

The Park also has an elite corps of game guards who are used primarily in an anti-poaching role. This corps consists mainly of

Shangaan men who, being native to the eastern lowveld, have the necessary bush knowledge to make them supreme trackers.

They are posted throughout the Park in the twenty-two game ranger sections where they live in staff villages near the ranger's residence. They are brave and loyal men who have, throughout the years, played a major role in the apprehension of poachers. When required, they also assist with some of the other duties of the section ranger, such as fire-fighting and the tracking of sick or injured animals. These Shangaan men have a particular grace and dignity about them and they walk tall and proud in their immaculate khaki uniforms. Some of them have been wounded in confrontations with armed poachers, and others have been injured in attacks by wild animals. But, like the game rangers, they are men who will never hesitate to perform their duty, no matter how harsh or dangerous the circumstances may be.

If one considers the energy, the expertise, the dangers and the hardships involved in the conservation of this vast stretch of wilderness, it seems that some credit is due to the people behind the scenes — and especially to those frontline troops of conservation: the game rangers and the game guards.

I salute them.

For some of the ideas expressed in this chapter, I am indebted to Edwin Dobb's review of *Discordant Harmonies* by Daniel B. Botkin in *The Sciences*, January/February 1992.

The Wives

Keeping house in the wilderness is a job that requires ingenuity and perseverance. I'm not too good at it. But the other game rangers' wives are.

They create gardens that look like settings for fairy-tales, and they carve, weave, quilt and sew, and decorate their homes with exquisite things. They make preserves, jams and jellies out of every kind of edible wild fruit and stock their pantries with a wide range of home-produced goodies that deepen my inferiority complex.

I also garden, bake and sew, of course, but only in a mediocre way and only because I have to. Considering the amount of trouble involved in getting to town, it seems easier to produce one's own food and clothes — except for the fact that I remain permanently behind schedule, no matter how hard I work. When I go out into the bush to collect wild fruit and berries to preserve, I discover that summer has already gone and that the trees are bare. My Christmas cake is never on time, and I can hardly keep up with making clothes for the children, let alone for myself. I often get anxiety attacks when I stand in front of my empty wardrobe, wondering what to wear.

Another task that requires stamina is the conservation of domestic food resources. I spend a lot of time and energy, for instance, screaming at the baboons and monkeys who raid my vegetable garden, and I have to keep a constant and watchful eye on my bantam chickens lest they get eaten by eagles, wild cats, civets or pythons. Since the bantams lay their eggs all over the garden, I also have to spend a fair amount of time egg-hunting.

And if I don't find the eggs in good time, they will be stolen by other egg-hunters such as genets, mongooses and servals.

Game rangers' wives also have to cope with solving problems on their own when their husbands are away. These include not only household problems (whimsical generators, snakes in the house, and so on), but also problems in the staff village (injuries, sickness, personal differences), as well as problems on the sections (bush fires, floods, refugees from Mozambique).

It's not easy to find the time for luxuries such as relaxation and boredom.

Although we, the wives, adjust well to solitude, that doesn't mean that we are dedicated hermits. We love to get together and always look forward to occasions when we can do so. Since these occasions are few and far between, we have devised our own personal infrastructure by means of which we stay in touch. This system is made up of our VHF radio transceivers as well as an institution referred to as 'the transport'.

'The transport', in short, is any official vehicle that is headed in your direction. But I'll explain this system in more detail later on.

Each ranger's house is equipped with a VHF radio transceiver. In fact, each ranger has three VHF transceivers: one in the house, one in his office, and one in his official vehicle.

The offices of the departments of tourism and maintenance services in the Park are also equipped with VHF transceivers, and since all of the people in these departments are also dependent on the radios for mutual contact, they may be used only for official business or urgent calls. But after one has lived here for a while, one acquires the ability to make an unofficial call sound official.

If, for example, your neighbour sends you a gift (such as a jar of marula preserve or some other home-made delicacy) by means of 'the transport' and you want to thank her, you call her on the radio. When she answers, you say, 'The parcel has arrived safely. Thank you very much.' No one is to know what the parcel contained. It could have been something urgent or official. Your neighbour may answer with something like, 'Glad to know. Have you had rain?' This doesn't mean that she is particularly interested in the weather, but rather that she is glad to hear your voice and wants to talk some more.

Now the weather does in fact play a major part in our lives here, and is therefore always regarded as official business. After giving her an extended weather report, you will of course enquire about the weather conditions in her area. When the weather has been exhausted as a topic, you will have to end the conversation, unless you can think of some other urgent or official-sounding topic. There are quite a number of these: sickness in the family (especially malaria), recent or current bush fires, the condition of the veld and the animals in the area, the water levels in rivers and dams, and the health of your dogs. (Game rangers' dogs have official status in the Park.)

Because our radios have to be left on day and night, we hear everyone's communications — which is nice because it enables us to stay in touch with what is happening in the Park. We know when a neighbour is ill with malaria, or has been bitten by a snake, or attacked by a wild animal, or when someone's dog was taken by a leopard. We hear when someone's vehicle got stuck in a swollen river, or when someone's garden was destroyed by elephants, and so on. One can even crack a joke on the air, as long as it sounds official.

When a ranger is away from home for a number of days, he is allowed to radio home to find out if all is well. The few words you exchange are really special, especially when you are missing each other. But because you know that your conversation is on an open channel for all to hear, you stick to generalities and try to keep your all too brief chat as formal as possible. The main thing, of course, is to hear each other's voice.

Often, when I hear a game ranger calling home in the evening to talk to his wife, I listen to their conversation with a lump in my throat — because I can picture the scene and imagine their feelings. Somewhere in the vast wilderness where he has to spend the night, he is about to build his camp-fire when something in the ambience — perhaps a beautiful sunset or the start of the evening bush serenade — strikes a chord of nostalgia and he misses his wife. So he calls home.

When she hears his voice calling her station number on the radio, she rushes to pick up the microphone. She has been thinking of him, wondering where he is, worrying about his well-being and safety — and wishing he would call.

So they talk, but not of the things they long to talk about. They stick to the formal code for radio conversation: Is all well? Are you OK? How is the work going? I think we may expect some rain soon. It was very hot today, wasn't it? Keep well. I'll call again. Take good care of yourself. Good night.

And as I hear their microphone buttons clicking out, I know that they are still standing there, with their microphones in their hands.

The transport system operates as follows.

Every week a large truck travels the length of the Park, stopping off at each tourist camp to deliver supplies to the shops and restaurants. The truck also brings the mail from Skukuza and drops it off at the various tourist camps.

Whenever we wish to send one another notes or parcels, we give them to the truck driver who then distributes them for us.

Many of us don't live within easy reach of a tourist camp though, and we don't get our mail very regularly. It depends of course on how often we, or our husbands, can manage to travel to the nearest camp. Fortunately, there are various staff members who do a fair amount of travelling in the Park and who visit us from time to time — such as the veterinary staff, the researchers and the maintenance staff (who do repairs to our radio transceivers and electric generators). As they travel through the Park, they stop at the tourist camps, pick up any mail that is waiting to be collected and bring it with them. In so doing, they become part of the system which we call 'the transport'.

I first learnt of the transport system from a neighbour, Sannie Espag.

When we arrived here in 1980, Ampie and Sannie Espag were stationed at Mooiplaas — a ranger station some fifty kilometres to the east of us. Ampie and Sannie had been in the Park for almost thirty years then and had been stationed at various game ranger posts throughout the Park before they came to live at

Mooiplaas. The house on the Mooiplaas section stands on a high koppie to the west of the tourist road which links Letaba and Shingwedzi. From the house and garden one has a magnificent view of the surrounding mopani plains.

Some weeks after we had moved in at Mahlangeni, Ampie and Sannie came to pay us a neighbourly visit. It was during this visit — while Sannie was telling me a story about trifle dessert — that I learnt of the transport system.

I would like to share her story with you.

One day, soon after they had moved in at Mooiplaas, Sannie discovered that the restaurant in the Letaba tourist camp serves the best trifle in the world. Ever since that day she has managed to persuade Ampie to take her to Letaba for dinner at least once a month. They dress up and travel the fifty-odd kilometres south to enjoy a 'night out'. After dinner, Sannie always asks for a second helping of the trifle which she then takes home with her.

Early the next morning, just before sunrise, Sannie carries her bowl of trifle outside and sits down in her garden to watch the sun rise over the plains below — and to enjoy her dessert. And, according to her, sitting there high above the rising sun and the surrounding plains while eating her trifle is almost like being in heaven.

Being a conscientious person, Sannie always takes care that the pudding bowl is returned to the Letaba camp. On the day that the delivery truck is due to pass on its return journey from the north, she takes the bowl and her rifle, walks down to the tourist road — about two kilometres from the house — and waits for 'the transport'. As soon as she hears the truck approaching, she steps into the road to flag down the driver and hand him the pudding bowl. And so the bowl always gets returned to Letaba by means of 'the transport'.

The annual gathering of game ranger families at Skukuza is always a very special event. It lasts two or three days, starting with the annual nature conservation conference which our husbands attend, and ending with our traditional family party on the last evening of the conference.

Although the party is the social highlight of the year, the preceding days are, in their own way, special to the wives.

While our husbands attend their conference and our children play with their friends, you will find us gathered in a quiet corner of the camp under shady trees, drinking tea and sharing our news. And should you listen awhile to our conversations, you will hear that we are women of the wilderness, for we talk of the hardships, the adventures, the troubles and the joys of our unique and eventful lives.

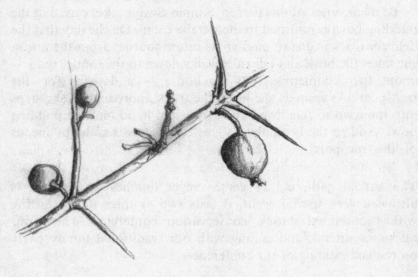

Mahlangeni's Shangaan Folk

Mahlangeni's field staff live in a little village to the north-east of our house on the bank of the Shibyeni creek. They are members of the Tsonga-Shangana tribe, they speak a language called Tsonga, and call themselves Shangaan people.

Most of the Shangaan people do not speak either English or Afrikaans, so we had to learn Tsonga in order to communicate with them.

Seven of the field staff are game guards, while six others are maintenance workers whose responsibilities include assisting with repairs to windmills and boundary fences, and the maintenance of patrol roads and firebreaks. They also assist with fire fighting.

Some of the men have their wives and families living here with them, but most of them have two or more wives and choose to have their families live in Gazankulu where they tend their farms and other family businesses. The families often come here to visit, and the men go home to Gazankulu at weekends and during their holidays.

Every year at Christmas, a party is arranged for the field staff in the village. Traditionally, the game ranger shoots a buffalo for them for the occasion, and lots of jabula (African beer) is ordered from Skukuza. The families in Gazankulu are invited to join in the festivities and they usually arrive some days before the party to help with the preparations. The women look striking in their traditional outfits (lengths of colourful cloth knotted over one shoulder) and the children come adorned in beads and trinkets.

To hear them singing at night to the accompaniment of their tribal drums is something special, especially when it is echoed by the wail of hyenas and jackals or the roar of lions. It's the music of Africa.

Because the Mahlangeni section is so large, the field staff is often away for days on end, camping in tents in the bush wherever they may be working. When Kobus is also away from home, he always arranges that one or two of the game guards remain at base to keep an eye on the homestead. They are brave, loyal people who have often and unhesitatingly helped me out when things have gone awry.

Since these men spend much of their time in the bush, they inevitably have their fair share of hair-raising encounters with wild animals.

Game guard Makasani Maluleke, for instance, recently landed under an elephant's belly.

Late one Sunday afternoon, after attending a jabula party in Gazankulu, Makasani was cycling back home to Mahlangeni in a happy, if somewhat too relaxed mood. After having crested a steep rise, Makasani was cruising downhill at a fair speed when he saw — rather too late — an elephant standing at the bottom of the slope, right in the middle of the road. Luckily, the elephant had its back to the oncoming bicycle and was either asleep or deep in thought. Makasani braked hard but the bicycle skidded, overbalanced, and ended up — together with Makasani — right underneath the elephant's belly.

Startled by the sudden noisy intrusion, the elephant screamed 'WHAZAT?' and swung around. Seeing nothing untoward, it realised that something must be amiss in the landscape down under, and it stuck its trunk under its belly to investigate. Makasani wasn't about to waste any time: crawling on all fours, he made a swift exit between the elephant's hind legs, took off, and sprinted up the hill — naturally in record time. He looked back only when he got to the top of the rise. The elephant had discovered the bicycle under its belly, had pulled it out and lifted it with its trunk. Holding it at eye-level, it was examining the bicycle with a puzzled expression. After a long, hard look, the elephant put the bicycle down and, according to Makasani, walked off into the bush shaking its head.

Game guard Samuel Nkuna once had a dramatic encounter with a leopard. He and his companions were tracking an injured waterbuck along the southern bank of the river, not far from the house. At one stage, Samuel wandered off some distance from the others to investigate something that had caught his attention in the undergrowth at the foot of a large mkuhlu tree. He was about twenty metres from the tree when a leopard burst out of the undergrowth and charged him in a blur of speed. Samuel told us that he had no time to cock and raise his rifle because 'in only two minutes' the leopard was on him. (Perhaps he remembers the incident in slow motion.) The leopard knocked him down and bit him in the shoulder before taking off into the bush. The other game guards rushed to Samuel's aid and helped him home.

We cleaned and disinfected the wound in his shoulder as well as some claw marks on his chest. Samuel didn't want to go to hospital, reasoning that Kobus and I had done a good enough job of doctoring his wounds, but Kobus explained to him that it's bad for a person's health to be bitten by a leopard because its teeth aren't very clean.

The truth, of course, is that septicaemia caused by carnivore bites can be fatal if not treated effectively. And so Kobus drove Samuel to the hospital at Phalaborwa for treatment. Luckily, the injuries weren't extensive and Samuel was discharged a few days later.

Million Mabunda, one of the maintenance workers, once had a terrible experience with an elephant cow.

Million and some other workers had gone to repair a stretch of boundary fence between the Park and Gazankulu. In the late afternoon, after they had finished their work and were cycling home, Million fell somewhat behind and was pedalling casually along at his own pace. Dusk had already settled and visibility wasn't too good, but apparently Million was in no hurry — until he suddenly found himself in the middle of an elephant herd. Braking furiously, he accidentally skidded right into a large cow and her calf. There is no elephant mother in the world who will tolerate such inconsiderate behaviour towards her calf. The cow wrapped her trunk around Million, plucked him from his bicycle, and tossed him high into the air. Million landed many metres away in a thicket of mopani scrub. Then the furious cow tackled the bicycle, literally tearing it apart and then stamping the pieces into the ground.

Million didn't wait around to find out what the cow was planning to do next. He crawled through the mopani scrub in the opposite direction as fast as he could until he reached a clearing, and then he leapt to his feet and took off — probably breaking several Olympic records in the process. Luckily, the incident occurred only some four hundred metres from the staff village. The elephant didn't follow him and he made it safely back home. When he got there, he was slightly hysterical and couldn't remember what had happened.

One of the Shangaan women came to the house to call me (Kobus wasn't at home). The woman couldn't tell me what had happened to Million except that, whatever it was, it must have been something really terrible. I grabbed the first-aid kit and ran to the staff village.

Million was sitting up, and although he appeared to be in shock, he showed no signs of serious physical injury — apart from an impressive collection of scratches and bruises.

After giving him a glass of sugar water to drink, I asked him what had happened.

He wasn't sure, he said, but he suspected that a whirlwind had blown him off his bicycle. Since it had been a clear, windless day, I expressed my doubts about his explanation.

He thought it over and agreed that it couldn't have been a whirlwind. In fact, he said, it had just occurred to him that it had been a buffalo that had knocked him over. I voiced my concern and asked if the buffalo had hurt him. He shook his head, saying that he didn't know; his body was numb.

But then he suddenly remembered that it hadn't been a buffalo: it had been a lion. The lion, he explained, had jumped out of a tree and flattened him. Although I didn't think this likely, I once again expressed my concern, adding that he was fortunate that the lion had not injured him seriously.

He agreed. But after a few moments he decided the lion story wasn't the correct one either. Two rhinos, he told me, had burst out of the bush and slammed right into his bicycle, knocking him off it.

I gave Million a couple of pain pills, just in case, and decided to go home. By then it was dark, and too late to investigate the incident for myself.

I went back to see Million early the next morning. The poor man looked a wreck. He informed me that he was aching from head to toe and that his blood was shaking. (It is common among the Shangaan people to complain of 'shaking blood' when they are feeling unwell.) Fortunately, though, his memory had returned, and he told me about the elephant.

Taking two game guards with me, I walked to the 'scene of the crime'.

Judging from the disturbed ground and broken vegetation, as well as the spoor and the pieces of bicycle lying around, the elephant cow had thrown a spectacular tantrum. Some eight metres from the wrecked cycle we found the spot where Million had landed and flattened the mopani scrub. His crawl marks, the upturned ground where he had leapt to his feet, and the running spoor combined to tell a dramatic story.

I hurried home and radioed a message to Letaba camp, requesting an ambulance for Million. (The Park has its own official ambulances.) Within two hours, the ambulance had arrived and Million was on his way to the hospital.

After a thorough examination, it was established that he had no serious injuries. He spent a few days in hospital, however, being treated for shock.

Although his physical response to treatment was good, no effective therapy has yet been discovered that will cure a person of an acute aversion to elephants. Even now, after many months, Million cannot so much as look at a picture of an elephant. It seems probable that he will suffer from elephant-phobia for the rest of his life.

In consideration of his mental health, he is no longer required to work in the bush if he doesn't want to. He is now officially the gardener and general caretaker of the staff village.

The Whims of the Generator

O n the day that we moved in to Mahlangeni, I found a letter waiting for me in the kitchen. It was from my predecessor, Marcia Botha. (She and her husband Cobus had been transferred to Satara — a ranger station in the central district of the Park.) The letter explained the whims of the generator, and read as follows:

Dear Kobie

Before starting the generator in the mornings, make sure that the refrigerator and freezer are switched off, else their engines might blow. Ten seconds after the generator is running smoothly, you can switch on the freezer, and another ten seconds later, the refrigerator.

If you have an automatic washing machine, you will have to disconnect or remove its water heating elements. They will draw too much power and trip the generator.

Don't use an electric kettle, electric cooking pot, coffee percolator, or anything that boils water — they will also trip the generator.

If you want to use a vacuum cleaner, switch off the freezer first.

Before using an iron, switch off the freezer as well as the refrigerator. Don't let your iron get too hot. If you hear a change in the pitch of the generator's drone, switch off the iron.

If you want to use an electric toaster, don't do so while the iron, vacuum cleaner or washing machine are running. If you hear the generator straining, switch off the refrigerator and freezer immediately.

When using a hair-drier, observe the same rules as for the toaster.

A sewing machine doesn't use much power, but at night-time when your electric lights are switched on, take care not to have more than two other appliances running at the same time as your sewing machine.

On the other hand, the generator doesn't like to run when no power is being drawn. As you know, the engines of a refrigerator and a freezer run only periodically. (As soon as a certain temperature is reached, they automatically shut down for a period of time.) When it happens that the engines of both the fridge and the freezer are resting at the same time, and no other electric appliances in the house are in use, the generator overheats. So it's best to keep at least some of the lights in the house burning during the day to make sure power is being used.

Call me on the radio if you have troubles.

Good luck!

Your predecessor

Marcia

As you can see, advanced qualifications in mathematics, engineering and philosophy are required to cope with the neuroses of an electric generator.

I am very grateful that I have a gas stove and don't have to run through the check-list before cooking.

Unfortunately, gas freezers don't work very well in a climate as hot and humid as ours, so we have an electric freezer. We also have one electric refrigerator and one gas refrigerator. In the summer months when the heat and humidity are at their peak, we have to put virtually anything edible — even maize meal, oats, flour, powdered milk and the like — into cold storage.

In the summer the gas refrigerator suffers from heat fatigue and hardly manages to keep its contents cool. The electric refrigerator works well — summer and winter — but only, of course, when the generator is running.

We can use the generator only for about ten to twelve hours out of every twenty-four, or it will overheat and use huge quantities of diesel. We find it best to run it from about six in the morning until midday, and then again from about five in the afternoon until nine or ten o'clock at night.

We are very dependent on our freezer. In the winter months I freeze as many vegetables from our garden as possible, to see us through the long summer months when vegetable gardens don't survive the onslaught of insects and heat. Whenever we manage to catch fish in the river, I freeze some of those as well.

When the generator is off, the freezer manages to maintain its freezing temperature for up to twelve hours — as long as you don't open it and let hot air rush in. But the electric refrigerator defrosts each time and has to be towel-dried before the generator is switched on again.

It took me many months to come to terms with the quirks of the generator. In the beginning, I often forgot some of the rules and accidentally caused the machine to fade, sputter and die. This frightened me, as I lived in constant fear that my mistakes might cause the generator to blow up or break down, or something. And it annoyed Filemoni, because to get the machine going again is no picnic. Two people are needed for the job: one to hold the switch in the start position and the other to turn the crank handle until the machine fires up. (Filemoni does the cranking, of course, being a lot stronger than I am.) When the generator is in a foul mood, you have to give it time and wait for it to cool off before you try again.

Luckily, it's easy to switch the generator off — merely a flick of a switch — except when the switch fails to disconnect (which happens fairly often) and you then have to disconnect the battery terminals to shut the machine down. It's not too difficult, but it's exasperating.

I usually read in bed before going to sleep, especially when Kobus is away. Reading relaxes me. Just when I'm feeling nice and drowsy and am about to put my book down before drifting into dreamland, I remember with a horrible start that I have to go out into the dark and fearsome night to switch off the darned machine.

By the time I reach the engine room, I'm wide awake and decidedly tensed up. I particularly loathe the moment when, on opening the door to the room, the full volume of the engine's roar hits me. I usually rush in and flick off the switch as quickly as possible to avoid being paralysed by the noise. When the switch fails, and I'm forced to spend some time in the company of that roaring machine while groping for its battery terminals in the dark, my heart rate increases to about four hundred beats per minute. Sometimes I do something wrong and the terminals give me an electric shock, stopping my racing heart in its tracks.

When eventually I'm safely back inside the house, my heartbeat is scrambled, my nerves are jangled, and I cannot sleep. I cannot read either, or do anything else for that matter, as the electricity is off and the house is as dark as the night outside.

One evening some years ago, while Kobus was hospitalised with malaria, I was sitting quietly in the house doing some sewing when I heard a sudden loud bang — like a gunshot — outside. The house was instantly plunged into darkness. Feeling panicky and disorientated, I groped my way towards the bedroom to find my torch and pistol. I heard one of my children groaning in her sleep but, mercifully, none of them woke up.

The 'gunshot' had come from the other side of the house, furthest from their bedroom. I thought of the Mozambican refugees who are sometimes found carrying AK 47s or other firearms. When I finally had both pistol and torch, I hurried through the house to the kitchen and peered outside. To my relief, I saw two game guards — armed with torches and rifles — running from the staff village towards our main gate. As they reached the gate and proceeded to unlock and open it, they called out to me, and I answered to let them know I was unharmed. A few seconds later they stood in front of me with puzzled expressions. Neither they nor I could think of a plausible explanation for the loud bang and subsequent loss of power. Even the dogs were confused and barking furiously.

The game guards took the dogs and walked along the perimeters of the garden to inspect the fences, but returned after a while to report that no signs of forced entry had been found.

We walked over to the generator room to see if we could determine why the machine had died. As we opened the door, there was a strong smell of burning inside the room. The generator itself looked undamaged. I shone the torch over the walls and it was then that we saw that the distribution board had exploded and burnt out. We came to the conclusion that a short circuit had probably been responsible for the explosion.

I thanked the game guards for their concern and their help, and made my way back to the dark house.

Early the next morning, I radioed Louw, the technician at the Letaba camp, requesting help. On his arrival at Mahlangeni, he was appalled at the extent of the damage. I apologised profusely, thinking that I might have been responsible in some way or another. (Perhaps too many, or perhaps not enough, lights had been burning while I was using my electric sewing machine.) But Louw kindly reassured me that it wasn't my fault that the distribution board had exploded. The bad news, however, was that it would take a number of days to put together a new distribution board. Parts would have to be ordered from Skukuza.

We would have to do without power for several days...

But the story has a happy ending. When the new distribution board was finally ready to be installed, Louw brought us a new and more powerful generator to replace the old one. And with the demise of that temperamental old machine that had exasperated and terrified me for so many years, most of Marcia's complicated rules mercifully became redundant. The new generator even has a switch that doesn't fail.

Malaria and a
Month of Mishaps

M alaria is caused by protozoal parasites of the genus
Plasmodium which are transmitted to man by female
anopheline mosquitoes. Four species of Plasmodium are known to
infect man, not all of them equally dangerous. Three of the species
cause repeated periodic attacks of fever, usually sudden in onset
and often with rigors. Although patients may become severely ill,
these cases don't always end fatally if left untreated.

The fourth recognised species that infects man, Plasmodium
falciparum, causes the severe form of the disease known as
pernicious (or malignant) malaria. Unless treated promptly and
energetically, most of the pernicious forms end fatally.

During the late summer of 1984, Kobus contracted malaria of the
Plasmodium falciparum variety. Even though we had carefully read
and studied the literature on malaria, we stupidly didn't recognise
the first clinical indications of the disease. I was just recovering from
a bout of tick fever and thought that Kobus was coming down with
the same thing, while Kobus maintained that he was immune to tick
fever and probably had a dose of influenza.

The trouble with Plasmodium falciparum malaria is that
initially one doesn't feel very ill until — suddenly — the disease
becomes so vicious that one finds oneself literally fighting for
one's life.

Kobus had been feeling slightly unwell for about two days
when I awoke one night to find him rummaging in the cupboard
for blankets. It was a particularly warm March night, and
certainly not appropriate to be sleeping under blankets. Even

when he was eventually well covered in blankets, Kobus shivered so violently that his teeth were chattering. I got up and fetched another blanket. Within minutes of covering him, he wanted to go to the bathroom, but was feeling too cold to get out of bed. Once he had motivated himself sufficiently to make the short trip, he dashed from the bed to the bathroom, almost freezing in the process. His teeth were chattering as he dived back under the covers and, idiots that we were, we both laughed at the scene. Even under three blankets, Kobus was still cold, so I fetched yet another. It was only then that it dawned on us that he could have malaria, and we resolved to visit the hospital for blood tests first thing in the morning.

But in the morning Kobus felt better and, dismissing his ailment as influenza, he went off to do his day's work.

Late that afternoon he came home feeling tired and dizzy, and decided to lie down for a while. He had hardly done so when he experienced some chilly sensations which soon progressed into a fully developed rigor. Shivering violently, his face blue and his teeth chattering, he complained that he couldn't get warm, even under the many blankets that I had piled on top of him.

I realised then that we were in trouble. He was very ill — too ill to walk down to the river so that we could row across and drive to Phalaborwa.

After about two or three hours the rigor subsided and his temperature rose to a burning fever. He had a severe headache, felt nauseous and complained of thirst, but couldn't swallow the water I offered him.

By sunrise the hot stage had finally passed, and the third stage — the sweating stage — began. Although he was perspiring freely, he felt much better and we made our way down to the river, rowed across and headed for the hospital at Phalaborwa.

A blood smear was taken, and *Plasmodium falciparum* malaria was diagnosed. Kobus was admitted without delay and treatment commenced immediately. By this time, however, he was critically ill and didn't respond to the treatment.

The fever attacks raged constantly and violently. When, after twenty-four hours, he still hadn't responded to the treatment, the decision was taken to administer chloroquine intravenously.

There was a staff shortage at the hospital at the time, but no reduction in the number of patients. When the ward sister realised that I could be of some assistance, she briefed me and allowed me to take over a major part of the nursing of my husband. I was grateful for this as it enabled me to stay at his bedside day and night. Pernicious malaria is a vicious disease and the patient is in need of almost constant care.

During the cold stage of a fever attack, I piled as many blankets as I could on to Kobus, sometimes rushing into other wards to 'steal' blankets from unoccupied beds. Even so, he shivered so violently that I had to hold him down to keep him from falling off the bed. When his face turned blue and he had difficulty in breathing, I held an oxygen mask over his face. The cold stage sometimes lasted as long as three or four hours.

As soon as the cold stage abated, the hot stage would begin. He'd discard the blankets, start flushing, develop a severe headache and often delirium, with his temperature rocketing to 40°C and above. During the hot stage, I put an oxygen tent over his entire bed, securing it carefully, and then sat down next to him and reached under the tent to touch his hand so that he knew I was still there. The hot stage is the worst part of each attack, being severe and long-lasting (four to six hours), and sometimes instilling in the patient the fear that the fight for life might become too exhausting. During the third stage, the patient perspires freely and his bedclothes become totally sodden, but he feels much better. During these stages, I took down the oxygen tent, helped Kobus to take a few sips of water and to rest for a couple of minutes — before the cold stage started again. Then the whole exhausting, frightening cycle would be repeated.

There was no time for sleep. Sometimes, during the sweating stages, I dozed fitfully in the chair next to Kobus's bed, never for longer than a few minutes at a time.

When, after forty-eight hours, he was still not responding to the chloroquine treatment, I became very frightened. At one stage, while he was resting for a couple of minutes between attacks, I rushed to the nearest telephone and called the Institute for Tropical Diseases in Tzaneen. I asked what treatment was available for a patient with pernicious malaria who was not responding to chloroquine. The director of the Institute informed me that quinine, given intravenously, would be the next step. He couldn't give any guarantee that this would cure an advanced case of pernicious malaria, but held out the hope that there was at least a chance of a positive reaction.

I found the ward sister and enquired whether the hospital had any quinine on hand. After checking, she found that they did not, and I implored her to order some right away from the Institute at Tzaneen.

Later, while the doctor was making his rounds and studying Kobus's fever charts, I heard him telling the sister to order quinine immediately. She answered that she had already done so and that it was on its way.

However, before the quinine arrived that evening, Kobus started to show signs of responding to the chloroquine treatment. I was immensely relieved. While quinine works faster than chloroquine and other derivatives, it has more serious side-effects.

This was our third evening in the hospital, and I think that it must have been mostly adrenalin that had kept me awake until then, for as relief swept over me at the first indication that Kobus was finally responding to the treatment, I found that I was desperately tired and in urgent need of sleep. I could hardly keep my eyes open and my thoughts were becoming so scrambled that I had trouble deciphering them. When I finally managed to convince myself that Kobus was only asleep and not comatose, I cornered the sister on duty and urgently requested that she keep watch over Kobus in my absence.

I barely managed to drive myself the ten-odd kilometres to the school hostel inside the Park. (I think I did so in my sleep.) It was close to midnight and the hostel was dark and quiet. Not wanting to wake anyone, I slipped inside and, quietly finding an unoccupied bed, collapsed on to it.

I saw our daughters early the next morning and told them about their father's illness, assuring them that he was on the road to recovery. The house-mother invited me to share breakfast with the children, but I was in a hurry to get back to the hospital to see how Kobus was doing.

Although he was no longer having the fever attacks, his condition was still serious. He was suffering from kidney failure as a result of the blockage of the capillaries by parasitised red blood cells. At least he was no longer experiencing the high levels of physical anxiety associated with the fever attacks, but he was uncomfortable and exhausted. One of the side-effects of chloroquine is insomnia. Anyone who has been treated for malaria will testify to the stress of lying awake while your exhausted mind and body cry out for sleep.

I spent that night at the hostel again but, before going to bed, washed my clothes and hung them on a towel rail to dry. When we had left Mahlangeni, we had been in such a hurry to get to the hospital that I hadn't even thought of packing any spare clothes.

The next morning it felt good to wear clean clothes again — even if they were unironed.

The schools had in the mean while closed for the autumn holidays and all the other children had left the hostel. After two more days I felt comfortable enough with Kobus's condition to take the girls home to Mahlangeni.

For the next week or so, I drove to Phalaborwa every morning, spent the day at the hospital, and returned home at dusk. The game guards kept a watchful eye on the girls in my absence, but they knew how to use the radio in case of an emergency. Hettie took care of the cooking, and there was always a plate of wholesome food waiting for me when I got home.

Ranger Ben Lamprecht of Letaba called on the radio every evening, both to enquire about Kobus and to make sure that I had arrived home safely. I really appreciated his concern — I knew that if I didn't answer his call personally, he would come looking for me.

As if things weren't bad enough with Kobus being so ill and in hospital, just about everything else that could have gone wrong at Mahlangeni did so during this period.

First, the gas ran out. I radioed the depot at Skukuza to order a new supply, but I knew that the transport wasn't due for another six days. Even then, it would go only as far as Phalaborwa gate, where I would have to fetch the bottle of gas myself. In the mean time we couldn't use the gas refrigerator or the stove.

Then the distribution board of the generator exploded, eliminating the use of the electric fridge and freezer. After the technician had been and had informed me that we would be without power for several days, I packed all our frozen food into empty maize meal bags and, with Filemoni's help, rowed the lot across the river and carried them to the car. I drove to the school hostel and asked permission from the house-mother to store our supplies in the hostel freezer. Each afternoon, on the way back from the hospital, I would decide on a 'menu' for the following day, retrieve the necessary items from the freezer at the hostel and take them home with me.

While we were without power, we lit candles in the house at night — it was actually quite cosy.

There is a little stove just outside our kitchen. It's in the niche where the hot water tank is installed. Filemoni lights a fire in it every morning to supply hot water to the household. While we were without gas, the girls used the little stove for cooking. Although it heats up slowly and has room for only one pot at a time, it was certainly better than no stove at all.

Meanwhile, a paranoid bull hippo decided to make life even more difficult for me. Each time Filemoni rowed me across, the hippo would pester us with loud threats and displays. One morning he surfaced some two metres from the boat and, with his enormous mouth wide open, narrowly missed plunging right into the boat. Then he disappeared into the water and proceeded to intimidate us by diving and surfacing repeatedly just below the bow of the boat. Afraid that he might decide to attack the boat, I cocked my pistol. I was sitting at the stern and had to lean past Filemoni to fire into the water over the bow. The hippo was so aggressive that he retreated only after the fourth shot. As he was retreating, I suddenly realised that I had been holding the pistol uncomfortably close to Filemoni's ear while firing. I apologised profusely to Filemoni — who couldn't hear a word I was saying. He had been temporarily deafened by the pistol shots. He looked at me with a puzzled expression, rubbed his ear, and informed me that his ears were going 'zzing'. I felt terrible.

Feeling apprehensive about rowing across the river again that afternoon while the hippo was in such a bad temper, I told Filemoni — loudly, so that he could hear — not to come across to meet me that afternoon. I would use the longer route via Shimuwini to get home.

Little did I know then that even more trouble awaited me at Shimuwini.

Shimuwini is a large dam in the Letaba River, some thirty-five kilometres south-east of our house. A huge weir makes up the eastern wall of the dam. The water spills over the weir on to a concrete strip some five metres below the top, and then into the lower reaches of the river itself. The concrete strip crosses the whole width of the river under the weir — a length of some 150 metres, and is about two metres wide. If you drive carefully and look where you're going, it's possible to drive across the river in comparative safety. It's important, however, to have your four-wheel drive engaged and to drive slowly, as the strip can become very slippery during times when only a thin trickle of water spills over it and a slimy growth of moss settles on the concrete.

Ampie and Sannie Espag once had an awful experience while attempting to cross the river on the concrete strip. They were heading for town (from Mooiplaas) and decided to use the short-cut via Shimuwini. Sannie had a doctor's appointment and was dressed up for the occasion. Behind them in the pick-up truck sat a Shangaan woman and her child, also on their way into town.

On this day the concrete strip was particularly slippery, and about half-way across their vehicle skidded, stopping with one wheel over the edge of the strip. On getting out to assess the situation, Ampie had trouble keeping his footing on the slippery surface and realised that there was no way that he could right the vehicle on his own. The only option was to abandon the vehicle and walk the rest of the way.

Sannie took off her high-heeled shoes and got out, but immediately slipped and fell down. The Shangaan woman fared no better. The only way to get across, they realised, would be on their hands and knees. Ampie tentatively led the way, with Sannie following. The Shangaan woman — her baby firmly strapped to her back — brought up the rear. The baby wasn't too happy with this mode of transport and hollered all the way.

By the time they reached the opposite bank, they were soaking wet and covered in slime. Feeling as wretched as they looked, they started walking along the patrol road which links Shimuwini with Phalaborwa.

As luck would have it, a Parks Board vehicle was out on the road that day and came across the bedraggled group some seven kilometres from Shimuwini. The driver loaded them into his truck and took them to the ranger's house near the Phalaborwa gate. There they got rid of their slimy coatings and enjoyed a welcome cup of tea. Sannie never did see the doctor that day. After all, her stockings were in tatters, her dress looked too awful for words and, to top it all, she was minus shoes and handbag.

On my way home from the hospital that afternoon, I drove via Shimuwini. Only a thin trickle of water dribbled over the weir. Thinking of Ampie and Sannie, I drove very slowly and carefully, and managed to make my way across the strip of concrete without incident.

When Ben called from Letaba that evening, he reminded me that the following day was pay-day, and that Mahlangeni's field staff were required to report to the Phalaborwa gate to receive their salaries, and then go into town to do their monthly shopping.

I walked over to the village to let the staff know that I would drive them to Phalaborwa the next morning. Not all the staff go along each time. Those who choose not to go to town authorise those who do to collect their salaries, and they also give them their shopping lists. On that day, six of the staff elected to travel to Phalaborwa with me.

We had to travel via Shimuwini again, as my car was now on our side of the river. Our other car (an old Land Rover), as well as Kobus's pick-up truck, always remain on our side of the river.

As I walked out on to the veranda early the next morning to enjoy a cup of coffee, a shock awaited me. The Little Letaba River was in spate, forcing a deluge of foamy brown water into the Greater Letaba.

I ran over to the village, calling to the men who were to accompany me to hurry. I wanted to leave immediately to get to Shimuwini before the flood waters reached the dam and started spilling over the weir. Within a few minutes, the men had arrived. They piled into the Land Rover and we were on our way.

When we arrived at Shimuwini some fifty minutes later, we found to our dismay that a thick sheet of water was already spilling over the weir. I got out of my vehicle and walked down to the bank to assess the situation.

The water running over the concrete strip was between ten and fifteen centimetres deep — deep enough to obscure the strip.

I considered my options. I could drive back to the patrol road linking Mahlangeni with Mooiplaas, and then turn east to link up with the tourist road which eventually crosses the Letaba River via the high water bridge (where it's always safe to cross the river). That route would take approximately four hours to Phalaborwa.

So I decided that I'd rather cross the river at Shimuwini (only one hour's drive from Phalaborwa). I convinced myself that if I drove as close to the wall as possible, I'd be able to stay on the strip (even though I couldn't see it).

I engaged the four-wheel drive, started the engine, and cautiously drove down the rocky path on to the concrete strip. And then I got really scared: the sheet of water spilling over the weir cascaded on to my car in a solid torrent. It was like driving into a waterfall. I turned the windscreen wipers on full blast, but they didn't really help much.

Once you're on the concrete strip, you cannot go back. To reverse on that narrow path is virtually impossible and, even if it were possible, it would be even more difficult to reverse up the rocky slope without missing the narrow track and crashing into the river below. I had no choice but to press on.

It was a living nightmare. If I kept too close to the wall, the water cascading over it pounded the car relentlessly, and if I moved too far from the wall, I risked being swept off the concrete strip and into the deluge below.

After what seemed like an eternity, we reached the half-way mark. At this point, the strip makes a slight deviation away from the wall because of an uneven rock formation. Since the strip was completely obscured, I had to rely on memory. I calculated the angle of curvature to be between thirty and forty degrees.

I miscalculated. With a thump, the left wheels of the Land Rover slid over the edge of the strip and we were balancing precariously over the swirling waters below.

I was still trying to recover from the shock and to consider my next move when the man next to me opened his door and got out, letting himself down on to some large rocks in the water below us. The other men immediately followed suit, clambering over the front seat to get out. (The rear door of the Land Rover was stuck and couldn't be opened from the inside.)

Within seconds, all six men stood up to their waists in the water on the uneven rock formation, leaning into the current and straining to lift and push the Land Rover back on to the concrete strip. I called out to them, begging them to come out of the water before they got taken by crocodiles or were swept away in the deluge. But they either couldn't hear me or were ignoring me.

I couldn't just sit there while their lives were in danger. I had to get out of the car and persuade them to get back on to the strip. We would abandon the vehicle and walk — or crawl — along the strip to the opposite bank, which wasn't too far away. First, I took my identity document and stuffed it into my blouse pocket. (I don't quite remember why I did this, except that it seemed like a good idea at the time.) Then I kicked off my sandals, opened my door — and was immediately drenched by the torrent of water cascading over the weir. Wishing that I was capable of feeling more courageous, I got out and stepped carefully on to the concrete — and was horrified to discover that the water rushing over it appeared to be several centimetres deeper than it had been at the start of the strip. This meant either that the level of the ground was slightly higher at the beginning of the strip, or — more likely — that the water level in the dam above us was rising rapidly. Taking care not to lose my balance in the current, I moved slowly around the car to the edge of the strip. Before I could say a word to the men they cried out angrily, commanding me to get back into the car.

I tried arguing with them, shouting above the noise of the water, but they wouldn't listen and insisted that I get back into the car immediately. Somewhat cowed by their authoritative manner, I meekly obeyed.

I watched with increasing apprehension as they battled against the current, straining to lift the heavy vehicle. Eventually they managed to get the two wheels level with the concrete and finally, with a tremendous effort, they lifted and pushed the Land Rover safely back on to the strip.

I got back behind the steering wheel, feeling both tremendously relieved that all had gone well, and absolutely terrified that I might drive over the edge again.

Two of the men apparently shared my fear, and decided to walk ahead in front of the car to show the way. They moved carefully along the strip, shuffling sideways like crabs for better balance against the current.

I followed slowly, grateful to find that it was a lot easier to stay on the strip in this way. A few minutes later we reached the far bank safely, and I felt deeply indebted to those strong and courageous men. Without their help, I would not have been able to get my car across the river that day.

By the end of the week, Kobus was begging the doctor to let him go home. He told the doctor that the hospital room was giving him claustrophobia. I don't know whether the doctor believed him, but I did. Game rangers are very prone to claustrophobia since they spend most of their lives out of doors. Eventually, the doctor agreed and discharged him.

Kobus had lost a lot of weight and had become a frightfully frail and pale version of the fit and strong man he used to be. But once he was back home at his beloved Mahlangeni he felt so much better psychologically that he soon started to regain his health and strength.

And so a difficult month of malaria and other mishaps finally came to an end.

Coping with Snakes

During that first interview in the chief ranger's office in Skukuza — when we were warned about the hardships and privations that a game ranger's wife could expect to endure — they forgot to mention snakes.

I think they ought to say something about snakes in these interviews.

During our first couple of years at Mahlangeni, it didn't occur to me that snakes have a right to live and I eliminated each one I came across. I did it with a shotgun, being too cowardly to use a stick or a whip. I didn't enjoy shooting the snakes. In fact, I hated it with all my heart. A snake that has been blasted with a shotgun looks like mincemeat afterwards and leaves the person responsible for obliterating it feeling wretched with guilt.

But the trouble was, I believed it to be my duty — as the mother of three young children — to dispose of all the snakes in the neighbourhood.

I also felt responsible for the safety of my brood of bantams. When a snake finds its way into a fowl run, it creates mayhem.

One night when Kobus was away, I was woken by a hysterical commotion in the hen-house and I knew right away that there was a snake around. Grabbing a torch and my pistol (a shotgun would have killed most of the bantams as well), I rushed outside.

When I reached the hen-house I found to my horror that there was an Egyptian cobra inside and that it had already bitten one of the hens and devoured all but one of her chicks. The snake was still engaged in the act of swallowing a chick when, startled by the gleam of my torch, it reared its head, immediately offering a good angle for an accurate shot.

Unfortunately, I got confused. I had the pistol in my left hand and the torch in my right hand and I tried to shoot the snake with the torch, while lighting the scene with the pistol. Of course, this didn't work. My muddle-mindedness enabled the cobra to escape into the darkness.

I wanted to try to do something for the bitten hen, but found that she was already dead. So I picked up her orphaned chick and took him inside with me. I felt sorry for the chick and so I let him sleep on the bed with me, in an empty shoe box lined with cottonwool. But, having shared my bed for just one night, the little bantam chick became convinced I was its mother, and it took me many months to persuade him that I wasn't.

He followed me around like a shadow and raised an enormous rumpus whenever I moved too fast and he couldn't keep up. I had to teach myself to walk more slowly and to have more patience. It was exhausting trying to be a good mother to a bantam chick.

When, after a few weeks, he became less dependent on me and started to scratch in the garden on his own, it was a great relief. I could enjoy some freedom again.

I often tried to introduce him to the other bantams, but he refused to accept that he was one of them. He continued to believe that I was his mother until he was quite grown up. Whenever he spotted me sitting in the garden, he would rush over to me and perch on my lap. I felt silly sitting there with a grown-up bantam on my lap, especially when we had visitors.

Even though he eventually accepted the fate of having to spend his nights in the hen-house with the other bantams, by day he would have nothing to do with them. He spent his time scratching around in the garden on his own.

One day I received a beautiful young red bantam hen from the wife of another ranger. All our bantams were white. I introduced her to our lone bantam, and although she was quite taken with him, he would have nothing to do with her and studiously ignored her. Feeling irritated with my stupid bantam cock for hurting the hen's feelings, I took her away from him and carried her over to the other bantams. But she, in turn, would have nothing to do with them. The moment I put her down amongst them, she ran off and made her way back to the loner. Although he continued to ignore her, she followed him wherever he went. Eventually, after a couple of days, her perseverance paid off: the loner fell in love with her. And so it finally dawned on him that he was a chicken.

Shortly after the episode with the Egyptian cobra, we enclosed the hen-house in a second layer of wire mesh, and fortunately no snakes have since gained access.

It took me the better part of two years to realise that, no matter how many snakes I eliminated, snakes were always around and would always continue to be. In any case, I couldn't go on with the warfare — it was too upsetting. By this time I had also come to realise that snakes are as scared of humans as we are of them and will only strike out in self-defence. So I finally came to the conclusion that the thing to do was to avoid snakes, not kill them.

I devised a set of ground rules on how to avoid snakes and taught them to my daughters. In case you are interested, here they are:

- ✗ Don't climb trees with dense foliage.
- ✗ Don't poke your hands into places where you can't see what's going on inside (for example, rock crevices, dense vegetation, holes in the ground).
- ✗ Watch where you place your feet. Don't walk through flower-beds, dense scrub or long grass.
- ✗ Don't walk under low branches without first looking up for snakes.
- ✗ Never leave the house at night without a torch. Light the way directly in front of your feet.
- ✗ Keep the gauze screens on windows and doors closed at all times to prevent snakes from entering the house.
- ✗ If you encounter a snake at close quarters unexpectedly, don't make any sudden movements. Retreat carefully and quietly.

My rules have proved to be successful. Throughout the years neither my daughters nor I have been bitten by a snake. Only Kobus has. (I'll tell you about that later.)

Shortly after I had resolved to avoid snakes rather than kill them, an unfortunate episode marred my good intentions.

One evening, while Kobus was away and only the girls and I were at home, Hettie came to tell me that she'd spotted a snake in the kitchen. She described the snake to me, and I assumed that it must be a mamba. (All snakes should be regarded as mambas until proved otherwise.) The mamba is the most feared snake in Africa owing to its considerable size, its speed of movement and ability to strike accurately. Its venom is neurotoxic and is rapidly absorbed, often causing death within less than thirty minutes.

I told the girls to stay out of the kitchen and I went off to investigate. I found the snake on the patio just outside the kitchen. (How it got inside and then outside again through the closed gauze screen is just one of the several mysteries of the bush.) In the faint light shining on to the patio through the kitchen window, the snake did in fact appear to be a young mamba. Kobus had only recently built the patio and a heap of left-over cement slabs still lay at its edge. I rushed over and grabbed one of the slabs. Aiming carefully, I hurled it at the snake's head. The patio is paved with the same cement slabs, and the snake lay in a groove between two slabs. My carefully aimed slab shattered on the paving while the snake — protected in its groove — was unharmed. I reached for another slab, deciding to wait for the snake to lift its head before throwing. As it did so, I hurled the second slab but the snake ducked and the slab missed, once more shattering harmlessly on the paving. This slab-hurling procedure continued for quite a while until the fifth slab finally hit the snake squarely (before it could duck) and it was killed outright.

By this time, however, I felt so despicable that I could have wept. I rushed inside to fetch my torch so that I could determine exactly what kind of snake I had killed. When I discovered that it was a red-lipped herald, a totally harmless little snake, and not a mamba, I loathed myself with all my heart.

Early the next morning when Filemoni arrived to light the fire in the stove, he took one look at the dead little snake lying amongst the profusion of shattered cement slabs, and muttered, 'Heeh!' Noticing me inside the kitchen, he added, 'You beat the hell out of him, huh?'

That did it.

I decided that I would never again in my life personally kill a snake.

If ever circumstances necessitated it, I would get someone else to do the killing.

I did just that a couple of months later.

I was alone at home and had just finished having a shower before going to bed. I opened the bathroom door and was greeted by the horrific sight of a huge Mozambique spitting cobra lying on the floor right in front of me. I leapt backwards and slammed the bathroom door. And then I couldn't decide what to do next. My clothes were in the bedroom, and the cobra was blocking my only way to get to them.

According to my textbook on snakes, the Mozambique spitting cobra is one of the most dangerous snakes in Africa, second only to the mamba. It is a nervous and highly strung snake that can move with considerable speed. It can also 'spit' its venom and reach its target (usually the eyes) at a distance of two to three metres with remarkable accuracy.

Despite the snake's reputation, I didn't feel like spending the night in the bathroom. Climbing out through the window in a state of undress didn't strike me as a good idea either. So I gritted my teeth and opened the door again — just a crack. The cobra was still there, but had moved slightly. Its head was some distance down the passage now, and only its tail section remained between me and the bedroom. Performing my very best high-cum-long jump, I reached the bedroom safely, threw some clothes on and ran to the village to ask for help.

Three game guards answered my call, and when I told them about the snake they quickly armed themselves with sticks, whips and an assegai.

I led them back to the house to show them where the snake was. It had moved into my bedroom by this stage, and when it saw us it disappeared behind a bookcase. I offered to help, but was promptly ordered out of the house. Not ungratefully, I complied and stepped outside on to the veranda.

It was easy to imagine the battle as I listened to the noise. Furniture was being moved about, plans of action were discussed and commands exchanged (accompanied by some colourful language). Suddenly the cracking of whips echoed through the house (accompanied by more colourful language). Finally, a brief silence indicated that the battle might be over. Sighs of relief and some self-congratulatory remarks confirmed that the battle had indeed been won.

The game guards came out of the bedroom with the dead snake impaled on the assegai. I shuddered at the sight, but was immensely grateful that I hadn't had to do it myself.

At times we are visited by other snakes, mostly small and harmless ones. Kobus simply catches them and releases them away from the house. When Kobus is away, I call the game guards to help me.

As our gauze screens remain shut day and night, we have never been able to explain how the snakes get inside — that is, until recently when another episode with a spitting cobra offered some explanation to the mystery.

Karin charged into our bedroom one evening and announced that she had discovered a snake in the most dreadful place: right inside the toilet bowl. We rushed to the bathroom and found the cobra with its head raised over the side of the toilet seat. On seeing us, it dived back inside and disappeared into the plumbing. We racked our brains, but couldn't think of any way to get the snake out of there. Eventually, we decided to leave the toilet seat up (in case the snake wanted to get out) but keep the bathroom door closed (so that we would find the snake there in the morning if it decided to come out). However, it didn't emerge and we never saw it again. We were decidedly skittish about using the toilet for quite a while afterwards, and didn't dally when we did.

Since then, we have heard that two other families in the Park have had the same experience. Apparently there is enough oxygen above the water levels in the plumbing for a snake to make its way safely along the pipes.

If that is the answer to our question as to how snakes find their way into our house, I don't like it.

Kobus got himself bitten by a snake in the winter of 1988.

It happened while Kobus and his colleagues were capturing zebras for translocation to another park. They were herding the zebra into a catching enclosure when Kobus spotted a purple-glossed snake lying in the path of the approaching zebras. Wanting to save the snake, he grabbed it by the tail and neck but, before he could toss it out of the way, the snake bit him on the hand. The attending veterinarian, Dr Cobus Raath, who was running directly behind Kobus, reached out to assist him and, in so doing, was also bitten on the hand. The purple-glossed snake is a seemingly harmless burrowing snake, and since it doesn't usually bite people, the properties of its venom are unknown. Neither Kobus nor the vet had the time just then to worry about their bites as they wanted to complete the capture exercise first. Once this was over, they decided that the snake probably wasn't poisonous but swallowed some antihistamine tablets just in case.

When Kobus came home that afternoon, however, his hand and arm were swollen to such an extent that the covering skin appeared stretched to capacity and looked almost translucent.

I was horrified and asked what the heck the zebras had done to him. He explained about the snake bite.

I rushed to the bedroom to fetch a sterile needle from the first-aid kit, and then to the refrigerator to find a vial of antivenom, but discovered to my dismay that the expiry date printed on the label was almost three months back. The trouble with antivenom is that its shelf-life is so short that it usually expires before a person has reason to use it. Once it has expired, it does more harm than good.

I hurried back to Kobus, planning to take him to the hospital. He was sitting in front of the television, watching a game of rugby.

Although our TV antenna reaches almost to the heavens, we don't get a very sharp picture and, since our viewing times are limited to the generator's time-table, neither of us are avid TV watchers. I know that Kobus is fond of rugby, but why would he want to watch a game while his life was in peril? It occurred to me that he might be delirious.

'We'd better drive to the hospital right away,' I told him. 'The antivenom has expired.'

'Not now,' he said. 'I have to watch the game.'

'You can't!' I exclaimed. 'You might die in the mean time.'

'I'll go afterwards,' he offered. 'It's a cup final.'

'What if you're comatose by then?' I asked. 'How do I get you to the hospital?'

'You'll find a way,' he said. 'Now please get out of the way so that I can see the screen.'

Feeling very sorry for myself for being married to a game ranger, I gave up, but insisted first that he take another antihistamine.

While he enjoyed the rugby, I studied all our medical literature on snake bites, as well as my textbook on the reptiles of the Kruger Park. To my dismay, I could find no information on the venom of the purple-glossed snake. According to the textbook, it is a shy snake that is seldom seen and it is not known to be aggressive. No records existed on the effects of its venom. Apparently Kobus and the vet were the first human beings in recorded history to be bitten by the purple-glossed snake. It occurred to me that the least I could do for mankind was to record my husband's reactions to the venom.

I rushed to the lounge to see how he was doing. His breathing was irregular and I could see that he was in pain, but that might have been because his team was doing badly in the match.

I remembered another book that might be helpful and ran to the bedroom to find it. It's called *Let's Get Well* and the author is an American nutritionist named Adelle Davis. I looked up the text on snake bite and found some valuable advice. Adelle Davis recommended that the victim immediately be given massive doses of vitamin C (at least 4 000 milligrams), followed by further frequent doses. According to the author, vitamin C inhibits the penetration of toxins into cells and reduces the toxic effects of poisons entering the system.

I grabbed a bottle of vitamin C tablets from the refrigerator and shook out eight 500 mg tablets. Bracing myself for the task of feeding them to the victim, I returned to the lounge. Fortunately Kobus was so involved in his rugby game that he swallowed the pills just to get me out of his hair.

When the game finally came to an end, I put my foot down and insisted that we drive to Phalaborwa right away. Kobus protested, saying that he was feeling much better, and he offered to go the following day.

It's no use arguing with a game ranger. They're the most bull-headed, stubborn species on earth.

It wasn't even dusk yet, but when I looked for him again, Kobus was fast asleep on our bed. The glands in his neck were swollen and his face had lost some colour. He certainly didn't look well. As I touched his swollen arm lightly he woke, groaned, and went back to sleep. Obviously his arm and hand were painful. Not knowing how to manhandle a sleeping husband, I distracted myself by preparing supper for our daughters.

An hour later I woke Kobus to give him another 500 mg dose of vitamin C. I repeated this procedure again before going to bed.

He had a good night's sleep, while I hardly slept at all. I lay awake, listening for changes in the rhythm of his breathing. If the poison proved to be neurotoxic, it could cause paralysis of the nervous system, and difficulty in breathing would be the first indication. If the poison had haemotoxic qualities, subcutaneous bleeding would be the first symptom to watch out for. Using my torch, I checked on his hand and arm at regular intervals throughout the night. I also woke him several times to feed him further doses of vitamin C.

The following morning Kobus looked and felt much better. (Only I looked terrible.) His hand and arm were less swollen than they had been the previous day and were apparently also less painful.

Three days later both hand and arm were back to their normal size and, had it not been for the puncture marks on his hand —

which also healed well — you wouldn't have been able to tell that he had been bitten by a snake.

We heard later that the vet, Dr Raath, had suffered from severe headaches and nausea for several days, his hand and arm had remained swollen and painful for more than a week, and the puncture wounds on his hand had turned septic. He had taken only antihistamine tablets.

It appears that Adelle Davis has a point about vitamin C.

A while ago, ranger Johann Oelofse came across a Shangaan woman in the bush who had been bitten by a puffadder. She was one of a group of Mozambican refugees passing through the Park on their way to Gazankulu. After she had been bitten she couldn't keep up with the rest of the group, and they went on without her. Johann helped her into his vehicle and brought her to Mahlangeni — the closest ranger station.

The woman's leg was painfully swollen by then and I doubted whether the vitamin C treatment would do any good at that late stage. The venom of the puffadder is mainly haemotoxic in its action, and the extreme swelling of her leg indicated that severe suffusion of blood into the tissues — through the breaking down of blood cells and capillaries — had already taken place. Wanting desperately to help her, I gave her 5 000 milligrams of vitamin C together with some calcium tablets to alleviate the pain. Before Johann drove her to the hospital at Phalaborwa, I gave her another handful of vitamin C tablets, and explained to her that she should take a couple of tablets every half hour or so. The poor woman was exhausted, but managed to communicate her gratitude with a nod and the shadow of a smile.

Two days later when Kobus came home, I told him of the incident. He radioed the official at the Phalaborwa gate, asking him to contact the hospital and enquire about the condition of the Shangaan woman who had been admitted for snake bite two days previously.

The reply from the hospital was that she must have been feeling much better: she had absconded from the hospital the previous day. It seemed that I had acquired another living testimonial for Adelle Davis's vitamin C theory.

Although I wouldn't rely solely on vitamin C to save a person's life in cases of mamba or even cobra bites, it does give some comfort to know that the vitamin appears — at least to some extent — to inhibit the progress of the poison.

Now that I have come to terms with the fact that snakes have the right to live, I feel a lot better about myself. I still don't particularly like snakes, but at least I now know how to cope with them.

One must (a) avoid them, and (b) take care never to be without a substantial supply of vitamin C.

The River – Part 1

Although both the rivers can be seen from our house, it is the Greater Letaba that plays the more influential role in our daily lives. The Greater Letaba is a perennial river, while the Little Letaba is a seasonal one that flows only in the rainy season. We call the Little Letaba by its full name, but we call the Greater Letaba simply 'the river'.

As the Little Letaba actually ends right here at Mahlangeni where it flows into the Greater Letaba, the latter is known elsewhere in the Park only as 'the Letaba River'.

The Greater Letaba is a beautiful and fascinating river that changes its colours and moods all the time. It has morning colours, noon colours and evening colours. In the winter it is placid and tranquil and its surface is as smooth and shiny as a mirror. In the summer, which is our rainy season, it becomes turbulent and restless, and its water level rises and recedes continuously according to the amount and frequency of rainfall in the catchment areas.

To us, the river with its alternating colours and moods, and the hippos with their sonorous voices, constitute the most lyrical features of the character of Mahlangeni.

Yet for many years, before the causeway was built, they also constituted the most troublesome aspects of life for us.

Rowing across the river was never the safest of ventures but, human nature being what it is, we adapted and sometimes even became nonchalant about it — until something happened to remind us once more that the unpredictable river and its paranoid inhabitants were never to be trusted.

One such incident that served as a reminder of the capricious nature of the river occurred some years back when we arrived home from a holiday in the Eastern Cape.

It had been a long drive — approximately 1 700 kilometres — and we arrived at the Phalaborwa gate late one afternoon feeling decidedly exhausted. It was early in January, and hot as blazes. As we drove along the lonely track through the mopani woodlands to Mahlangeni, we could hardly wait to get home. We talked excitedly about the familiar and welcome sight that would greet us when, on reaching the southern bank of the river, we would be able to see the house in its oasis of shady trees on the far bank. We would park our car in its lean-to under the jackalberry trees and sound the hooter to let Filemoni know we were there. Then we would carry our luggage down the bank to the waterside and wait for Filemoni to bring the boat and take us home.

We forgot to consider that the river might not be in a hospitable mood that day.

As we turned the last bend — where the track arrives at the southern bank — we gasped with surprise and dismay.

The river was in spate.

Between us and the opposite shore was a two hundred metre wide torrent of restless water that seemed to be in a particular hurry to reach the ocean.

It is highly frustrating when you can see your home but don't know how to get there.

We discussed our options. There were really only two choices. We could drive back to Phalaborwa gate, go on to Letaba camp to cross the river on the high water bridge, then continue north along the tourist road, and finally east along the patrol road to Mahlangeni. Or we could risk a crossing in the boat. The first option would add at least four hours to an already exhausting day's drive.

We all voted for the boat. Actually, initially I abstained — the coward, as usual. But as I contemplated the exhausting alternative, I changed my mind and added my vote in favour of the boat.

Kobus sounded the car's hooter to alert Filemoni. But Filemoni apparently wasn't there, and because of the noise of the water it took a while before anyone responded. Eventually, José (one of the game guards) appeared on the far bank and made his way down to the water's edge.

Kobus signalled José to drag the boat about a hundred metres upstream before launching it. (We've developed an efficient signalling system between the shores over the years.) José dragged the boat upriver but, deciding that a hundred metres wouldn't be enough to compensate for the downstream current, he dragged the boat at least another hundred metres upstream, right into the mouth of the Little Letaba. As I watched him climbing into the boat, I lost my nerve and started gesturing frantically to José not to come. But he was already in the boat and on his way. He'd hardly left the shore when the torrent gripped the boat and started sweeping it downstream. The flow was stronger than we had suspected. Fortunately, José is a strong man and he managed to keep the bow of the boat aimed towards our shore. Even so, it didn't seem possible to me that such a flimsy looking vessel could be manoeuvred safely through the turbulent water, and I could hardly bear to watch as José battled with the oars while the current continued to sweep him downstream.

Realising that the boat would eventually be swept far past the usual anchoring spot where we were waiting, Kobus started running downstream along the water's edge. Eventually he managed to grab hold of the bow of the boat as it finally came within reach of the shore. He helped José out, and together they dragged the boat ashore and then some two hundred metres upstream.

By now I was convinced that the four-hour journey via the high water bridge would have been bliss compared with the troubles that we were about to encounter.

Kobus decided that we would have to row across in instalments. (The more heavily you load the boat, the more difficult the rowing becomes.)

Kobus, Karin and I made the first crossing.

I tried to stay calm and enjoy the 'adventure', but my heartbeat became a pounding crescendo that competed with the roar of the

river. The water pummelled the boat mercilessly as Kobus battled to row upstream against the current. I held on to Karin, telling her that if the boat capsized, she was to hang on to it as best she could — it would get washed ashore sooner or later. The torrent continued to sweep us downstream at a relentless pace while Kobus struggled to keep the boat moving towards the opposite bank. I shut my eyes every now and then in the hope that when I opened them the shore would suddenly appear a lot closer. It didn't work though — it took almost for ever to reach the other side.

The boat finally beached more than two hundred metres below our usual landing place in an almost impenetrable thicket of reeds.

After we'd disembarked, Kobus dragged the boat upstream again while Karin and I made our way carefully through the dense reeds to higher, open ground.

Some four hundred metres upriver, Kobus launched the boat and braved the waters again to fetch our other two daughters. Karin and I sat down on the sandy shore, rubbing the bruises which the reeds had inflicted on us, and kept our eyes on the boat.

When it finally came within reach, Hettie and Sandra rushed towards it to grab the bow and, with José's help they steadied the boat and managed to drag it ashore. Once again, Kobus and José hauled the boat a couple of hundred metres upstream.

My heart started beating a steady allegro fortissimo as I watched my two older daughters climbing into the boat. Within seconds of its leaving the shore, the torrent gripped the boat again and started sweeping it downstream at a dizzying pace. As a mere onlooker who could do nothing at all to help, I felt even more frightened now than when I had been in the boat myself.

The current was particularly strong in the area between the middle of the river and the northern shore, because of the inflow from the Little Letaba. As the boat reached this area it suddenly careened dangerously, and I jumped to my feet, signalling frantically to my daughters that they should cling on to the boat if it capsized. They signalled back that they understood and that I wasn't to worry. Happily the boat didn't capsize and, after I'd aged several years, they finally beached safely.

But the crisis wasn't over yet. Kobus had to repeat the whole exhausting exercise once more to fetch José and our luggage. I noticed that he was beginning to show signs of exhaustion, and I was worried that he might not have sufficient strength left to complete this third round trip. I was beginning to suffer from panic fatigue.

Fortunately, Kobus held his own against the raging river and finally returned safely with José and our luggage. I noticed, though, that his shirt was soaked with perspiration and that he was short of breath. It hadn't been easy.

Although we were immensely relieved to be safely home, we also felt rather guilty about our rash behaviour. We resolved to have more respect for the river in future and never again attempt a crossing under such adverse circumstances.

One particular incident that most effectively reminded me of the ever-present danger of paranoid hippos occurred on a Friday morning some years ago when I set out to fetch the children at the hostel.

Filemoni was away on leave and I had rowed myself across. After securing the boat, I started up the winding footpath leading through thickets of croton bushes and jackalberry trees to the car shelter at the top of the bank. I'd walked only a short distance up the path when, less than fifteen metres ahead of me and to my right, the undergrowth exploded and a hippo came crashing through the crotons. Instinct commanded me to turn and bolt for the safety of the boat, but my mind screamed: 'Wait! Never get between a hippo and the water.' At that moment I was right between the hippo and his aquatic haven. For one terrible second we stood looking at each other, and I realised that if we both opted to dash for the safety of the river, the hippo would almost certainly overtake me and probably annihilate me in the process. So I put my head down and ran straight into the dense tangle of croton bushes to my left, creating an impressive tunnel through the almost impenetrable thickets. I didn't slow down until I'd almost reached the top of the bank. There I changed direction to find the footpath again. When I came out of the thickets on to the footpath at the top of the bank, I turned to see where the hippo had gone. Surprisingly, he hadn't fled into the water. He had chosen a direction directly opposite to mine and had steamrollered a highway through the croton jungle to the west of the footpath.

Apparently the sight of me had given him such a fright that he'd forgotten that a hippo feels safe in the water. I guess I hadn't looked too good that morning.

After this incident, Kobus and the game guards went across the river and chopped a wider clearance through the croton thickets on either side of the footpath to reduce the chances of another close encounter of the same kind.

Apart from the risks involved in crossing the river, the operation also entails a lot of effort.

The Letaba River has a wide bed that is flanked on either side by high banks. A narrow stone stairway leads from our front gate down the bank to the riverbed. In the winter, when the water level is low, the sandy shore between the bottom step and the water's edge usually covers some eighty metres. In the summer the water's edge can be anywhere, sometimes reaching right up to the stairway or even higher.

On the far side of the river there is no sandy shore between the water and the bank. The bank rises directly out of the water at an angle of approximately thirty-five degrees and then undulates in even and uneven slopes until it flattens out at the top into mopani savannah.

Hauling the girls' hostel luggage down the steep stairway every Monday morning, across the sandy beach to the boat, and then finally up the opposite bank to the car is an exercise that keeps us all in good shape. In the summer, when the humidity often reaches intolerable levels — even before six o'clock on a Monday morning — the exercise is far too exhausting to be fun.

One Monday morning, as the girls and I were making our way up the opposite bank, I slipped on the dew-covered grass and went crashing down, losing my grip on the suitcase I was carrying. It slid down the bank and crashed into the river. (It was Sandra's suitcase, containing all her school clothes for the week.) I sprinted down the slope, jumped back into the boat and rowed furiously after the drifting suitcase. Fortunately I managed to reach it and retrieve it before it sank or emigrated to Mozambique.

On Friday afternoons the whole luggage-hauling routine is, of course, repeated in the opposite direction. And once a month or so, when I combine a trip to the hostel with a trip into town to buy groceries, the latter adds considerable weight to the load that has to be ferried over. Sometimes the groceries don't all fit into the boat and a second trip has to be made to get everybody and everything across.

Whenever Kobus replenishes our supplies of diesel, petrol and gas, these also have to be conveyed by boat. Rowing the heavy, awkward containers across isn't easy.

It is in the rainy seasons especially that the boat trips entail a lot of effort and trouble. Each time it rains in the catchment areas, the water level of the river rises, and when the inflow ceases it ebbs — leaving a broad strip of muddy sludge behind. It also leaves the boat stranded in the mud, usually some distance from the ebbing waterside. It's not too difficult to drag a boat across dry sand, but dragging it through sludge is a very messy and exhausting business. On Monday mornings, at times such as these, we carry our decent shoes in a bag and wear old canvas shoes on the trek through the muddy morass. We also take a container of water and some towels along so that, on reaching the far bank, we can wash the mud from our feet and legs before putting on our respectable shoes.

One Saturday morning — while the river was ebbing after a flood — our new chief ranger, Bruce Bryden, arrived at Mahlangeni to pay us a visit.

Bruce was eager to show Kobus a new pistol which he had recently acquired, and the two men made their way down to the riverbed to test the weapon.

Karin was feeding some titbits to a tame tortoise in the front garden while, some distance from her, Hettie was stroking the head of one of our horses who was grazing on the lawn.

As Bruce fired the first shot down by the river, its sudden echoing report startled the horse and it reared, jerking its head upwards and smashing it into Hettie's jaw. She lost consciousness and collapsed on to the grass. As the frightened horse turned to flee, one of his hooves came down on the side of Hettie's head, opening a deep gash in her temple.

Karin, who had turned towards the river when she heard the shot, swung around as she heard the horse whinnying. She saw him taking off in fright, and then she noticed her sister lying slumped on the grass. She ran to her as fast as she could. Finding her with her head in a pool of blood, she was very shocked and concluded that the shot that had been fired had hit her sister. Remembering that she had seen the two men leaving through the front gate a short while before, she turned and ran towards the gate, shouting for help with all the volume her young voice could muster.

The men responded immediately and rushed up the stone stairway. I was busy in the house at the time. When I heard Karin shouting for help, I knew that something serious had happened and I ran outside.

When I reached the scene, Kobus and Bruce were already in attendance, feeling Hettie's pulse and lifting her eyelids to check her pupils. She was still unconscious and her long blonde hair was soaked in blood.

Realising that the wound was still bleeding, I rushed back into the house to fetch bandages. After we had bound the wound, Kobus lifted Hettie gently and carried her down the stone stairway to the riverbed.

There was no time to bother about fetching canvas shoes, towels or water. We hurried through the mud to the boat, sinking almost half-way to our knees in the sludge. Bruce helped us drag the boat through the deep mud to the water. I got into the boat and sat down so that Kobus could hand Hettie to me. While Kobus took the oars and Bruce helped launch the boat, I turned to look at my other two daughters who stood on the shore — ashen-faced, but bravely waving us goodbye.

Bruce volunteered to stay with them until we returned.

When we reached the opposite bank, Kobus carried Hettie up the steep bank to the car. I sat in the back of the car with Hettie, cradling her head in my lap. She had in the mean time regained consciousness but was as white as a sheet and lay very still. The wound was bleeding through the bandages and I registered vaguely that my clothes, arms and legs were covered in mud and blood.

Kobus drove as fast as he safely could, and we arrived at the hospital just over an hour later. Bruce had meanwhile radioed ahead to Phalaborwa gate, and the official on duty there had in turn contacted the hospital to let them know we were bringing in an injured child.

When we arrived at the hospital the staff was waiting for us with a gurney in place to rush Hettie inside. When they saw that Kobus and I were also covered in blood and mud they concluded that we, too, had been injured. It took some explaining to convince them that they needn't bring gurneys for us as well. While Hettie was wheeled to the theatre, Kobus and I located a tap in the garden where we quickly rinsed off the worst of the dirt before going back inside.

When Hettie came out of the theatre some thirty minutes later, she looked a lot better. The deep gash in her head had been stitched and dressed, her hair had been washed, and she had regained some colour in her face. She was even smiling at us. At least, it was a brave smile, if not a very successful one. Her jaw was severely swollen where the horse's head had struck her and most of her front teeth were broken.

A series of tests was carried out to determine whether there had been any brain damage, but thankfully the results were negative. She'd suffered only a mild concussion.

After a couple of days in hospital for observation, she was allowed to come home. I took her to a dentist, and when the repair work to her teeth had been completed, she looked as good as new.

After five years of crossing the river by boat, we received the exciting news on the VHF radio one morning that the Parks Board had decided to construct a causeway across the river at Mahlangeni.

Some five hundred metres downstream from the boat's usual mooring, there is a place where the river runs wide and shallow over a rocky shelf. It was the ideal place to build a causeway.

As soon as the construction of the causeway was under way, Kobus borrowed the Park's grader and cleared a road from our back gate around the north-eastern corner of the garden and down to the site of the causeway. On the far side of the river he cleared a road slanting up the bank to meet the patrol road at the top.

We were tremendously excited when the causeway was finally completed in August 1985. After the construction workers had left, we had to wait a couple of days for the cement to dry.

And then, at last, the big day dawned.

For the first time in the earth's history as we know it, human beings would cross the Letaba River at Mahlangeni via a causeway. (It was almost like that first small step on the moon.)

We all got into the car and drove down to the river along the new road that Kobus had cleared. Then we drove slowly across the river on the two hundred metre causeway. We waved like royalty to the watching hippos. Then we got out and walked the full length of the causeway to see how that felt. It felt just great. The hippos swam up close and stared at us with quizzical expressions. I explained to them that, through the technological and engineering achievements of mankind, the river had now been tamed. Never again would its unpredictable moods, nor the paranoia of its inhabitants, cause us grief.

The River – Part 2

Not only did the causeway bring a great deal of change to our own lives, it also brought new dimensions to the lifestyle of the entire neighbourhood.

A herd of elephants were the first to discover the causeway.

Before I can tell you how that happened, I have to explain about the 'no entry' sign.

Kobus had, some years previously, found an official 'no entry' sign lying in the bush in the middle of nowhere. It is known that elephants have the habit of pulling out official signs and then abandoning them somewhere deep in the bush. As Kobus did not know where the sign had originally belonged, he brought it home with him and put it in our storeroom. On the day of the opening of the causeway, he remembered the sign and fetched it. He carried it across the river and planted it on the far bank at the entrance to the causeway. It made our causeway look more official, he said.

That night the herd of elephants visited the southern bank. Apparently they took offence at this sign of officialdom in their territory. They pulled it out and discarded it some distance away in the riverine bush. Then they all filed across the causeway.

The next morning we found our brand-new causeway covered in elephant droppings. We could see by the spoor that the elephants had not really wanted to come and graze on our side of the river. After they'd walked the full length of the causeway, they had made a U-turn and returned to the southern bank. Apparently they had merely wanted to satisfy themselves as to the purpose and user-friendliness of the causeway. Or perhaps they had wanted to show us what they thought of the no entry sign.

Many other species of game, such as waterbuck, kudu, impala, bushbuck and warthog have since discovered the benefits of the causeway and now use it regularly to get to whichever side of the river they wish to be. The traffic on the causeway tends to be particularly heavy early on Monday mornings when we're in a hurry to get to school.

The baboons who sleep in the jackalberry trees on the opposite bank are especially delighted with the causeway and use it daily to get to our vegetable garden and papaw trees.

When they see us watching them on their way across, they promptly strike up a relaxed pose and make themselves comfortable on the causeway, pretending that they merely wish to sit there and enjoy the view from that particular vantage point.

Although the view of the river from the causeway is in fact very beautiful, you must not be taken in by the baboons for one moment. The only kind of view they appreciate is one with food in it.

Although life has become a great deal easier with the causeway, I was wrong when I believed that the river had been tamed.

It hasn't.

Floods still occur, of course, and when there's a really heavy flood it submerges the causeway completely so that we have to make the huge detour to the high-water bridge near the Letaba camp to get to Phalaborwa. For a few years we still had the option of rowing across when the causeway was submerged (as long as the current wasn't too strong), but that option expired in 1988 when our boat disappeared in a flood — which, I guess, was final proof that the river cannot be tamed.

Then there are the times when everything around us is in spate: the Little Letaba River, the Greater Letaba River, and the Shibyeni creek as well. At such times we are effectively cut off from the outside world. This usually happens at the most inconvenient times — such as the long weekend when we had visitors from the city.

Our guests arrived on a Wednesday afternoon, planning to stay with us until the Sunday. Having only received their message on the Wednesday morning (due to our irregular mail deliveries), we were caught unprepared: our food stocks were very low and would not last through a long weekend with four extra people to cater for. Since the Thursday was a public holiday and the shops would be closed, I decided that I would go to Phalaborwa on the Friday to restock our pantry.

Early on the Thursday morning it started to rain heavily on the escarpment and over most of the lowveld. By Friday morning both the Letaba rivers as well as the Shibyeni creek were in spate. We were cut off from the outside world.

I started stretching our meagre food supplies. I stretched them every which way by adding bits of everything to anything else that was edible. By the Saturday my pantry shelves and refrigerators looked depressingly empty and I was running short of ideas. I walked over to our vegetable garden, but the recently planted vegetables had hardly started growing. There were no frozen vegetables left over from the previous winter either — the freezer was empty except for a few cans of frozen fruit juice. Luckily, there were some papaws on a tree in the garden. I remembered that someone had once told me that cooked green papaw tastes almost the same as pumpkin.

For lunch, we had ripe papaw with fruit juice. For supper, I chopped a tiny piece of left-over buffalo meat into microscopic portions to make a stew, but it ended up as a feeble gravy. I served it with cooked green papaw disguised as pumpkin, and bread which I'd baked with maize meal since I'd run out of flour. (It tasted not unlike sawdust.)

By the Sunday morning the Letaba River was still in spate, but the Shibyeni creek had ebbed sufficiently to allow our guests to take the long detour via the high-water bridge. They planned to leave right after breakfast.

Breakfast?

Feeling at a total loss, I stood in my kitchen, pondering. Looking through my empty refrigerators I found three eggs (not enough for nine people), a small piece of butter and a lick of jam (no bread to go with it), and about one cupful of milk powder — sufficient to make a litre of milk (but no oatmeal or maize meal to make porridge).

Resolving to stay calm, I decided to tackle the problem scientifically. First, I made a list of everything in the kitchen that was edible. Apart from the above-mentioned items, I found some sugar, spices, salt, baking powder and about half a cup of flour. Then I sat down at the kitchen table and methodically paged through my recipe book.

A scientific strategy never fails. I found a recipe for a crustless milktart which required three eggs, a litre of milk, two tablespoonsful of butter, baking powder, sugar, cinnamon, and one cup of flour. I had everything except one cup of flour. (I had half a cup.)

The milktart was a great success — apart from the fact that it was a little soggy owing to the shortage of flour.

After our guests had left, the problem was what to feed my family the rest of the day. I discovered one last ripe papaw in the garden and we shared that for lunch. I searched all over the garden for bantam eggs, but apart from a few eggs upon which a brooding hen was sitting aggressively, I couldn't find any.

Later in the afternoon we tried to catch some fish in the river, but when the water is muddy after a flood the fish don't bite. Kobus volunteered to go out and shoot a francolin or a guinea fowl, but was delayed by a problem in the staff village.

We went to bed ravenously hungry.

Early the next morning I could only offer the girls some weak black coffee before taking them to school, but I promised them a big breakfast at the Letaba camp en route to Phalaborwa. The causeway was still submerged and we had to take the high-water bridge detour.

Before leaving, I radioed the official at the gate and asked him to contact the girls' schools to explain that they would arrive late because of the floods.

We left at about half past five and reached the Letaba camp just before eight. I told Mishak, the waiter in the restaurant, not

to bother about a menu — we'd eat anything. He promptly served us the best breakfast that we had ever had in our lives.

When I dropped my daughters off at their schools later that morning, I was grateful to know that they'd had a decent meal.

Although floods occasionally disrupt our daily lives, it is always a thrill to see the river in spate.

There is something about a massive roaring body of water, rolling on relentlessly to its distant destination, that has the same kind of exalting qualities as music.

In times of protracted drought, when the river dwindles and loses much of its force, we always long to see it in all its dramatic splendour again.

The heaviest flood we have ever experienced at Mahlangeni occurred in February 1988. I was alone at home on the day that it started.

I woke up shortly before sunrise, knowing that something had disturbed me but not sure what it was. The wild geese hadn't yet arrived to startle me out of my sleep with their raucous trumpeting, and it isn't normal for me to wake up before they do. I then realised that it was the sound of aircraft above the house that had woken me. It seemed to hover there somewhere, and it bothered me a great deal as I couldn't think of any reason why it should do so — or why it should be there in the first place. We seldom see or hear aeroplanes in our part of the world. I was still trying to figure out a logical answer to these troubling questions when it dawned on me that I wasn't listening to the sound of hovering aeroplanes, but to the thundering roar of a raging river. I rolled over in bed to look out of the glass doors — and my mind reeled at the sight: the river had flooded its banks and the violent torrent had risen to the level of the garden. Uprooted trees and huge logs were being tossed about in the spuming surf like matchsticks. I leapt out of bed, dressed in half a second, and ran outside.

The impact of the spectacle was so overwhelming that it took my breath away and for a while I found it difficult to believe and comprehend what I saw.

I was relieved, however, to find that the water level wasn't quite as high as it had seemed from the bedroom. It was in fact still a couple of metres below the top of the bank, which meant that at least the garden and the house would not be flooded before I could make myself a cup of good, strong coffee from which to derive support. I opened the front gate and walked down four steps to the edge of the torrent — forty-two out of the forty-six steps were submerged. I wondered whether the sandy shore at the bottom was still there.

Only the crest of the opposite bank was showing and it appeared to be out of reach for ever. I looked across the awesome expanse of water towards the east where the causeway was supposed to be, but I couldn't even imagine where its exact position was. The whole landscape was alien. Every familiar landmark had disappeared under the stupendous waterscape. I was worried that the causeway might have completely disintegrated under the weight of the deluge.

That suddenly reminded me of the boat. I scanned the water carefully but could see no sign of it. I looked to the side of the stairway along the bank for the iron pole that holds the long anchoring chain, and was relieved to see that part of the pole still showed above water. I wondered, though, why the chain seemed to be dangling loosely in the current and my heart missed several beats as I realised that our boat, which had stood us in such good stead for so many years, had broken its anchor and was at that very moment probably speeding headlong towards the far-off ocean. I could hardly bear the thought of never seeing our boat again, but there wasn't time to stand there and agonise. It occurred to me that if I didn't hurry up and do something right away, I might even end up in the ocean myself — something I'd hate to have happen before I'd had my first cup of coffee. I quickly found a stick and stuck it into the bank to mark the water level.

I enjoyed two cups of strong coffee, which put my mind into a more functional gear and enabled me to start thinking logically. First, I decided that if the garden and house were eventually flooded I couldn't make my escape by car and drive off without the dogs, horses and bantams, not to mention the people in the

151

village. If evacuation became necessary, it would have to be on foot. It was going to be quite an exodus.

I decided to go outside and check on my marker before losing my calm unnecessarily.

As I stepped outside, I was immediately bowled over anew by the spectacular sight. (This happened to me several times throughout the rest of the day. Apparently my mind had trouble registering the scene.)

When I reached my marker I was relieved to find that the water level had remained constant. Perhaps evacuation wouldn't be necessary after all. As I stood gaping at the thundering river, I noticed that the dogs and horses were as stunned as I was. Ears pricked, noses to the wind, they stared at it with acute incomprehension. I decided to make another cup of coffee before checking on the marker again.

When, some twenty minutes later I found the stick still standing safe and dry just above the water level, I concluded that — mercifully — the flood had reached its zenith and had stabilised. It was time to call Kobus on the radio and report the news of the flood to him. Although it seemed as if several days had gone by since I had first woken up, it was now only half past six in the morning.

Kobus had spent the night in Olifants camp where he had attended a meeting the previous day. When I told him about the flood, he could hardly wait to get home to see it for himself. It being a Friday, he told me that he would drive to Phalaborwa to pick up the girls and bring them home with him via the high-water bridge.

After talking to Kobus I radioed the officials on duty at Phalaborwa gate and Letaba camp to tell them about the flood so that they could warn tourists not to use the low-water bridge between Phalaborwa and Mooiplaas.

Then I rushed outside again to check whether things still looked the same out there (just in case I had been hallucinating a little). If anything, the scene appeared even more dramatic than I had remembered it.

I hurried to the site of my marker. It was still as it had been. This eased my mind a great deal. Feeling a lot more relaxed now, I started walking along the crest of the bank to appreciate the awe-inspiring beauty of the scene. As I approached the mouth of the Shibyeni creek, I saw a torrent of water cascading from the Shibyeni into the Letaba. Worried that Kobus and the girls might be cut off from home by the Shibyeni, I decided to check the depth of the water. As the dense vegetation on the bank of the creek makes it difficult to get close enough for a good view, I had to walk all the way to the site where the road dips through the creek to the north-east of the staff village.

There was a lot of water in the creek and, at that stage, it would have been impossible to drive through it. But a strip of mud on either side of the water indicated that it might be ebbing, and I placed a marker at the water's edge so that I could check on it later in the day. After I had done this, a movement on the opposite bank caught my attention. A magnificent nyala bull stepped from the thickets and walked down to the water's edge. Not wanting to startle the animal, I immediately froze. He caught sight of me but, because I remained as frozen as a statue, he couldn't decide what I was. We stood staring at each other across the water — a distance of barely five metres. The nyala was so beautiful that it brought tears to my eyes. I had never before had the privilege of looking a nyala straight in the eye. Enjoying every second of our unique encounter, I held my breath as the animal studied me thoughtfully. Satisfied eventually that I was merely a funny-looking shrub, he lost interest in me and proceeded to contemplate the flooded creek. After a while, he decided that he wasn't thirsty after all, and sauntered gracefully off into the bush.

I went back home to divide the rest of my day between gaping at the river and checking on my markers. The Shibyeni creek was ebbing at a reasonable rate, holding out the hope that Kobus and the girls might be able to get through it in the late afternoon. At about noon I discovered that the river had also started to ebb: the water level had fallen to some three or four centimetres below my marker.

Meanwhile, Kobus and the girls were having a tough time trying to get home. Kobus had collected the girls at their schools several hours early, explaining to their headmasters that they faced an enormous detour and wanted to get home before nightfall.

They crossed the high-water bridge in the early afternoon, but when they reached the Tsendze stream an hour later, they found it in spate. Unable to get through it, they had to alter course and drive many kilometres along firebreaks and patrol tracks to circumvent the Tsendze. More than once the vehicle was bogged down in muddy watercourses and they had to dig their way out. Luckily the Shibyeni creek had ebbed sufficiently to let them through.

They finally arrived at Mahlangeni just before seven o'clock that evening. Dusk had already settled, but it was still light enough to see the flooded Letaba from our garden. Although the earlier ferocity of the flood had abated somewhat, I was happy at last to be able to share the spectacular scene with my family.

For several weeks after the flood the causeway remained hidden under the water and, since our boat had disappeared, the only way to get the girls to school was by the vast detour over the high-water bridge. As soon as the water dropped to a level where we could at least see, or rather guess, where the causeway was, we parked our car on the opposite bank again and walked across the causeway. We did this for the better part of three weeks before the water level had ebbed sufficiently to allow a vehicle across. Walking across wasn't an easy matter. The water came right up to our knees and the current was still so strong that we had to shuffle sideways like crabs to avoid being swept off the causeway. It was certainly not a very safe thing to do either — because of the presence of crocodiles — but it was just so much quicker than making the 160-kilometre detour.

Although the causeway has changed our lives, it hasn't tamed the river. The river still reigns supreme and — what's more — it has abducted our boat. It was such a faithful little vessel, having conveyed so many supplies, groceries and humans (sometimes sick or injured ones) for so many years.

We really miss our boat.

Fire

K obus came home late one afternoon and, having nothing of immediate urgency to attend to, agreed to accompany me on my habitual late afternoon walk. I was elated as he had been very busy for several weeks and we had spent little time together.

It was a beautiful afternoon. Winter had almost gone and the first hints of spring were in the air.

We walked along the dry bed of the Shibyeni creek for some distance and then crested its eastern bank. As soon as we reached the top of the bank, Kobus suddenly stopped. Studying the sky above the eastern horizon, he pointed to one of several clouds and announced: 'There's a fire.'

I looked up at the clouds and asked, 'Where? You mean in heaven?'

Still gazing at the cloud, he said thoughtfully, 'Fifteen, maybe twenty kilometres away.'

'It can't be,' I murmured. 'Heaven can't be that close.'

Kobus turned and started back down the bank, saying, 'I'd better get there. Sorry to cut our walk short.'

'Don't they have their own fire fighters in heaven?' I asked hopefully.

My little joke wasn't appreciated. I guess it wasn't even heard. Kobus had already crossed the bed of the creek and was hurrying up the opposite bank. I stood gazing at the clouds above the eastern horizon for a while. I wasn't even sure which cloud was the culprit. They all looked pretty much alike to me. It always amazes me how a game ranger can spot a telltale cloud — sometimes almost on the other side of the world. And even if the whole sky is overcast, he will point out one common-looking, unoriginal cloud amongst the many and tell you it's a smoke cloud.

I'd never before accompanied Kobus on a fire-fighting exercise and I suddenly decided that, for once, I'd like to do so.

I hurried home. Kobus and the field staff had already loaded their fire beaters and were boarding the pick-up truck. (The 'fire beater' is a flat square of perforated, fire-resistant rubber attached to a long stick.)

I jumped into the passenger seat, announcing that I was going along to help.

After having travelled some ten kilometres, I could see the distant, orange-red glow of the fire. Soon grey smoke filled the air, and some fifteen minutes later we reached the edge of the fire. It looked like a veritable inferno to me, but Kobus assured me that it was a relatively small fire. It was burning to the north of the road and, driven by a southerly wind, was advancing rapidly.

Using grass torches, Kobus and the game guards immediately started setting a backburn.

I looked up at the veil of white smoke that boiled skyward and felt small and threatened. I climbed on to the back of the pick-up in order to feel a little bigger. Up there, I also had a better view of the activities going on around me.

Driven by the wind, the advancing fire had a lot more momentum than the backburn, and I worried that the backburn wouldn't spread fast enough to stop the advancing blaze from jumping right over it. I watched as a large flame from the major fire licked at the undergrowth and lower branches of a tree and then leapt suddenly to the top, turning the tree into a twenty-metre-high torch.

While some of the men hurried along the track setting the backburn, the others collected their fire beaters and began extinguishing the rearmost flames of the backburn to stop them from leaping across the track.

Ash rained down on me and swirled in the churning air as the roar of the advancing fire grew louder. The flames of the backburn danced leisurely on through grass and scrub, advancing slowly, yet steadily towards the main fire. But even as the backburn advanced northward, segments of its rear line continued to arch southward, licking at the sky above the track, and I watched with concern as the men battled to extinguish the errant tongues of flame.

Every now and then I would notice one of the men being surrounded by flames and I would shout urgent warnings to him, or scream instructions to the others to go to his aid. Nobody paid any attention to me, however, and after some time I realised that these men were experts and didn't need my advice. A gust of wind suddenly brought a curtain of flames tearing towards the truck (and me!). I jumped from the back, got in behind the wheel and switched the engine on. Jamming the truck into reverse gear, I pressed down hard on the accelerator. But instead of reversing, the truck shot forward — almost into the wall of flames. I'd engaged the wrong gear. Slamming the brakes on, I managed to find the reverse gear and got out of the way.

After about half an hour, large gaps started to appear in the advancing fire line. Its momentum had been broken by the backburn. Within another half hour, the fire was fading and dying. The men relaxed their pace and, using their fire beaters, mopped up the remaining pockets of flame.

By dark, the job was done and we headed for home.

Kobus was curious to know why I had tried to drive the truck into the flames. I pointed out that I wasn't very familiar with the gears of his pick-up and that, anyway, I'd saved his truck from incineration. He thanked me, but forgot to comment on my brave deed.

A network of firebreak roads (which includes the tourist roads and patrol tracks) divides the Park into three hundred units in such a way that each one of these units is contained within safe lanes for backburning. These units are called 'blocks'.

When a fire is driven by a strong wind, backburning can become a difficult and dangerous task. Smouldering debris, such as dried elephant or buffalo droppings, gets blown across the firebreaks, setting adjacent blocks alight.

It is especially in the late winter and early spring (just before the start of the rainy season) that conditions often become extremely conducive to devastating, high temperature fires. At times like these, the rangers depend heavily on their VHF radios — both for reporting major fires and for calling for assistance if needed, as well as for reacting to such reports or calls.

During September of 1985 the Park radio mast developed problems, cutting off all communications for almost two months. The situation was critical. The previous summer had brought good rains and abundant growth of grass. Throughout the warm, dry winter, the sun had turned the grass to straw, and the straw to tinder. Now the air was hot and dry, and there was enough flammable material in the veld and bush to start a conflagration. The refugee problem (people crossing through the Park from Mozambique to South Africa) was at its peak, and the risk of man-made fires ran high. The rangers patrolled their sections day and night — watching and waiting.

In the early hours of a Saturday morning near the end of September Kobus walked out into the garden and saw the eastern sky was flushed orange-red. It was not the rising sun.

Within minutes Kobus and his field staff had collected their fire beaters and were on their way.

They found the fire forty kilometres away to the east. It was burning along a vast front from east to west and, driven by a strong wind, was advancing southwards. They immediately set a wide backburn, but the wind retarded the backburn while sweeping the major fire relentlessly on through grass and bush as far to the east and west as they could see. Realising that they couldn't set a wide enough backburn in time to stop the advancing line of fire, they drove some twenty kilometres downwind — on to the next firebreak road — and hurriedly set a new backburn. The advancing fire beat them to it and jumped their backburn in several places. Retreating once more, they drove on to the next firebreak road to set yet another backburn, but the wind carried smouldering debris across that backburn into adjacent blocks, creating a number of new, uncontrollable blazes.

As the VHF radios were out of order, Kobus could not call for help. He sent one of his game guards to the Mooiplaas ranger station to ask for assistance. The guard returned a while later to report that

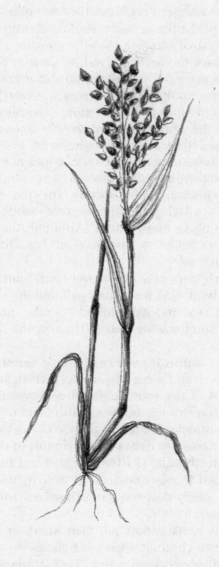

the ranger wasn't home — he and his field staff were fighting another fire in the northern region of the Mooiplaas section.

The wind swept the fire across many backburns and firebreaks throughout the rest of the day. Aided by his loyal team, Kobus fought back, but for the first time in his career as a game ranger, he was unable to get a fire in his section under control.

In the early afternoon the wind changed direction and started sweeping the fire in an easterly direction, towards our house. At dusk I could see the distant glow of the fire intensifying into an orange-red corona that stretched across most of the eastern horizon. The birds in our garden fell silent, and not even the chirp of a cricket disturbed the eerie quiet.

My sister's children were visiting for the spring school holidays. Luckily all the youngsters were inside playing card games and listening to noisy music. Although they knew about the fire, they didn't yet know that the wind had changed and was bringing it towards us.

I slipped quietly out of the house every half hour or so to check on the fire. By about nine o'clock, high fountains of colour were surging into the sky and ash started to rain into the garden. Except for the distant, steady roar of the fire, the night remained strangely quiet.

Hettie and her cousin Hennie (my sister's eldest son) were the first to get worried and went outside to investigate. When they saw the high glow of the approaching fire, they called me. I tried to play down the seriousness of the situation and told them calmly of the plans I had made. If the fire got too close, we would all go down to our boat and row right into the middle of the river, where we would be perfectly safe. (In 1985 we still had the boat.) I also reminded them that Kobus and his staff were fighting the fire and that they would surely do everything they could to stop it from reaching our house.

Apparently my reassurances put their minds at ease, and they went back inside to continue their card games.

I remained outside to keep watch. Having made up my mind that we would evacuate as soon as the fire reached the opposite bank of the Shibyeni creek, I tried to estimate the remaining distance between the fire and the creek. I guessed it to be about three kilometres. But I wasn't sure. It's difficult to estimate the distance between oneself and inferno. Fear tends to cloud the mind. I knew that the creek would not stop the fire, nor even slow its progress. The strong wind and the dense, dry vegetation on the banks of the creek would spur the flames on and send the fire sweeping across in no time at all.

The sound of an approaching range fire is as frightening as the sight of it. First there is the low steady drone, then a distinct swelling of sound that increases gradually in volume until it becomes a violent shuddering roar.

When the crescendo-ing roar began to frighten me, I went back into the house to call the children together and to tell them of my plans. In answer to their questions about what they could take with them in the boat, I told them that only the firearms and some drinking water could be taken aboard. There were seven of us. There wouldn't be room for anything else in the boat. My youngest nephew, then about six years old, asked if he could take some clean clothes. They would be flying home in a couple of days' time and he didn't think he should board the plane in the dirty clothes he was wearing. (This lad played so vigorously during the day that by nightfall his shiny blue eyes were the only clean thing about him.) I assured my nephew that his clean clothes wouldn't take up too much space in the boat and that he could bring them with him.

Sandra — always my most pragmatic child — was the most upset of all the children and wanted to know what would happen to our dogs, horses and bantams. I told her that we would take the dogs with us and release the horses and bantams before the fire reached the creek, allowing them to make their escape in good time.

Secretly, I felt profoundly sorry for her, knowing how much she hates dramatic events that have potential emotional impact.

We decided that we would all go outside and watch the fire. As soon as it reached the opposite bank of the creek we would set our plans in motion.

High torches of orange flame licked at the sky across the Shibyeni. The sight was as spectacular as it was frightening. But, strangely, the fire seemed to be standing still, almost as if pausing to reassemble its forces and choose the right moment to surge forward and sweep across the creek.

I held my breath, watching and waiting.

Minutes passed. The fire didn't make its move.

What was it waiting for?

And then the answer hit me: the wind had changed direction. It was no longer blowing east to west, but south to north. The fire would not cross the Shibyeni. It was being swept northwards.

Since all of the landscape within sight was already aflame from south to north, the southern edge of the fire would eventually die in its own ashes. It was the northern edge of the fire that would sweep on, incinerating the veld and bush and blackening the earth in its terrible wake.

I felt immensely relieved at the realisation that the children and I were safe and that evacuation would not be necessary, at least not for the time being. But I was desperately worried about Kobus and his men. They had been away from home fighting the fire for more than sixteen hours. I wondered where they were, and if they were safe.

After the children had gone back inside to prepare for bed, I fetched a long ladder from our storeroom and climbed to the top of our water reservoir, which stands on the roof of Kobus's office. From there I could see the northern edge of the fire creeping — like some gigantic glow-worm — relentlessly on and on across the landscape to the north. I wished desperately that the wind would drop and give the men a break.

I went to say good-night to the children, but could not go to sleep myself. So I boiled a dozen eggs, sliced up two loaves of bread and made sandwiches. Then I filled two thermos flasks with strong, sweet coffee and packed everything into a basket — just in case Kobus or one of his men might find the time to come and fetch it. None of them had eaten since the previous day.

At about midnight I lay down to rest for a while. I must have dozed off as I was woken shortly after midnight by the drone of a vehicle. I rushed outside. It was Kobus. I hardly recognised him. He was blackened from head to toe by soot and smoke. Only the whites of his eyes showed. He told me that they desperately needed more men to help them get the fire under control and he asked me to drive to ranger Dirk Swart's house near Phalaborwa gate to ask for assistance.

Taking the basket of food I had packed, as well as a large container of drinking water, he left immediately to get back to the fire. I ran inside, woke Hettie and asked her to take responsibility for the other children's safety while I was gone. I reminded her of the plan to row into the river should the wind change direction again and bring the fire across the creek. She promised that she would keep an eye on the situation and take good care of her sisters and cousins.

For a moment I considered taking all the children along with me, but then I remembered that my little Suzuki jeep wouldn't take seven people. (We no longer had the old Land Rover — it had expired the previous year.)

Before I left, I checked the wind direction again: it was still blowing due north, and would probably continue to do so.

I drove to Dirk's house as fast as I safely could, taking just over an hour to get there.

His wife answered my knock on the door. When I told her about the fire, she woke Dirk immediately.

Dirk suggested that I head back to Mahlangeni and the children while he assembled his field staff. He assured me that they would get to Kobus as soon as humanly possible.

While driving back, I watched the tall grasses bending in the wind — and was relieved to note that the wind was still blowing south to north. Far ahead on the horizon, I could see the orange-red glow of the fire. From my vantage point it seemed to be standing still, which meant that it was moving in the same direction as I was — from south to north.

Some twenty kilometres from home a sudden gust shook my jeep, and flurries of dust and leaves swirled across the track in front of the car. It took me a couple of seconds to register that the wind was changing direction. Soon steady gusts of dust and debris were dancing and tumbling across the road in the beam of the headlights.

I looked long and hard at the distant glow on the horizon. The gigantic glow-worm had started to creep slowly but steadily westwards.

I pressed hard on the accelerator. The dangers of speeding through the bush at night were secondary now to the safety of the children.

If the fire rose again on the far bank of the Shibyeni, the wind would quickly sweep it into the high trees inside the eastern fence of the garden.

I knew I was driving much too fast, but terror gripped me at the thought that Hettie might have fallen asleep again.

The glow crept relentlessly westwards along the horizon. I sped through the night, intermittently slamming on the brakes to avoid collisions with impala and other game, and swerving dangerously as rabbits zigzagged crazily across the track in front of the jeep.

Some ten kilometres from home, I knew that I would not be able to outpace the fire: it had expanded into a blazing front that stretched across most of the northern horizon from east to west. I could not help but believe that it had already swept across the garden and house.

Only when I reached the last bend in the road — where it turns into the track that leads alongside the river — could I see that the fire had passed some distance behind the house.

Tears of relief stung my eyes as I turned down the bank on to the causeway.

Some time during the early hours of the morning, the men finally succeeded in getting the fire under control. Dirk and his team returned to their base, and Kobus and his men arrived home shortly before dawn. They were so exhausted that they could hardly walk.

After only a few hours of rest they left again to extinguish smouldering tree stumps and mop up other remaining pockets of fire. It took them the whole of that day.

The period immediately after a devastating fire is one of the most distressing in any ranger's life. Injured animals must be tracked down and, if necessary, destroyed. Since the fire had ravaged such a huge area, Kobus requested that a helicopter be sent from Skukuza to aid him in the search for injured animals.

For many weeks after the fire the bush lay charred and desolate over vast stretches to the north and east of our house. It was a severely depressing scene.

One day shortly after the fire, as I was driving towards Shingwedzi, I came across an injured honey badger stumbling along at the side of the road in the blackened veld. I stopped next to him and, watching him intently for a while, realised that he had been blinded by the fire. As he struggled painfully to find his way to wherever he hoped to go in the vast, dead landscape, he kept stumbling and bumping into burnt-out stumps and rocks. A lump settled in my throat as I cocked my pistol and got out of the car. Aiming carefully, I released him from his agony.

Shaking with misery, I sat down beside the dead creature and stroked his scorched fur.

'I love honey badgers,' I told him softly. 'I once raised one.' I sat there for a long time, staring at the ruined landscape and trying to get my sorrow under control.

Trumpets in the Morning

T he riverine bush at Mahlangeni is home to several Egyptian
goose families. We often see parent birds with their downy
youngsters waddling across the sandy shore to the water.
Egyptian goslings are the cutest little creatures.

Karin's wish to see some goslings close up was realised when
one of our game guards brought her a clutch of five abandoned
eggs he had found.

We tricked one of our bantam hens into hatching the eggs, and
before long the bantam mother was proudly marching her five
'chicks' around the garden. The fact that her children bore no
resemblance to their cousins made no difference to her. The other
bantams stared suspiciously at the clumsy-looking brood who
waddled when they walked, but fortunately a mother's love is blind.

When a bantam cock spots a hawk or an eagle overhead, he
crows his danger warning, whereupon the hens rush their chicks
under the nearest cover (any low-growing vegetation) and then sit
over them with wings spread to protect them. Since goslings grow
much faster than chicks do, the bantam mother soon found it an
exhausting exercise to bully her chubby charges under a bush and
then try to get them all under her wings.

It must also have frustrated her that her children ignored her
clucking calls whenever she'd caught a nice worm or grasshopper
for them to eat. They preferred to snack on the grass from the
lawn. Nevertheless, she remained a loyal and caring mother and
spent her days clucking and fussing around her brood.

I believe her identity crisis reached its peak on the day that the
goslings discovered the joys of swimming.

Right outside our bedroom is a large meandering fish-pond. Kobus built it shortly after we moved in at Mahlangeni. He'd hoped that the watery scene amongst the shady trees and plants would create a feeling of coolness on those long, hot summer days. It does. And the fish-pond is really beautiful. But when stepping out of the sliding doors at night you have to watch your step, or you risk falling into it. We tried to keep some fish in the pond, but the resident kingfishers caught and ate them all. A horde of frogs has since taken up residence in the pond and they drive us crazy with their nightly choir practice.

The goslings were only a few days old when they discovered the fish-pond. They promptly plunged right in and started swimming happily around. Their astounded mother was unable to comprehend the scene. She froze on the spot, neck stretched forward, her eyes blinking rapidly in confusion. As realisation dawned, she had a fit. Clucking hysterically, she commanded her children to get out of the water immediately, but they were enjoying their swim far too much to pay any attention to her. She started flying from one side of the pond to the other, flapping her wings furiously and begging her children to come out of the water, please. Her frantic behaviour brought the bantam cock rushing over to see what was happening. He couldn't believe his eyes and stood gaping at the sight, unable to decide what he should do.

From that day on, the goslings frequented the pool daily, and their poor distraught mother could do nothing but stand at the edge of the pond, watching anxiously over them.

One day another bantam hen and her brood of chicks turned up at the pond to view the strange scene. As the hen looked on, she expressed her bewilderment with a series of nervous nods and eye-blinks. One of her chicks, however, appeared particularly interested in the proceedings and apparently decided that if his cousins could do it, so could he. He walked to the edge of the pond, leaned over and was readying for the plunge when he lost his nerve and decided to stick to dry land. I'd been watching him from my bedroom and was about to rush outside and save the silly chick from drowning when I saw with relief that his bantam instincts had prevailed.

Soon the fast-growing goslings were as big as their bantam mother. And when they discovered their vocal cords and started honking like hoarse trumpets, she'd had enough. She decided then and there that she could no longer tolerate her children's embarrassing behaviour and that she would, from that day on, simply get on with her own life and ignore the brats.

Egyptian geese are gorgeous birds. They are chestnut and auburn-coloured above and fawn to tawny underneath. They have beautiful coloured wings with white shoulder and black flight feathers, and a striking emerald green line along the edge of the wing.

At the age of about eight months, two of our geese — no longer goslings — decided to move house. With a honking farewell fanfare, they flew over the fence and east along the river until they finally disappeared from sight. We trust that they have found a comfortable new home and breeding place somewhere in the riverine bush to the east. About a month later, a third goose took wing and, with a loud parting salutation, left us to seek a new home amongst the other Egyptian goose families along the river banks.

The remaining two geese stayed with us for another two months before they, too, decided to emigrate. They took off and flew high over the fence — also with a loud farewell fanfare. But they didn't fare far. They landed in the riverine bush along the sandy shore right in front of the house, fell in love with the setting, and promptly made it their new home.

Although they spend their days grazing along the river bank, they come to dinner at the Mahlangeni restaurant just before sunset every evening. We notice them on the lawn, waiting for their bowl of porridge to be served. If the service isn't prompt, they start screeching like hoarse trumpets until one of us rushes outside with their meal.

Even when they were goslings, they didn't take to the dry maize kernels which we feed our bantams, but chose rather to share the dogs' dinners (maize meal porridge with meat and gravy). It was the porridge they were after. We noticed that the dogs became nervous when they were watched by the hungry

geese while they were eating, so we got into the habit of putting out a plate of porridge for the geese every time we fed the dogs.

It has been several years now since those last two geese 'emigrated' and they have since produced and raised their own brood of goslings, but they still turn up every evening at mealtime to enjoy their plate of porridge. While they were hatching and raising their brood, the parents took turns to come and feed. One of them would stay with the eggs, and later with the young goslings. They also took turns to come and take their daily swim in the fish-pond. Only when their youngsters had become self-sufficient did they start turning up together again to feed and swim.

Another habit that these two maintain is to arrive just before dawn each morning, swoop to a landing on the rock in the fish-pond outside our bedroom, and startle us awake with raucous trumpeting. The purpose of their trumpeting is, of course, to broadcast their proprietorship of the Mahlangeni pond and restaurant to all other Egyptian geese in the neighbourhood and to warn them that trespassers will be prosecuted.

If you take into account the distance that their voices have to travel to reach all the goose families along the river, you can probably imagine the volume of noise that hits us in our bedroom early each morning.

Hyenas

There is probably no other sound in Africa that is as evocative and as sinister as the whooping howl of a hyena. It rises from nowhere in the deep of night and drifts over the landscape in rising and falling echoes — a haunting chant that lingers in the darkness to stir ancient memories of witches and ghosts.

Although the hyena is more closely related to the cats than the canines, he looks more like a dog. He is part scavenger and part predator and eats anything that his powerful jaws and teeth can mangle — which is just about everything. He has a massive head and upper chest, and a sloping, seemingly half-crippled rear. He moves with a shuffling, shifty gait, he drools a lot and he giggles. He also steals.

One night, some years ago, a hyena dug his way under our main gates and sneaked into the garden. He ate the leather saddles of the girls' bicycles, a brand-new pair of Karin's shoes which she'd left outside, and a pair of boots which Kobus had left on the patio behind the kitchen. He also discovered my vacuum cleaner in the garage and ate the dust bag.

Kobus had been out on patrol that night and had taken the dogs along with him. Had they been home, the hyena would never have ventured into the garden. Despite his strength and stealth, he's something of a coward.

I wrote a letter to our insurance company to enquire whether we could claim compensation for our losses.

They replied that, although our insurance policy covers theft, it doesn't specify anything about hyenas. But they were willing to pay us out if I sent them a sworn statement which I could make at any police station.

Luckily, I had some hyena hairs as evidence. I had found the hairs in the wire of the gate on the morning after the incident. I had gathered them carefully and sealed them in an envelope. Just in case.

Taking the envelope with me, I drove to the police station at Phalaborwa. I showed the hairs to the constable on duty and told him the story. He misunderstood, thinking I wanted to lay a charge against the hyena. I had to explain to him that I only wanted to swear that it was the truth.

I eventually acquired the sworn statement and mailed it to the insurers.

Not long afterwards we were fully compensated.

We were very grateful.

This was not, however, the end of our hyena problems.

Some months later, Kobus and I were driving home late one night after attending a function at Olifants camp. When Kobus became sleepy after two hours on the road, I took over while he catnapped in the passenger seat. Somewhere on a winding stretch of track near the Shabarumbi creek a hyena suddenly dashed out of the darkness, right in front of the car. I slammed on the brakes, swerving, but couldn't avoid hitting the animal. We collided with a thud. Kobus and I leapt out of the car to see whether the hyena was hurt — but he'd disappeared. All we could hear were his crashing sounds as he ran away through the bush. Kobus said that he did not think that the hyena had suffered any injuries other than perhaps a bruised hip. Even so, I felt terrible. I had never before collided with an animal.

And one of the car's headlights was completely smashed.

Again, I wrote to our insurance company, enquiring whether we might claim compensation for the headlight, and again they were sympathetic to our problem. They sent me a motor accident claim form to fill out. I answered the questions as follows:

(1) Speed before accident: *35 kph.*
(2) Road surface: *Bumpy (dirt track).*
(3) Width of road: *2 metres.*

(4) Weather conditions: *Good.*

(5) Visibility: *Bad (pitch dark).*

(6) Street lighting: *Poor. (No moon. Only stars.)*

(7) Was any warning given by you, e.g. hooting, indicator, etc? *No. (Animals are not acquainted with these.)*

(8) Give details of any road safety signs or warning signs in vicinity of scene of accident: *None.*

(9) Damage to other vehicles: *None.*

(10) Personal injuries: *(A hyena was injured.)*

(11) Name of injured: *(Hyena.)*

(12) Address and phone number: *Shabarumbi creek, Kruger Park. (No telephone.)*

(13) Details of injuries: *Unknown. Possibly bruised hip.*

(14) Name of hospital where treated: *(He was not treated.)*

(15) Connection with accident, e.g. pedestrian, driver or passenger: *Pedestrian.*

Then followed a blank space where a sketch of the accident was required. I didn't know how to draw a picture of a hyena dashing out of the pitch-black bush in the dark of night. I considered colouring the whole space black and writing an explanation underneath to the effect that the nights up here are so dark that one can't see a thing. It didn't seem a good idea, however. It's true that the nights in the bush are terribly dark, but I'm nervous of taking any chance with the truth in a legal document that requires the whole truth and nothing but the truth.

I asked Kobus to help me with the sketch. He made a simple graphic drawing indicating the direction of travel with arrows, the relative position of the hyena when first sighted, and an arrow to indicate its direction of movement across the road, with a cross indicating the point of impact. I had not thought of that. I thought they wanted a realistic drawing of a hyena dashing out of the bush in front of the car.

Again, we were fully compensated.

And again, we were extremely grateful.

Soon after this, there was a third hyena incident, but I didn't have the courage to write to our insurance company again. I was afraid that they might suspect me of fabricating hyena stories for insurance claims.

During the winter school holidays, the girls and I accompanied Kobus on a field trip to Shipandani, a ranger outpost on the eastern boundary of Kobus's section. As our house is situated on the western boundary of the section, Kobus often sleeps over at Shipandani when he is working in the eastern area. It's a beautiful little camp on the bank of the Tsendze stream. To the south of the camp is a boulder-strewn koppie where baboons often play and where impala lilies bedeck the hillside in a blaze of pink blooms during the winter months. Three thatched rondavels, a lean-to storage kitchen with an open camp-fire area, and two reed structures housing a toilet and a shower make up the camp.

Since the camp is not fenced we let the dogs sleep inside one of the rondavels whenever there are leopards in the area.

One night during the winter holidays, a hyena sneaked into camp and stole our best iron cooking pot as well as a beautiful orange blanket which one of the girls had accidentally left outside on a chair near the camp-fire.

The spoor told us that only one hyena had been responsible for the thefts. It didn't look as though he had made two trips, and we are still wondering how he managed to carry away both the heavy iron pot and the blanket.

The spoor disappeared in the reeds along the river bank, and although we searched the area for our pot and our blanket we never found them.

A few months later, while doing an aerial census, Kobus flew over the area south of Shipandani and spotted an orange-coloured object in the veld to the south of the koppie. He asked the pilot to decrease altitude so that he could see what it was. It was our orange blanket. Unfortunately the area is particularly rocky, and there was no nearby place suitable for a helicopter landing so Kobus couldn't retrieve our blanket. I often wonder whether it is still lying there all by itself, and why the hyena had carried it such a long distance before discarding it.

We still don't know what became of the cooking pot.

A good blanket and an iron pot aren't exactly cheap any more, but I couldn't bring myself to write another letter to the insurance company. Even if they believed my story, I felt too embarrassed to go to the police station again to make a sworn statement to the effect that a hyena had stolen our blanket and our pot.

A couple of years ago while he was in town, Kobus bought himself a pair of canvas boxing boots. They are thin-soled and light, and Kobus had fancied a pair for a long time, reckoning that his long walks in the bush justified the purchase.

Shortly after buying the boots, Kobus was part of a team camping at the site of a zebra-catching enclosure, busy with the relocation of some of the animals.

The other game rangers teased Kobus a lot about his boxing boots, but he ignored them. They were the most comfortable shoes he had ever possessed. The only problem was that they tended to smell a bit ripe after a day's hard labour. At night, he had to leave his boots outside in order to preserve the fresh air in his tent.

True to form, a prowling hyena discovered the boots one night. He picked up one of them and made off with it — only to drop it again some thirty metres into the bush. Apparently the smell had overpowered him. If you consider the rotten, putrid carrion that hyenas feast on, you can probably imagine how offensive the boots must have been to put a damper on the hyena's appetite!

When the other rangers saw the hyena spoor in the morning and found the saliva-covered boot close to the camp, they had much to say. One of them suggested putting together a search party to look for the hyena, in case he was lying dead in the bush. Another suggested hanging the boots on the zebra enclosure at night to keep marauding lions at bay. This idea was unanimously rejected on the grounds of cruelty to the zebras.

Kobus still defends the virtues of his boxing boots. Not only are they comfortable, they're also hyena-proof.

Getting to know Baboons

Although baboons, with their capacity for primitive reasoning, are recognised as animals of superior intelligence, they look more like members of the riff-raff than the intelligentsia. They have no natural grace or dignity, and they're not particularly handsome. They're not even photogenic — their dull, blurry coats make them look out of focus. But, unlovely as they may be, they are the entertainment stars of the animal kingdom.

Our former chief ranger, Dirk Ackerman, once told us the following story.

One evening on his way home to Skukuza he stopped on the bank of the Sabie River to watch a troop of baboons that was preparing to retire for the night. The mothers were engaged in the usual battle of persuading the youngsters to stop playing, get up the trees and go to bed. Meanwhile, the subadults (or teenagers) were whooping it up, chasing one another all over the trees and shouting at the tops of their voices, much to the annoyance of the tired adults who were longing for some peace and quiet.

As he sat watching the baboons, Dirk noticed a large adult male who had found himself a comfortable spot in the fork of a wild fig tree. The baboon was contentedly settling in for the night when he noticed a guinea fowl calmly perched on the same branch, just an arm's length away. The baboon's first reaction was to studiously ignore the bird, but the longer he did so the more resentful he became of the intruder. The guinea fowl was cluttering his personal space and the idiotic bird wasn't even aware that it was doing so. It just sat there dozing. The more the baboon tried not to think about the bird, the more agitated he became. His eyes flickered involuntarily towards the fowl every now and then and he started fidgeting uncontrollably. The tension in the tree mounted until the baboon's frustration exploded. In one swift movement, he reached out, grabbed the dozing guinea fowl, rumpled its feathers aggressively and threw it out of the tree straight into the river. The bird's hysterical squawks resounded in the dusk as it hit the water.

Luckily it didn't drown, but it looked pretty bedraggled as it struggled ashore and was visibly shaken by its experience.

Hopefully that guinea fowl has learnt its lesson and will in future respect a baboon's right to some privacy.

The baboons who sleep in the jackalberry trees across the river from us are a bunch of insomniac chatterboxes. They often shriek, mutter, grunt and natter at full volume late into the night, only to start up again in the early dawn. One wonders what it's all about. (It's like having noisy neighbours whose language you don't understand. For all you know, they could be discussing you.)

One day I decided that I had better find out a thing or two about baboons, so I travelled the 260 kilometres south to Skukuza and borrowed a good selection of books from the library. There are not many publications on baboons, but a fair number exist on primates in general and on the big apes in particular, especially the gorillas and chimpanzees.

What I read fascinated me so much that I decided to do some research of my own and make a documentary film about the baboons of the Kruger Park.

My first task was to find a troop of baboons to use as subjects. Naturally, the local troop seemed the obvious choice, but I soon discovered that their daily foraging expeditions took them to areas that were inaccessible to my Suzuki jeep. Despite its four-wheel drive capacity, the little vehicle was not designed for hill climbing, river crossings and heavy bundu-bashing. I could have followed the baboons on foot, of course, as Dian Fossey and Jane Goodall did with their gorillas and chimps, but I'm not designed for heavy bundu-bashing either — at least not while single-handedly lugging along a tripod and 16 mm camera with a heavy zoom lens, plus sound equipment, and the inevitable firearm.

I had to find a troop whose territory took into account the limitations of my jeep.

For weeks on end I followed various troops throughout the Park. Some of them covered upwards of twenty kilometres on their daily excursions, and all the troops I tried to follow frequented areas that posed impossible conditions for me.

One day, ranger Cobus Botha of Satara suggested that I follow a troop that lives in the Sweni region south of the Satara camp. The area consists mostly of open savannah and flat woodlands that are easily accessible. I set off eagerly and soon found the troop. The whole of their foraging area was indeed accessible, and I was very excited. But, after observing the troop for a number of days, I was put off by their incessant in-troop squabbling and quarrelling. They weren't a very nice lot, and their uncivil behaviour jangled my nerves.

I resumed my search.

Near Skukuza I found a troop of loafers whose whole territory was less than half a kilometre in extent. At night they slept in trees on the banks of the Nwatitshaka creek where they had a view over Skukuza's rubbish dump. In the mornings they would tumble out of the trees and stroll up to the dump where they spent their days picnicking amongst the rubbish, or waiting for the dump truck to arrive with new provisions (mostly left-overs from the Skukuza restaurant and the kitchens of the personnel village). They seemed generally mild-mannered and good-tempered, and they didn't mind my presence. I filmed some footage of them for its entertainment value. It would have been easy to make them the subjects of my entire film, but it didn't seem a good idea to use a bunch of lower-class tramps as my star actors. They were certainly not representative of the baboon troops of the Park.

Once again, I resumed my search.

Finally, one day, I found the perfect troop in the perfect setting: the whole of their foraging territory was easily accessible, and the general character of the troop appealed to me.

This particular troop lives on the southern bank of the Shingwedzi River, only a few kilometres from the Shingwedzi tourist camp. They spend their nights in the riverine trees, and their daily expeditions take them along a patrol track up to a dry creek, then along the banks of the creek for some distance, and eventually to a perennial water-hole in the creek. They spend the midday hours relaxing at the water-hole before making their way back — more or less along the same route — to reach their sleeping places in the riverine trees by dusk.

I was elated. I had found everything I could possibly have wished for: a nice, friendly-looking troop, an accommodating area set in beautiful photogenic surroundings (riverine bush and mopani woodlands) and, as a special bonus, the close proximity of a tourist camp to use as a base. Kobus had bought me a little caravan, and I obtained permission from the Shingwedzi camp manager to park it in the camp. I would sleep there during the week and return to Mahlangeni at the weekends to be with my family.

Everything was set, and I couldn't wait to start filming.

First, however, I had to gain the confidence of the troop members and make them comfortable with my presence. As long as I stayed in my jeep they ignored me — they are used to tourist cars. But the moment I got out to mount the camera on the tripod, the troop leader would bark a command and the females with their babies and youngsters would vanish into the bush. The troop leader and his ministers would then sit around, silently and suspiciously watching my every move. It frustrated me a great deal. I wanted to film the activities of the whole troop, not just a silent and suspicious minority.

The next few weeks were a test of my own resolve and patience. I followed the troop on their daily excursions, and whenever they settled down to rest for a while I would get out of my car and put on my 'look-how-friendly-I-am' act. Looking casual and relaxed, I would talk to them in my most cordial tone of voice. As the days and weeks went by, they started getting used to me until, eventually, the troop leader and his ministers concluded that I was harmless. Their suspicions changed to a cautious acceptance of my presence and I was elated when the troop leader, whom I had named 'Big Boss', finally stopped giving his command to the females and children to disappear.

The youngsters were the first to want to make friends with me. Initially, they merely sat watching me with curiosity, occasionally venturing up closer for a better look. Before long, they started communicating with me in baboon language and even invited me to play with them. I was slowly learning to understand their language and even to react to their communications in a way that made some sense to them.

Their language consists of gestures, sounds and facial expressions which they combine in a variety of ways in order to tell each other how they feel, what they want, and what they intend to do. One of the first gestures I learned to recognise was the 'come and play' gesture. If a baboon approaches you with a clumsy uncoordinated gait and a comical expression on his face, he's saying, 'Let's play!'

While actually playing with the baboons was far from my intentions, I encouraged their playful behaviour by using voice intonations to express my pleasure. They soon recognised my appreciative tone of voice and reacted by performing all sorts of silly antics for my benefit. They would bound about and somersault, and if I responded enthusiastically, they would repeat the antics over and over again, stopping each time to observe my reactions.

While the toddlers and youngsters entertained me with their skylarking, the teenagers seemed fascinated by my camera equipment and tried to fiddle or tamper with it whenever I turned my back. My harsh tone of voice and admonishments would send them shying away, but only until I dropped my guard again. Eventually I had to resort to arming myself with a stick with which I rapped their knuckles if they got too mischievous. They were terrified of the stick and soon learnt to treat my equipment with respect.

One of the teenagers (whom I nicknamed 'Silly Grin') was particularly sensitive to my 'angry' tone of voice. Whenever I scolded him, he stopped what he was doing, sat down and flashed a toothy grin at me, ears flattened against his head — the gesture

which, in baboon language, means 'I'm sorry'. Silly Grin's apologies always touched a soft spot in me and I couldn't bring myself to rap his knuckles but had none the less to scold him regularly as he was forever making a nuisance of himself. And no matter how often I reprimanded him, he always apologised.

While the youngsters and teenagers tried to involve me in their playful activities, the adults treated me with aloofness and paid me scant attention. It was only Big Boss who seemed to be constantly aware of my presence. Whenever and wherever I turned, he would be there somewhere, watching me quietly. For many weeks it unsettled me, until eventually I realised that Big Boss was merely doing his job as supreme guardian of his troop's safety and that he was, in fact, allowing me many privileges. He let me get quite close to the toddlers and youngsters, and he let me scold them and even rap their knuckles if they tampered with my equipment. But there was one privilege that remained off-limits to me: I was not to touch nor even approach a nursing female or her infant. Whenever he noticed me approaching a mother with a baby he would give a warning grunt, jerk his head and raise his eyes. I had no doubt that he was saying, 'Don't you dare!'

I respected his wishes and kept my distance from the babies.

The troop consisted of forty-six baboons and, as time went by, I learned to recognise each one's particular attitudes, facial features and personality traits. I grew fond of the clowns and became especially attached to the playful toddlers and youngsters. There was one specific quintet of toddlers who spent all their days inventing antics to amuse me.

The toddlers and youngsters form playgroups with their peers, and they remain in these playgroups until they're teenagers (about four years old). Then the girls separate from the group to practise the arts of grooming and baby-sitting. But the boys remain in the playgroup and their games become rougher and wilder as they test one another's strengths and abilities. They know that one day the strongest and cleverest of them will become the new troop leader.

At the age of about eight years they are adults, and each of them has a job to do. The females bring up the children and the males are responsible for the safety of the troop.

The troop leader is chief minister, but he is also responsible for law and order. Then there are a number of deputy ministers. Their shared portfolio is mainly defence. The younger males do duty as sentries and are responsible for raising the alarm when danger is spotted. The sentries are usually seen sitting in the tops of trees, looking serious and official as they conscientiously scout the landscape for signs of predators. They always advance ahead of the troop to take up their positions. As soon as the troop approaches, the sentries come down from their vantage points and move on again to take up new positions ahead.

As the weeks and months went by, the baboons grew so accustomed to me, and I to them, that we eventually lost all distrust of each other and I was more or less accepted as a member of the troop. It happened so slowly, and in a barely discernible way, that I didn't actually realise it was happening at all until one specific day when it dawned upon me like a sudden revelation.

In the late morning of a particularly hot summer day, after I'd followed them on foot for quite a distance, the baboons decided to take to the shade and rest rather than continue their journey in the blazing sun. I was as hot and bothered as they were, and gratefully slumped down on to the sand to share a shady spot under some lala palms with a group of females and their babies. The males rested in the shade of some nearby mopani trees, while the ever-energetic youngsters played tag all over the place.

It was so hot that the perspiration was streaming from my forehead into my eyes. Having nothing with me with which to wipe my stinging eyes, I wondered whether the baboons would take offence if I used my shirt to mop my face. I looked about, but the baboons weren't taking any notice of me and, as I lifted my shirt and wiped my face, feeling embarrassed about exposing my midriff, it occurred to me that I was being silly. None of the baboons was wearing any clothes. What's more, a female sitting within an arm's length of me was nursing her infant, totally unperturbed by my presence. It was then that the uniqueness of my situation suddenly struck me: I was sharing a spot of shade in the middle of the wilderness with a troop of wild baboons!

I was so exhilarated by my discovery that I laughed out loud — and momentarily startled the resting adults.

A few minutes later, I developed an urge to visit the bathroom. I got up and walked to another stand of lala palms some distance away. As I walked around the large, low-hanging fronds to get behind them, I suddenly found myself face to face with an enormous hyena. He'd apparently been sleeping behind the palms and, when he heard me approaching, had jumped to his feet.

I sprinted back to the safety of my troop. When I got there, still shaking with fright at the surprise encounter, I found Big Boss staring at me.

'Listen,' I said, 'do you realise that your sentries are sleeping on the job? I almost walked right into a hyena!'

Naturally, Big Boss couldn't understand what I was saying, but he didn't like the accusatory tone of my voice and he glared at me as if to say, 'Careful how you talk to me! OK?'

I realised that I had come to trust Big Boss and his ministers and sentries as my personal bodyguards. Not that I expected them to physically protect me from harm, but I relied on their effective warning and defence systems to give me sufficient time to reach the safety of my jeep whenever primate-eating predators lurked in the area.

I usually parked my jeep a fair distance from the troop, not wanting it to appear on camera while I was filming. Often the baboons would wander off and I would follow them with my camera until the distance between me and my safe haven grew too far for my comfort. Rather than lugging my heavy equipment back to the car, I'd leave it where it was and, after a stern warning to Silly Grin and his mates to leave the camera alone, I'd dash back to fetch my jeep and bring it closer.

During the times I spent with the baboons there were several occasions on which the sentries raised the alarm. Big Boss and his ministers always reacted instantly to the high-pitched, two-phased barks of a sentry. Big Boss would herd all the females and young into the safety of the nearest trees and then charge off, together with his ministers, to investigate the cause of the alarm. I, of course, bolted for the safety of my jeep as soon as an alarm sounded, not wasting any time finding out the cause of the alarm until I was safely in my car.

Baboons at war kick up a terrific noise. They bark, roar and screech with such vigour that twenty baboons sound more like two hundred. Often, as I sat in my car listening to the hysterical commotion, I worried about the possibility that my friends were actually being attacked, but they always returned from the battlegrounds unscathed. Apparently the violent cacophony of their war-cries unnerved even the most formidable of transgressors. On the few occasions that I managed to catch sight of the fleeing intruders, they turned out to be hyenas and, on one occasion, the culprit was a leopard.

Unfortunately I was unable to film the scene with the leopard as dusk had already settled and the riverine bush was very dense. In fact, apart from a brief glimpse of the leopard's rump and tail, I hardly saw him at all. But I had my tape recorder with me and I managed to record the sound.

Barking, screeching and roaring with a fury that frightened even me, the baboons chased the leopard from tree to tree, surrounded it, allowed it to escape, and then surrounded it again and again until, finally, it was so intimidated that it fled. The defence operation lasted a full forty minutes. By that time I was almost deaf and I'm sure that the baboons must have been hoarse from the prolonged strain that their vocal cords had to endure.

Although lions will prey on baboons, it is rare for them to do so. Leopards have the advantage that they can climb trees. Apart from the occasional acrobatic individual, most lions can only manage to jump into the lower branches of a tree and not actually climb it. Even so, baboons have a healthy respect for the kings of the bush.

Around noon one day, while the baboons and I were resting at the water-hole, two sentries simultaneously sounded the alarm. I knew from the intensity of their calls that the situation was serious and I dashed for my jeep even faster than I normally did (which is pretty fast anyway). I had to cover a distance of almost two hundred metres as on that particular day I had kept on postponing the decision to fetch my jeep and bring it closer.

As I sprinted towards my jeep, I heard Big Boss barking and barking, and I wondered whether he was chasing not only the females and children to safety, but me as well.

Once inside the jeep, I drove back to the troop and found to my surprise that, unlike other occasions, Big Boss and his ministers were also up the trees. A few seconds later a pride of lions appeared and made their way to the water-hole. The baboons were very quiet as they waited patiently — high up in their trees — until the lions eventually made their way off.

On another occasion I visited my troop after dark to record some evening chatter. At dusk, after the troop had settled in for the night in the riverine trees, I'd returned to the camp to get a bite to eat, and I drove back to the troop a little while later. They were so quiet, up in their trees, that it took me a while to locate them. When I parked under the stand of trees where I'd last seen them, there was not the slightest sound to indicate that they were still there. Believing that they might have moved to other trees in my absence, I drove slowly along the river bank for a while, straining to detect some baboon sounds, but I heard nothing. This puzzled me, as I'd expected to hear their usual insomniac chatter, interspersed with occasional shrieks from argumentative young-sters and grunts of admonishment from the adults. But it was abnormally quiet.

After a while I returned to the spot where I'd initially believed them to be, and as I switched off the engine to listen for them, I heard a stifled cough from one of the treetops. They were there after all. I quickly switched on my tape recorder, put my earphones on and stuck the rifle-mike out through my window, holding it an arm's length from the jeep so that it wouldn't pick up the soft hum of the tape recorder on the seat next to me. The sensitive directional microphone picked up some more muffled coughing and some throat-clearing from the treetops, but no other baboon sounds. I couldn't understand why they were so quiet.

And then, to my surprise, I heard the sound of approaching footsteps. I moved the microphone in a slow half-circle to locate the direction from which the footsteps were coming, wondering what on earth anyone could be doing out in the bush at this time of night. Didn't he realise there might be lions around?

The directional microphone indicated that the footsteps were coming from directly behind me. The person appeared to be walking on the grassy cover along the bank. I turned to look behind me through the rear window of my jeep. The footsteps seemed very close. The light of the half-moon enabled me to see some twenty metres into the bush but I could see no signs of the owner of the footsteps. It was very spooky.

Then the sounds of the footsteps disappeared altogether. That was even more spooky. I turned to look through my side window, and found myself looking straight into the eyes of a large lioness. She was standing within an arm's length of me, staring at my microphone. As I jerked my microphone and arm back into the jeep she made a sniffing noise which, picked up by the microphone, resounded fortissimo through my earphones.

The footsteps I'd been listening to had been hers. I couldn't believe my own stupidity. I, who had been studying baboons for so long, should immediately have interpreted their silence as an indication that there were lions in the area.

I never did get my baboon sounds that evening and had to return on another occasion to record them.

Big Boss's sense of responsibility and loyalty to his troop often impressed me. He was constantly vigilant and he reacted instantly whenever the alarm was sounded. On one occasion a toddler was separated from its mother during an alarm and was running frantically about, looking for her and screaming with panic. Big Boss charged over, gathered up the terrified infant in the gentlest manner and carried it, pressed close to his chest, up the nearest tree. After placing the infant on a high branch, out of harm's way, he dashed down to assist his ministers in seeing the intruder off.

I once read an article about baboons in which they were described as 'brutal fighters'. During the eighteen months that I spent with the troop, I never once saw any behaviour that could be described as 'brutal'. I found them to be generally good-natured and tolerant, displaying genuine affection for their offspring and for one another.

Baboons are social animals, and they are in many ways almost human. This doesn't mean that they are angels, of course. The strict rules and traditions of their complex society can cause a lot of personal stress and frustration. Social status, for instance, plays an important role in their lives and when this subject comes under debate, it results in a chaotic spell of arguing and yelling. They chase each other, hurling insults and threats, but they never actually come to blows.

I often found myself in the midst of such an episode of chaos, and in the beginning I used to flee and hide in my jeep until it was over. Eventually, however, I grew used to these outbursts and remained right behind my camera, filming the scene. On a few occasions I was almost run over by the feuding animals, but I never personally came under attack. Not being a baboon myself, I had no social status, and the baboons knew of course that it would be pointless to contest the rank of a non-ranking individual. I was therefore quite safe in their midst, even in the heat of the battle. These stormy exchanges often ended as suddenly as they'd started, and life would get back to normal again with everybody feeling better for having settled their differences.

The troop that I had observed some time before in the Sweni area south of Satara was far more quarrelsome and unsettled than the Shingwedzi troop. I put this down to the fact that their leader was not as strong a personality as Big Boss. I believed that their behaviour reflected an almost constant leadership struggle, with the leader having to stamp his questionable authority on the pretenders to his throne. But, in fairness, even their most heated displays of force never reached 'brutal' levels — at least not while I was with them.

If I were asked to describe baboons in a single phrase I would choose 'charming clowns' — certainly not 'brutal fighters'.

Baboons as
Movie Stars

F ilming baboons isn't as much fun as you might think. While you're busy setting up the tripod and mounting the camera, reading the light, setting the exposure and adjusting the focus, they perform as if they were competing in the finals of a chorus line audition. But the moment you start the camera rolling, the idiots either freeze and behave like bored statues, or start dashing crazily all over the place — and out of your light and focus range. And no amount of pleading or yelling will coach them to stay in shot.

If you don't have infinite reserves of patience and resilience, you must not try to film baboons. It wouldn't be good for your health.

I worked so hard for so long that I sometimes found myself losing courage and wanting to quit. But after having spent our precious savings on film, I had no choice but to complete the movie and get it on to the market.

After a long day of hard work with the wayward actors, I would stumble into my caravan in the evenings and collapse on to the bed. I was often too exhausted to prepare supper for myself and I survived mostly on a diet of wheat biscuits, tinned fruit and coffee.

My days started early. At first light the baboons would be up and about, performing the most awesome trapeze acts and other acrobatic feats high up in the riverine trees. Circus-time lasted only from dawn until approximately one hour after sunrise, and I resolved to capture on film as much of their early morning activity as I possibly could. This was tricky because it was almost impossible to know ahead of time exactly where and in which tree the next astounding act would be performed. I had to rely mostly on luck, focus my lens on a possible candidate, and let the camera roll. Often the chosen candidate would stand there doing nothing for minutes on end, wasting my precious film. As soon as I gave up on him and switched the camera off, he'd leap up like a flash of lightning, grab a branch and perform the most breath-taking trapeze act ever witnessed, and exasperating me almost beyond endurance.

Because I attended the early morning circus-hour every day of the week (barring weekends) for almost eighteen months, I did eventually succeed in capturing a fair number of fantastic scenes on film.

At approximately one hour after sunrise, Big Boss would utter a couple of bass grunts, indicating that the circus was over and that it was time to be on the move. His command would be relayed by his ministers to the rest of the troop until everyone had received the message. The performers would come down from their trees and the sentries would depart to take up their positions ahead of the troop. As soon as the foraging safari was under way, I would follow the baboons in my jeep, stopping whenever they paused and setting up my camera in case something interesting happened.

The movement formation of the troop was noteworthy. The mothers with babies always walked in the centre of the group accompanied by strong adult males (usually the troop leader with a number of his ministers). The youngsters stayed close to the centre group and were kept from straying by the adult males. The juveniles and subadults made up the flanks, while two of the senior ministers – who appeared to be the oldest males in the troop – usually followed as a rearguard.

They seldom moved at a consistent pace. A lot of time was spent dawdling along the way, hunting for roots, berries and insects and, while doing so, they'd often sit about for a while, socialising, chatting and grooming each other's coats. Whenever they dallied or moved at a leisurely pace, I'd get out of my car, mount the camera on the tripod and follow them on foot in case something interesting happened that I'd want to film. (The camera, mounted on the tripod, wouldn't fit into the car and many precious minutes were wasted getting out of the car and setting the camera up.)

I had to discipline myself to double back to the jeep regularly to bring it closer. It was hard work – following the baboons on foot and then doubling back to fetch the vehicle every now and then. I often considered leaving the car behind and following them on foot all day long. It would have been less exhausting in the end, but I didn't have the courage to spend so many hours out in the bush with no safe haven to flee to during an alarm. I would have considered climbing up the nearest tree along with the baboons, but getting up a mopani tree isn't as easy as you may think. Apart from the mopani trees — which constitute the dominant species in the Shingwedzi area — there are a number of other tree species as well, but most of them, like the leadwood and fever trees, have tall, straight trunks with their lowest branches several metres from the ground, making it pretty difficult for a human being to climb them.

By late morning the troop would reach the water-hole, settle down and spend the midday hours lazing about and relaxing — mercifully offering me a respite from the strenuous morning safari. Often, however, there wouldn't be much time to rest because, even while relaxing, baboons can be very entertaining and I couldn't afford to let any worthwhile shots slip through my fingers. Baboons seem to be constantly occupied with the undercurrents and complexities of their political affiliations and social relationships and there is hardly a moment of boredom in the daily life of a troop.

It was during these hours spent at the water-hole that I eventually succeeded in filming some of my best shots of the social behaviour of the adults and of the youngsters at play.

A number of zoologists and other scientists agree that every activity of a wild animal is functional, relating in one way or another to its survival. According to them, the function of play is to learn. If that is true, then young baboons are the most avid students I have ever come across. From the age of three months to about six years they seem to do little else but play, and while it may be educational for them, the curriculum appears to be aimed at turning them into professional acrobats and comedians.

I spent many delightful hours watching them gambolling, jesting, somersaulting, running and leaping — one after the other — over the same water puddle, chasing round and round a tree trunk, dashing up a tree and charging with perilous speed to the furthest reaches of the highest branches, leaping — one after the other — through the tree tops, and swinging precariously from spindly twigs or vines, hanging upside down or dangling from one hand in the air many metres above the ground.

During the hours spent at the water-hole I also learned that the babies and toddlers in a baboon society enjoy a very privileged status. They are admired, cuddled and pampered by every member of the troop — even by their older siblings who are obliged to play second fiddle to them for parental attention. By the time the babies become toddlers (from three to twelve months) they are dreadfully spoilt and, being very much aware of their special status, can make life pretty uncomfortable for their older siblings. The slightest provocation from a sibling (whether real or imagined) can send a toddler into a screaming rage and mom or dad will often come running to comfort the brat and send the older child to the doghouse — regardless of whether he is guilty or not. On the couple of occasions that I witnessed a toddler screaming with rage until it choked, it gave me an almost perverse pleasure to watch the little imp gasping for breath.

The hours at the water-hole always passed too quickly. Sometime after midday, usually around three or four o'clock, Big Boss would grunt his familiar bass command and the sentries would set off to take up their positions for the homeward journey. The mothers would call and collect their children, and soon the troop would be on its way, with me following in my usual tedious mode — alternately by car and on foot.

On the few occasions that I felt too weary to follow them on foot and opted for the luxury of my jeep, unique and exciting things happened and were lost to my camera for ever. Once a scene worth filming starts happening, it won't wait for you to unload and set up the camera. It just goes right on happening and by the time you're ready to roll, you'll capture only the tail-end of the story.

So, I carried my camera — already mounted on the tripod — over my shoulder, shifting it from one aching side to the other and setting it down at intervals to dash back to fetch my car. During my initial months with the baboons many priceless shots went a-begging as I struggled to adjust the focus, read the light and set the exposure, and my frustration often bordered on tears.

As time went by, however, I became more familiar with the behaviour of the baboons and gradually learned to anticipate some of their actions. I also became quite adept at setting my camera down in a flash, finding focus and rolling within seconds of having sensed the prelude to an exciting event. Sometimes, however, my instincts were wrong and nothing interesting happened, but at other times my luck held and I succeeded in getting some valuable footage.

It sometimes happened that I managed to capture only part of an interesting incident on film. To be able to show the whole story I had to wait and hope that a similar event would eventually present itself in one form or another, enabling me to film the missing scene.

I recall one such incident, where I needed but a single shot to complete a particular sequence of events.

Big Boss had given the signal for the return journey and the mothers started calling and collecting their youngsters. Two little devils, who were playing tag in the branches of a bushwillow tree, were having too much fun to pay any attention to their mother's call. She stood at the bottom of the tree, pleading and calling, but to no avail: her children had become deaf. She decided to take a more direct course of action, and climbed up after them. As she reached out to grab one of the brats, she lost her balance and fell out of the tree. Standing at the bottom of the tree once more, she looked up into the branches, trying to devise another plan. One of the youngsters — swinging from a lower branch — momentarily appeared within her reach and she leapt up, stretching out to grab him by the tail, but she missed and landed flat on her back. Big Boss came over to see what the trouble was. Looking up into the tree, he spotted the two little devils and, with an authoritative bark, ordered them to get down right away. They lost no time in obeying his command and promptly fell out of the tree, hastily joining their mother and hurrying to catch up with the rest of the troop.

I had captured the whole sequence on film, except Big Boss's approach to the bottom of the tree. Without that scene, I'd have continuity problems with the editing. All I needed was a shot of Big Boss striding purposefully up to a bushwillow tree. It didn't have to be the same tree — any other bushwillow tree would do. (In a long shot, viewers wouldn't know the difference.) It didn't seem like a difficult shot to get, and for the next couple of days I kept my lens aimed at Big Boss, anticipating that at any moment he'd stride up to a bushwillow tree in his usual authoritative manner.

He wouldn't and he didn't. He became allergic to bushwillow trees and steered clear of them.

I decided that any other tree would do. It needn't be a bushwillow. The viewers probably wouldn't know the difference.

Big Boss acquired an aversion to trees in general and wouldn't go anywhere near any tree, at least not during the daytime.

I decided that I'd be contented without a tree. A shot of Big Boss striding in an authoritative manner in any direction would do. I'd make it a medium close-up. The viewers would conclude that the tree was just outside the frame.

Big Boss lost the ability to look authoritative. He didn't stride anywhere — he plodded — and a dull, aimless look settled on his face.

I could have murdered him.

One day, while I was aiming the lens at Big Boss as he sat doing nothing, my patience started to run out. The light was beautiful, the setting was just right, and within a short distance of Big Boss stood a perfect bushwillow that looked exactly like the one in which the little devils had played. I begged Big Boss to get up and walk to the tree. He ignored me. By this stage I had been filming for more than a year and I desperately wanted to start wrapping it up — not only for financial reasons but also because I was getting homesick. I was suddenly convinced that Big Boss was being difficult on purpose, and I lost my temper.

'For heavens sake, just get up and walk to the damned tree!' I yelled at him.

Big Boss was furious. He flew up and charged at me. He was so angry that he didn't run, but approached with stiff-legged bounces, his fangs bared. He bounded right up to me and swiped at me with his paw. He missed — perhaps deliberately —

and glared at me for some seconds before walking away with a stiff, imperial gait. I was scared almost out of my wits and resolved then and there that in future I would treat Big Boss with the respect due to him.

As luck would have it, one of the other large males provided me with the shot I had been waiting for. He strode purposefully to the bottom of a mopani tree (it looks like a bushwillow tree from the distance) and paused at the bottom to look up into the branches above. It was perfect. I could have kissed him. I filmed the shot from an angle which excluded his tail. (Big Boss had a broken tail and its distinct kink was a dead giveaway.) So, using a stand-in, I finally managed to can the shot which had caused so much friction and unhappiness between Big Boss and me.

As soon as Big Boss realised that the lens was no longer constantly being aimed at him, he stopped behaving idiotically and regained his authoritative style. I guess the steady stare of the lens had temporarily unhinged him.

When at last I had all the shots I needed for my film, I packed my camera away with a profound sense of relief. I was ready for the second — and much easier — phase of the job: the sound recording. Armed with a tape recorder borrowed from a friend, I followed my troop to their water-hole. I hung the microphone in a tree, switched the recorder on and watched as the whole troop became mute. They sat staring either at me or at the microphone, refusing to utter a single sound. By this time I was really fed-up with the idiots and I was desperately longing to get some normality back into my life. I'd been worrying about my movie and thinking of nothing but baboons and baboons, day and night, for what seemed like an eternity. There were days when I didn't feel so very sane any more. Almost eighteen months had passed since I had embarked on the project, and masses of work still lay ahead. Sixteen thousand feet of developed film had to be viewed, edited and shaped into a presentable documentary movie. I really didn't have either the time or patience to hang around watching the bloody-minded baboons staring silently at the microphone. If they wanted me to believe that they'd lost the power of speech, then that was that. I wasn't going to plead or argue with them. I'd simply have to come up with a trick to get their voices recorded. I packed up my sound equipment, drove to the camp and spent the rest of the day in my caravan, concocting plans to outwit the baboons.

The following morning I went out to the water-hole ahead of them. I hid the tape recorder under the sprawling fronds of a lala palm, and suspended the microphone from a stem higher up where it was hidden from sight by another of the fan-shaped leaves. When the baboons arrived, they found me sitting in the shade of the lala palms looking bored and aimless, and doing nothing. It fooled them. They paid little attention to me. I slipped my hand under the palm leaf and surreptitiously switched the recorder on. They suspected nothing and continued with their normal conversations.

At last the day dawned when I had enough baboon sounds on tape and could pack up and return to Mahlangeni. I took an almost perverse pleasure in saying goodbye to the troop.

Although editing is physically less taxing than filming, it's a pretty major job in itself. I sat at my editing table in my makeshift studio at Mahlangeni for many months on end, viewing and reviewing, cutting and splicing and, of course, worrying.

When I'd finally completed the visuals, I started laying the sound-tracks. And then, much to my dismay, I discovered that I didn't have enough baboon sounds on tape to complete the sound-tracks. I needed some more barks, grunts and shrieks. Having learned to understand a fair amount of the vocal index of the baboon language, it was important to me that I use the correct vocal cues with every visual.

Different kinds of barks, for instance, have different meanings. There is the high-pitched, two-phase bark (alarm call), the dog-like bark (contact call), the roaring bark (war-cry), and the shrill, single-phase bark (call for help). There are also different kinds of grunts, such as the snort-grunt (warning), the cough-grunt (reprimand), the sigh-grunt (endearment), and a whole range of casual grunts (friendly, relaxed conversation). Other vocal expressions include lip-smacking (sweet talk), tongue clicking (complaining), screeching (arguing), and chattering (idle talk).

I packed my sound equipment and set off for Shingwedzi once more. As I drove, I wondered whether the troop would remember me after the many months that had passed since I had last seen them, and I worried that they might not allow me close enough to them to record their voices.

When I found them later that day, relaxing in their usual spot at the water-hole, I realised that I needn't have worried. They had not forgotten me. As I got out of the jeep, Silly Grin was the first to approach me with a welcoming gesture. Soon the youngsters bounded up to me and invited me to play with them. The adults regarded me in their usual aloof way, paying me little attention. I had a wonderful surprise, however, when Big Boss got up and came sauntering towards me. For a fleeting moment I had the impression that he wanted to shake my hand in formal greeting. But he sat down a little distance from me and, folding his arms, contemplated me in a friendly way. And then he said: 'Huh-huh. Huh-huh.' It seemed to come straight from his heart, and I understood it to mean: 'Welcome back. Make yourself at home.' I appreciated his cordial renewal of our acquaintance so much that it brought a tear to my eye.

Within three days I'd recorded all the sounds I needed and I packed up for the last time. This time I made a much nicer farewell speech than on the previous occasion and I felt genuine regret as I made my way home.

Some months later my movie was finally completed and I sold it to the national television network. They still broadcast it approximately twice a year and they sell video copies of it through their marketing department. It gives me immense pleasure to know that many thousands of people are able to share my affection for the Shingwedzi troop with me.

The Thoughtful Elephant

O nce, while still working on my movie, I took two weeks' leave of the Shingwedzi baboons to visit the troop in the Sweni area near Satara. I wanted to film some scenes of their daily behaviour in order to illustrate the contrasting characters of the easygoing Shingwedzi troop and the quarrelsome Sweni troop.

I waited for them one afternoon on the northern bank of the Sweni creek. They usually turned up somewhere between four and five o'clock. Not wanting the troop to see me, I had chosen a hiding-place in a thicket of undergrowth between a concrete water reservoir and a jackalberry tree at the edge of the creek. From my hide-out I had a view over a stretch of marshy savannah bordered by a stand of Delagoa thorn trees. My jeep was parked some distance away, well hidden from the approach route of the baboons.

Presently, I heard the troop approaching. Judging from the barking and screeching they were, as usual, in an unpleasant mood. That was good. I aimed my lens at a spot between the Delagoa thorn trees where I expected the baboons to make their appearance and busied myself setting the exposure and adjusting the focus. The afternoon sun filtered through the trees, streaking the grassy marsh with splashes of gold. The light was perfect and I wished the troop would hurry up and come into shot.

I was so busy peering through the lens and anticipating the possible movements of the baboons that I'd more or less forgotten where I was — until a sudden splash in the reservoir beside me made me jump. I looked over my shoulder and, to my horror, saw a bull elephant about the size of a mountain standing a couple of metres behind me, drinking from the reservoir.

199

My heart almost stopped. I sank slowly to my haunches, trying to blend into the foliage of the dense undergrowth around me. I barely breathed as I sat there, waiting for the elephant to finish his drink and take his leave. The more I worried that he might hear the pounding of my heart, the louder it seemed to get. When at last he'd had enough to drink, he didn't leave but hung around for a while and then decided to have a shower. I was becoming light-headed from all the adrenalin racing through my system as I peered at him through the foliage, wishing fervently that he would finish his shower and leave. But he was obviously enjoying himself and was in no hurry. I was so close to the darned elephant that I was practically sitting in his shadow.

When he was finally satisfied that he was clean enough, he didn't turn and head back to wherever it was he had come from, but began walking directly towards me. It was my worst elephant nightmare come true. There was definitely not enough space between the wall of the reservoir and the jackalberry tree for both of us, and I knew I'd get trampled if I didn't remove myself promptly. Summoning every ounce of adrenalin in my system, I burst from my cover and sprinted to my jeep — a distance of some sixty metres.

I suppose my sudden take-off must have startled the elephant, but I wouldn't really know because I didn't look back until I was safely in my jeep. He was still standing at the spot where I'd been hiding, sniffing at the undergrowth and trying to establish what kind of creature had launched itself so suddenly and disappeared so swiftly. And then he discovered my camera and tripod. I could hardly bear to look as he started sniffing and feeling the camera with his trunk. The camera had been a gift from Kobus and was very precious to me. It was hard to sit there and watch my camera meet its end. I wondered if the insurance people would believe my story.

But then the most amazing thing happened. After the elephant had finished his inspection of the photographic equipment, he stood thinking for a few seconds, and then stepped — oh, so very, very carefully — around the camera and tripod, taking care not to bump against them with his massive bulk in the narrow space between the reservoir and the jackalberry tree. I could hardly believe my eyes.

I'd expected him to walk right over it, stamping it into oblivion, or to wrap his trunk around it and toss it out of his way, or — at the very least — to knock it over while moving past it.

Whatever his reasons for deciding not to damage my precious camera, I shall always be grateful to the thoughtful old elephant. The sight of him stepping carefully past the fragile equipment is indelibly marked in my memory.

I once heard a similar story from ranger Paul Zway. He had absent-mindedly left a pair of binoculars on the wall of a reservoir. When he returned to fetch them, he found an elephant bull busily inspecting them. After sniffing and touching them carefully with his trunk, he peered at them with myopic eyes for a while, and then eventually ambled off into the bush, leaving the binoculars unharmed on the wall.

You may remember that game guard Makasani Maluleke had a similar experience when he and his bicycle landed underneath the belly of an elephant. The elephant had pulled the bicycle out from beneath its tummy, held it at eye-level for inspection, and then put it down carefully before walking away.

But if these incidents give you the impression that elephants are by nature gracious and considerate creatures, then please read the next chapter.

Elephants
in the Night

O ne of the reasons why tourists are not allowed to drive in the
Park after dark, and why the Park's personnel prefer not to,
is because elephants become invisible at night. Even if you shine a
light on them, they seem to merge into the blackness of the night.

Mishak, the driver of the transport truck, once had the
following experience with elephants in the night.

Having been held up by engine troubles, he had left his truck at
the Shingwedzi camp and borrowed a pick-up truck to deliver the
last of the provisions. By the time he was back on the road and
heading for his last delivery stop, dusk was already settling, and it
would be dark before he reached Punda Maria. Some twenty
kilometres from his destination, Mishak suddenly found himself
on a direct collision course with the derrière of an elephant. In the
dark, the elephant had remained invisible until the truck's lights
were actually shining through its hind legs. It was a young bull,
presumably in his teens. As Mishak slammed the brakes on, the
startled elephant's hind legs buckled at the knees and he sat down
on the bonnet of the truck, screeching like a tornado.

Fortunately, within a couple of seconds, the young elephant
recovered sufficiently from his shock to get up off the bonnet and
flee into the bush. In response to the youngster's screams, an entire
breeding herd appeared on the road to investigate the source of the
commotion. Mishak relates that one moment they weren't there,
and the next moment they were everywhere. To avoid infuriating
the short-tempered cows, Mishak switched off the engine (which,
surprisingly, was still running despite the damage to the bonnet).

Mishak decided it would be politic to wait for the herd to take its leave before attempting to move on himself.

The cows, however, weren't thinking of leaving just yet. Trunks in the air, they ambled over to the truck. Something smelled good. It was the sacks of maize meal on the back of the pick-up. Soon the truck was surrounded by cows, tearing the sacks open and helping themselves. Others unloaded sacks on to the ground, and the calves came over to join in the fun. With his truck surrounded by elephants, Mishak could do nothing but sit and yell at the looters. They paid him no attention whatsoever and proceeded to enjoy their glorious maize meal party.

For many days afterwards tourists reported that they'd spotted white-powdered elephants, and enquired about strange white marks and white elephant spoor along the road some twenty kilometres from Punda Maria.

As a rule, I avoid driving at night but, one Friday evening, after attending a school function with the girls, I had no choice but to drive home in the dark. Remembering the time I had collided with the hyena, I drove carefully and slowly.

About ten kilometres from home, the massive bulk of an elephant suddenly loomed in the beam of the headlights. He was standing with his head in the bushes alongside the road, with his behind on the track directly in front of us. As I slammed on the brakes, the jeep skidded to a halt right under the elephant's rump. He got such a fright that his hind legs buckled at the knees (this usually happens when an elephant is startled suddenly) and his enormous posterior started descending on to the bonnet. We steeled ourselves for a colossal crunch but − to our immense relief − the elephant managed to right himself and charged off into the bush, screaming with consternation. We could feel the landscape shuddering as the bewildered giant crashed destructively through the bush.

I don't know which of us got the bigger fright − the elephant or us. I guess I probably did, because my teeth chattered the rest of the way home.

One night, long after we had gone to bed, Kobus and I were woken by the resounding clanging of steel in trouble. My first thought was that a hyena was trying to get in through our main gates, but Kobus flew up, saying, 'It's an elephant breaking the fence. He's going to plunder the vegetable garden.' As he scrambled out of bed, groping for his torch and rifle in the dark, he urged me to get up and go with him. He wanted me to shine the torch on the elephant so that he could fire a shot over its head to frighten it away.

I tried to think of an excuse to stay safely indoors but, failing to come up with a good one quickly enough, I found myself reluctantly following Kobus outside into the pitch-dark night.

We could hear the elephant stripping branches off a wild fig tree in the vegetable garden. I shone the torch in his direction but saw nothing. The closer we got to the fig tree, the more the feeding noises of the invisible elephant ruffled me, and I had trouble keeping the trembling torch steady.

Suddenly, Kobus said, 'There he is!'

I still saw nothing.

'Shine towards his head!' Kobus urged.

'I can't see him!' I insisted.

'But he's right in front of you,' said Kobus.

Then I realised with an awful start that I'd been shining the torch on the elephant's body all along, but had mistaken it for the darkness of the night.

'Light his head!' Kobus repeated.

I moved the beam towards where I thought his head would be, but it was his tail.

'His head's on the other side,' hissed Kobus. 'And where are you going?'

'I'm lighting it as well as I can,' I protested. 'And what do you mean, where am I going? I'm right here!'

But as I said that I suddenly realised that I wasn't right there any more. I'd been walking in reverse gear. The confounded elephant was calmly tearing the tree to pieces, even though he'd heard us approaching.

I didn't like it.

But, despite my apprehension, I steadied myself and finally managed to light one of the elephant's ears, and Kobus fired a shot over its head. The elephant got the message and wheeled around. As he hurried through the vegetable beds, heading for the break in the fence, his feet obliterated scores of seedlings and pulped vast quantities of tomatoes, pumpkins, marrows and other vegetables. He climbed gracefully over the broken fence, treading carefully to avoid getting his feet caught in the tangled wire, and disappeared into the night.

When Filemoni saw the damage to the vegetable garden the next morning, he said something in Tsonga about elephants which I'd rather not translate for you. It's a bit unprintable, I think.

Horses, Dogs, Pigs and All The Rest

W e ordered our first horse by mail in 1982. On the day that he was due to arrive, Kobus drove to the Phalaborwa railway station to fetch him while the girls and I waited at home in excited anticipation. The girls had already decided that they would name him Prince.

When Kobus finally arrived home that evening, a scrawny, scruffy, feeble-looking creature stepped from the pick-up. He looked more like a slovenly mule than a horse and had the bearing of a frightened donkey. The name Prince didn't seem quite so apt any more.

The girls weren't as disappointed in the horse as one might have imagined. They felt sorry for him and were determined to make a happy and dignified animal out of him. The horse was terrified of us and wouldn't let anyone near him, but the girls were not to be put off. At first they could only talk and croon to him from a distance, but after some time he allowed them to stroke his head and eventually to brush and groom his coat. Finally, their love and care — coupled with a course of medication and a healthy feeding regimen which Kobus provided — produced results and the horse started to look like the dignified animal he deserved to be. He gained weight, his coat started to shine and his manner became relaxed and affectionate.

Sandra christened him Aznar (an Arabic name which she found in a book). Filemoni, finding it difficult to pronounce the Arabic name, calls him 'Azzenaz'.

Aznar is an intelligent horse. Not only does he respond well to the vast number of commands which Sandra has taught him, but he also understands that he lives in a wilderness area where it's not safe to venture far from home. He spends most of his time grazing along the river bank or in the reedbeds in front of the house. Whenever he senses potential danger, he comes charging back inside the fence. There are days when he will not venture outside the fence at all, and we take that as a sign that there are predators in the area.

Aznar was very nervous the first time he encountered elephants. Kobus had gone riding in the bush when they came across the herd, and Aznar trembled like a reed as he stood watching the great beasts. When, after some time, he realised that the elephants posed no threat to him, he calmed down and became very interested in the herd's activities. He has no fear of elephants now, only an intelligent respect for their size. Whenever elephants come grazing in the riverbed, Aznar moves a respectful distance away from them and then continues grazing peacefully. When the elephants sense him, they put their trunks in the air to smell him and, after some discussion among themselves, usually conclude that he's an odd-looking but harmless creature who is not worth their attention.

Some two years after acquiring Aznar, we got a second horse. His name was Apollo. He was a handsome Anglo-Arab colt who became good friends with Aznar. Unfortunately, he had a stubborn streak and wouldn't heed our warnings about the dangers of venturing too far into the bush. Aznar fell under the influence of Apollo's obstinacy, and we often had to go looking for the horses and bring them back closer to home and relative safety.

On a day that I was alone at home, I noticed that the horses were missing again. I was about to go to the staff village and ask the game guards to help me find them when I heard the thundering of hooves.

It was Aznar, galloping homewards, wide-eyed and whinnying. I knew right away that something was dreadfully wrong. Before I could even call for help from the village, two game guards who had heard the thundering of the horse's hooves came rushing over, already armed. They hurried down the river bank, following the horses' spoor. While I tried to placate Aznar, the game guards ran along the shore in an easterly direction and eventually disappeared into the riverine bush. I led Aznar to his stable and talked to him in a comforting tone, but he was terribly upset and kept whinnying and pawing the ground as if trying to tell me something.

Some minutes later I heard three shots coming from the direction the game guards had taken. My heart started beating a lively crescendo. We'd had Apollo for only two years. He was still so young — only four years old. It wouldn't be fair if he was dead.

As I waited nervously with Aznar, I wished desperately that the game guards would return, leading Apollo with them.

When they finally returned, Apollo was not with them. They approached me with sombre faces, and I almost fainted when one of them held out Apollo's tail, offering it to me as a keepsake. They told me that they had come across four lions who had killed the horse. They had fired some shots into the air to chase the lions from their kill, and after having determined that Apollo was indeed dead, they had cut off his tail to bring to me.

I wasn't brave enough to take the tail, but I thanked them for their trouble and concern and asked them to put the tail in Kobus's office.

I went inside and radioed Kobus. Just talking to him was therapeutic. My call was heard by several other people in the Park, and their messages of condolence also helped me to absorb the shock.

That night I had an awful nightmare. I dreamed that the game guards had brought Apollo back to the house, alive but severely mauled — and with a missing tail. I tended to his wounds and tried to stitch his tail back on with needle and thread. When I finally woke up I was drenched in perspiration.

The girls were terribly upset about the loss of Apollo, and Aznar missed his companion so much that we decided to buy another horse as soon as possible.

We bought an American saddle horse named Kirby. Filemoni — unable to pronounce the name — calls the horse Kobie, which is, of course, my name. Actually, I can't blame him. 'Kobie' does sound very much like 'Kirby', and most English-speaking people I know call me either Coby or Kirby.

Kirby is a handsome, intelligent animal, and I believe he will never fall prey to lions as Apollo did because, if anything, he is even more cautious than Aznar.

The first time Kirby saw an elephant he was terribly shocked, even though the elephant was way off on the far side of the river. He galloped home as fast as he could and spent the rest of the day hiding in his stable. Although we've explained to Kirby time and again and as best we can that elephants pose no threat to a horse, he doesn't believe us and refuses to trust them. When elephants come to graze along the river banks, Kirby hides in his stable until they leave.

Recently a lone elephant bull turned up for a swim in the river right in front of the house. Entering the water until only his head and trunk remained above the surface, he cavorted and splashed about, really enjoying himself.

When Kirby saw the elephant he dashed home but, unlike other occasions, he didn't head for his stable. He ran through the garden to the front fence and stood there, watching the playful elephant from behind the safety of the wire. He trembled with apprehension, but couldn't tear his eyes away from the elephant. Every now and then he rushed away from the fence and, snorting and prancing, went looking for Aznar — no doubt to tell him about the daft elephant. Having done that, he returned to his vantage point once more to stare at the elephant with fascination.

The nicest thing about having horses is that one can ride up close to herds of game. Apparently the animals interpret the horse and rider as a single being and, although they may wonder about the strange-looking creature, they seem to know that it's not a predator and have little, if any, fear of it.

Our first Kruger Park dog, Simba (a ridgeback bitch), gave us many years of pleasure and companionship before she died of heat exhaustion one hot summer day. We had been out riding, and Simba had run along with us. We hadn't ridden any considerable distance, but Simba had run several zigs and zags as dogs usually

do, and when we got home she lay down panting under a shady tree, never to rise again. We felt terrible when the vet diagnosed heat exhaustion as the cause of her death. We are wiser now: we leave the dogs at home whenever the mercury rises above 38°C (101°F). They can then laze away under the shady trees and jump into the fish-pond to cool off whenever they want to.

Another of our dogs was a fox terrier named Otto. He was very friendly and lovable, but he wasn't a particularly bright dog. He spent most of his days barking furiously at squirrels, tortoises, frogs, lizards, geckos, and even grasshoppers. Kobus called him a 'small game hunter'.

One of our resident squirrels took a dim view of Otto and teased him mercilessly at every opportunity. He almost drove the poor dog out of his mind. I believe Otto's greatest wish was to be able to climb trees so that he could sort out the squirrel. He often tried to run up the trunks of various trees in pursuit of his nemesis, but the law of gravity always won and brought him back to earth.

There is a spot in the south-western corner of our garden under a spreading umbrella thorn tree where I love to sit and read. The branches of the tree form a natural canopy above one, and the view of the confluence of the two rivers is panoramic. Otto used to come and curl up at my feet as I sat there, at peace with the world — until the squirrel arrived. Positioning himself on a branch directly above us, he would start teasing the dog, shrieking, 'Cheeky-cheeky-cheek! Cheeky-cheeky-cheek!' Otto would come to life like a bolt of lightning and have a barking fit. The louder he barked, the louder the squirrel shrieked. It was like a noise pollution competition. As the level of Otto's frustration rose, so did the pitch of his barking until he woofed away in a soprano voice. The noise of their hysterical rumpus was quite blinding, and I'd be forced to retreat to a quieter place to continue my reading.

A few years ago we all went for a walk along the southern bank of the river, the dogs accompanying us. We have always taught our dogs to stay away from the water's edge, and Otto knew the rules. But on this day he must have been preoccupied, forgetting all he had been taught.

Kobus, the girls and I were strolling along, chatting, and we realised that Otto had strayed from us only when we heard him yelping some distance behind us — down by the river. We heard only two yelps, then a loud splash followed by an eerie silence. We ran down the bank to the waterside. The water was calm with barely a ripple to show what had happened. We didn't want to believe that a crocodile had taken our dog, but the imprints of his little paws leading to the water told the story. We stood gazing at the dark water for a long time, almost as if our silent staring might bring Otto back.

Our dog Janna is an Australian cattle dog. He is pitch-black in colour, resembles a ridgeback in build, and has the kindest eyes and the most disarming smile. Because his forebears were bred for cattle herding, Janna's herding instinct is quite overpowering. He believes it to be his duty to herd the bantams to the hen-house and the horses to their stable every evening.

When the horses start coming home, Janna flattens himself behind a convenient bush and waits for them, trembling with anticipation. Once they're in range, he launches himself in their direction, does his herding act, and then hides behind another bush. He repeats this action as many times as is necessary to see the horses into their stable. Of course the horses know full well where their stable is and don't need any help to get there but, being the dignified animals they are, they simply ignore Janna's antics.

The bantams become hysterical every evening when Janna herds them to the hen-house, but that's only because they're too dumb to realise that Janna is a kind-hearted dog who would never harm even the smallest of creatures.

During the winter months Janna is kept occupied by the resident baboons on their forays to raid our vegetable garden. Lying in ambush between the vegetables, he waits until the raiders climb over the fence and come within range. At exactly the right moment he bursts from his cover and does his herding act. Screaming with fright, the baboons retreat, scaling the fence a lot faster than they did on their way in.

Whenever we go walking in the bush and come across herds of animals, Janna becomes very tense — not out of fear, but because he has to suppress his herding instincts. We are fortunate that he is an obedient dog. Imagine our predicament if he drove a herd of buffalo back to the house!

A few months after Otto was taken by the crocodile, ranger Johan Steyn brought us a beautiful puppy that looked very much like a wolf cub. His mother was a border collie and his father a cross Australian dingo/cattle dog. We named the pup Wolfie. Now that he is fully grown, he bears a remarkable resemblance to a Canadian wolf and people who visit us are instinctively terrified of him. Wolfie does look rather serious, but actually, once you get to know him, you will find that he is a loving and gentle dog. He only puts on his fierce-looking-wolf act because he's a conscientious dog who takes his responsibilities as a bodyguard seriously. He relies on this performance to discourage anyone from getting too close to the girls or me — especially when Kobus is away from home. When he bares his fangs and growls softly and ominously, no one who doesn't know him will dare to come within hand-shaking distance of us.

When Kobus realised that our field staff had become terrified of Wolfie, he devoted some time to helping them lose their fear of the dog. He taught them to look the dog straight in the eyes, stride confidently up to him, greet him by his name and pat him on the head. Each one of the staff got a few turns to practise the act until eventually the poor dog became totally flustered by this extended show of confidence and amiability. It worked, though. Our field staff are no longer afraid of the dog. But sometimes it strikes me as comical when I see the game guards and other staff members all greet the dog in this formal fashion. Striding purposefully up to the dog, they say: 'Awusheni Wolfie. Kunjani?' (Good day, Wolfie. How are you?) and give him three polite pats on the head — while Wolfie stares resentfully into the distance, pretending to be too preoccupied to pay any attention to the exasperating greeting ritual.

I am always grateful for the dogs' company when I am alone at home. They love our daily late-afternoon walks and view them as standard procedure. From about five o'clock in the afternoon they wait impatiently for me to make my appearance, and if I linger too long they will bark and yelp at the door to remind me of our standing appointment.

Recently, on one of our walks, the dogs and I almost met our neighbour the leopard.

We were walking along the bank of the Shibyeni creek when both Wolfie and Janna suddenly froze and, with their hair bristling, stared intently into the undergrowth ahead of them. I was about to turn and backtrack quickly and quietly, but the dogs' strange behaviour fired my curiosity. They were staring into the undergrowth like apprehensive statues.

I cocked my pistol and moved cautiously forward to try to see what it was they were staring at. I couldn't see anything in the dense vegetation and as I moved carefully on and past the dogs they unfroze and followed me, growling softly and warningly. My heart started beating in my ears, but I had an overwhelming urge to know the reason for their strange behaviour. Why didn't they bark or charge into the undergrowth to investigate? And then I saw it. An impala ram, lying very still on his side, half hidden under a shrub. I crept carefully up to him, wondering why he was lying so still. I bent down and touched his eyelids. They didn't move. He was dead, but his body was still warm. He was such a beautiful ram and evidently in good shape, so it didn't seem logical that he should be dead. It also puzzled me that the dogs kept some distance from the ram. Why didn't they come up and sniff him properly as dogs are supposed to do? They remained tense and strangely aloof, while continuing to growl. Lifting the ram's head, I noticed two fine, deep fang marks in the side of his neck — and I suddenly came to my senses. He had been killed by a leopard! I dropped the ram's head as if it were a poisonous snake and, as I turned, I caught sight of the leopard's pug marks in a sandy spot right in front of me.

'Let's go!' I told the dogs, and we vacated the scene with impressive speed.

The leopard must have retreated when he heard us approaching, but he would be lying up somewhere close by, guarding his kill. I certainly didn't want to give him the impression that I was planning to steal his kill.

That is the closest I have ever come to meeting our neighbour and, to tell the truth, in hindsight I'm a little disappointed that I didn't catch a glimpse of him that day.

The dogs have their sleeping mats on the patio outside our bedroom, next to the fish-pond. They lie there at night, but they don't really sleep much. There are too many night sounds to be listened to and barked at. When lions roar somewhere in the distance, they bark furiously, but if the roars come closer, their barking decreases in volume until it becomes a cautious, muffled woof that escapes their lips every once in a while. If the lions roar just outside the fence, the dogs become totally mute and lie very quietly, pretending to be some place else.

You can't blame them. When lions roar close to you the earth trembles and you feel very vulnerable, even behind the safety of high fences. It certainly doesn't seem wise to let the lions know where you are by barking at them.

In December 1989 Kobus's brother, who is a farmer, gave us two cute black piglets as a Christmas present. Actually, we are not supposed to keep domestic animals in the Park (other than dogs or horses) but my brother-in-law didn't give us the piglets as domestic pets. The idea was for us to fatten them up for a couple of months and then eat them.

It didn't strike me as a nice idea. In fact, I could hardly bear the thought of doing such a dreadful thing. Although I admire vegetarians, I am not one myself but I eat only the meat of animals with whom I was never personally acquainted. And when I think about even that, it bothers me a great deal to know that I'm a predator. I don't feel like one. I feel like a harmless and vulnerable primate.

As it happened, we fed and cared for the pigs, but we never ate them and we don't intend to. They have become part of the family.

Since we didn't have any other place for them to sleep, we put them in the hen-house with the bantams. For three or four nights the poor bantams didn't sleep a wink. They were terribly upset by the intrusion into their domain of the fat little black blobs, and they discussed the situation nervously throughout the nights. Eventually, though, they learnt to accept the piglets in the hen-house and managed to get some sleep again. But as the pigs grew older they started snoring, and the poor bantams' insomnia began anew.

As the piglets grew fatter and fatter, my daughters — being acquainted only with warthogs — accused me of over-feeding them and suggested that I put them on a diet. I didn't feed the piglets too much, of course — only a bowl of porridge in the mornings and evenings, and a few left-overs from the kitchen. They grazed on the lawns in the garden during the day, and I don't believe they ate any more than pigs normally do. I explained to the girls that, although pigs bear some resemblance to warthogs in general appearance, they are not really related. Pigs are fat slobs by nature.

In point of fact, the pigs looked totally overweight to me as well. I guess I'd also grown used to the slimmer, neater shapes of warthogs and had forgotten how fat pigs can really get.

We all grew very fond of the big black blobs. Winston Churchill once said: 'Dogs look up to us, cats look down on us, pigs treat us as equals.' He must have known pigs well. They are intelligent, amiable creatures and since they look neither down on you nor up to you, they are totally undemanding — like easy-to-be-with friends in whose company you can relax.

We named the boar Fritzie and the sow Fiela. Fritzie tends to spend most of his time eating and he pays little attention to us as a rule. If you go up to him and stroke his head or scratch his ears, he will simply acknowledge your presence with a friendly grunt and go right on eating. (The girls call him Fat Fritzie.)

Fiela is more winsome and demonstrative and likes to be fussed over. (The girls call her Friendly Fiela.) Whenever she spots one of us in the garden, she comes trotting over, presses her big wet nose into your hand and, leaning against your legs, waits for you to scratch her ears. While you scratch her ears, she falls asleep and topples right over on to your feet. Since she's astoundingly heavy, it takes some doing to get your feet extracted from under her sleeping body.

The older and fatter Fritzie and Fiela got, the louder their nightly snoring became. Fritzie's snoring is particularly offensive and at times tends to sound like the grumbling and snarling of feeding lions. When the bantams couldn't stand the clamorous snoring any longer and started to spend most of their daylight hours catching up on lost sleep, we built a little reed enclosure with a tin roof for the pigs to sleep in — at a fair distance from the hen-house. The hen-house, the stables and the pig-house all stand in the north-western corner of our premises, and the whole area is fenced in. The reason we fenced it was to prevent the horses from roaming the garden at night. Their stable isn't very roomy and on hot nights they need more space in which to move about. The enclosed area is approximately 300 square metres in extent, giving the horses a fair amount of roaming space at night.

When the pigs were about six months old, Kobus's nephew Cornelis and his wife Bianca came to visit and brought us a magnificent present: a beautiful four-year-old Anglo-Arab stallion named Tangle.

Cornelis and Bianca arrived fairly late in the evening. It had been a long journey — towing a horse-box all the way from Pretoria — and the last fifty-kilometre stretch on the bumpy dirt track had been especially taxing. The horse appeared nervous as he stepped from the horse-box, but the girls helped to feed him and make him feel welcome, and he soon calmed down. Then we led him to the camp to introduce him to Aznar and Kirby.

Aznar, being a kindly soul, greeted the newcomer in an amiable way. But Kirby was not at all impressed with the handsome stallion and behaved abominably towards him. He whinnied and neighed, kicked and reared, throwing a disgraceful tantrum. Tangle kept a respectful distance from Kirby and gave voice to his offended feelings with a fair amount of whinnying and neighing of his own.

Kobus suggested that we go inside and leave the two horses to sort out their problems in their own time. He predicted that the animosity between them wouldn't last long and that they would soon become friends.

By the time we all went to bed that night the two horses could still be heard neighing and whinnying, but there were longer intervals of silence in between. Obviously they still didn't like each other, but at least the animosity between them appeared to be fading.

Shortly after midnight that night Kobus and I were woken by the hurried footsteps of game guards approaching our bedroom across the patio. The chief guard, Corporal Manhique, called to us through the mesh screens: 'Ngala yi khomile hashi!' (A lion has taken one of the horses!)

Kobus leapt out of bed, grabbed his rifle and torch and rushed outside. I fumbled for my torch and pistol in the darkness, threw on my dressing gown and sandals and rushed after them. My heart was beating an agonised fortissimo as I wondered which horse had been taken. It would be dreadfully unfair if a lion had caught our new horse on his very first night with us. I thought of Aznar and Kirby, and knew it would break my heart if it was either of them.

It was one of those pitch-black, inky-dark nights and as I approached the camp I saw only the dim spots of light from Kobus's and the game guards' torches. They were already entering the camp, and I was certain that they would stumble right into the feeding lion in the darkness. I dashed into Kobus's office, found his spotlight and, uncoiling the lengthy cord, rushed outside, shining the strong beam into the camp. The light picked out Aznar, standing safely under a mopani tree; then another horse, standing behind an umbrella tree: it was Kirby, also unharmed. So the lion had taken our new horse! But where was the confounded lion?

I played the light from one side of the camp to the other, letting it pause briefly under trees and shrubs to double-check the shadows. Kobus turned and, shading his eyes against the sharp light, signalled me to shine the spotlight into the south-western corner of the camp. I did that. And there stood Tangle! Also unharmed. I moved the beam of the spotlight in zigzag fashion over the whole of the camp area. There was no lion.

Kobus and the game guards were talking and laughing now. Relieved, I rushed over to them to listen to their conversation and to learn what had happened.

The game guards had been asleep when our guests had arrived with the new horse and had consequently been unaware of the newcomer. Around midnight, one of the game guards, Wilson, had been woken by the sound of a neighing horse. Realising that he had never before heard one of our horses neigh in such a weird way, he suspected that the horse was in trouble. His suspicion was confirmed the very next moment by the distinct growling and snarling sounds of a feeding lion. He grabbed his rifle and torch, rushed outside and called the other game guards.

Apparently, there had been another flare-up of tempers between Kirby and Tangle at that time, and Kirby's eerie neighing had indeed sounded like a horse in agony. The 'growling lion' was, of course, Fritzie and Fiela snoring their heads off — especially Fritzie, whose snore can carry over a long distance on a quiet night.

When the game guards had stormed into the camp, rifles at the ready, they had expected to find only one horse alive. Naturally they were astounded to find not only two horses alive, but three.

Nevertheless, Kobus and I were very grateful to them for their concern and speedy action.

In October 1990, when Fritzie and Fiela were almost a year old, we became the foster parents of three orphaned baby warthogs.

The game guards had been out on patrol when they found the three tiny piglets lying close together in the middle of the road. They were barely a week old and they were nearly dead from starvation. The game guards had found the spoor of the piglets leading from a hollow anthill nearby, and they discovered that the mother had been taken by a hyena a day or two previously. It appeared the babies had left the safety of their anthill to search for their mother. Being so weak from hunger, they had managed to get only as far as the road (some fifty metres from their anthill) before they'd collapsed in a little heap. The game guards gathered up the starving piglets and brought them home to us.

Over the years I have been foster mother to an array of orphans and strays: the honey badger, several birds, a banded mongoose, a squirrel and two scrub hares. So I always keep baby feeding bottles in the house for such emergencies. When Kobus brought me the three starving piglets, I immediately made up a milk mixture. Then Kobus and the girls lent a hand to help me coax the frightened little animals to drink from a baby's bottle. Of all our foster children, only the honey badger had taken to the bottle immediately. Getting the others to feed from a bottle hadn't been easy.

The little piglets were terrified of us, and no matter how hard we tried, they would not take the bottles. By ten o'clock that night they still had not fed, and we gave up the struggle. We gently put the babies in a box and tried to make them as comfortable as possible. We went to bed, feeling sad with the knowledge that they would probably die soon.

I couldn't sleep, and at midnight I jumped out of bed, warmed up their milk again, and sat down on the veranda floor with the box of babies at my side. Determined to force-feed each one of them, I took the strongest-looking one from the box. Holding him securely in my lap, I pried his clenched little mouth open with my fingers and forced the bottle teat into it. Miraculously, he started to suckle right away. Pausing for breath every once in a while, he managed to drink almost 40 millilitres before falling asleep in my lap. By this time his sister had woken and was squealing. I stuck the bottle teat into her open mouth and quickly clamped her mouth shut with my other hand. Surprisingly, she also suckled right away, pausing occasionally for breath and finally drinking almost as much as her brother had before falling asleep. I was so relieved I could have wept.

The trouble with the maternal instinct in human beings is that it extends to the babies of all other mammal species. And once you feel responsible for the survival of another baby, you have no choice but to fight the battle to the end.

The third piglet was my greatest worry. He was the weakest and smallest of the three. It was obvious that he couldn't survive much longer — at least, not without nourishment. I lifted him gently from the box. He crawled about in my lap, moaning and wailing, but refused to take even a drop from the bottle. I forced the teat into his mouth, but it was evident that he'd suffocate if I continued to try to force-feed him. It occurred to me that the teat of the bottle might be too large for his mouth, and so I went off and found a medicine dropper.

After a while I succeeded in dripping several drops of milk into his little mouth. He liked that and wanted more. When I'd finally managed to feed him 25 millilitres of milk, I was confident that he, too, would survive.

Feeding the piglets remained a struggle for another day or two but, as they grew accustomed to the bottle, they started enjoying the feeding routine so much that they wanted milk every couple of hours.

I introduced them to Fritzie and Fiela, hoping that Fiela might display some motherly or sisterly love towards them. But the pigs didn't take to the little warthogs at all. In fact, they ran away from them. I've no idea why. I had thought they would be interested in making their acquaintance since pigs and warthogs appear to speak the same language.

As the little warthogs grew older, feeding them turned into an exasperating exercise. Whenever they spotted me, they started screaming for their bottles. Their shrill, grating little voices jangled the nerves of anyone within hearing distance. Even the dogs fled from the noise. Being allergic to noise myself, I'd become so flustered that I'd spill milk all over myself while trying to fill the three bottles. It occurred to me that a mother warthog must have nerves of steel to put up with such rowdy, demanding babies.

During the school holidays, when the warthogs had arrived, the girls had been available to help me feed them, but when they went back to school I had to manage the feeding routine single-handedly, except in the evenings when Kobus was home and, mercifully, helped me. Feeding three impatient little warthogs — all at the same time — requires some expertise. (It was impossible to feed them one at a time. The other two hollered their heads off while waiting their turn and even climbed into my lap and started bullying the one being fed.)

To be able to hold three bottles at the same time, you have to hold one in each hand and grip the third one between them, holding all three bottles tightly together. The trick then is to get all three teats into the yelling little warthog mouths without dropping the bottle in the middle.

Luckily the warthogs soon learned to find the teats without help, so that all I really had to do was to grip the three bottles tightly and hold them out to the screaming little hogs until each one of them had a teat in its mouth. But if I dropped the middle bottle there would be an instant fight, as the one who'd lost his bottle would immediately start bullying the other two to get their bottles from them. For the first couple of minutes, the little hogs would suckle contentedly (as long as I didn't drop the middle bottle) and then, as their tummies started to feel full, they'd start having all kinds of problems with their teats.

One would suddenly decide his teat was no longer to his liking and would want to change it for his brother's or sister's teat. The brother or sister wouldn't want to go along with the deal, and the two of them would start a fight, striking each other with their heads while squealing and screaming as if they were being murdered.

The third piglet (the weaker one, who suckled more slowly than his brother and sister) would meanwhile suck away contentedly, minding his own business — until it suddenly occurred to the other two that what they really wanted was their little brother's bottle and, attacking the poor little fellow from both sides, they would grapple for his teat.

I eventually realised that the other two only fought when they were no longer hungry, and from then on I would put their bottles down as soon as they started fighting, and take off with their little brother to some place where we wouldn't have to listen to the other two fighting over nothing.

When the warthogs were six weeks old I stopped feeding them from bottles and taught them to drink milk from a bowl. It was a very messy business at first, as they'd all fall into the milk, start fighting with each other and splash milk all over the place. But eventually they learned to drink milk from the bowl and, later, to eat porridge.

The little warthogs are two months old now and graze on the lawns with Fritzie and Fiela. Strangely, the pigs remain totally indifferent to the warthogs and will have little to do with them. Fat Fritzie is, of course, too busy eating to have time for other interests. Friendly Fiela does occasionally allow the piglets to snuggle up to her when she lies sleeping under her favourite shady shrub, but I suspect that she sleeps so soundly that she is oblivious of the presence of the piglets. When she wakes, she gets up unceremoniously and walks right over the startled little hogs.

Feeding time at Mahlangeni has become a complicated ritual. In the late afternoons shortly before dusk, the horses, dogs, pigs, warthogs, Egyptian geese and bantams, as well as numerous uninvited guests, all turn up at the Mahlangeni restaurant for their dinners. (The guests who invite themselves are the resident squirrels, together with flocks of hornbills, starlings, sparrows, loeries, doves, bulbuls, and other birds.)

If you know anything about the pecking order in feeding routines where animals of different species are involved, you will probably realise that the managers of the Mahlangeni restaurant have no easy job. Each animal believes that the other animals get more and better food than he does. It makes me really mad, because we go to a considerable amount of trouble to prepare each animal's dinner according to his particular needs and tastes.

The horses get lucerne; the dogs get porridge with meat and vitamin-enriched gravy; the geese get dry porridge; the pigs get porridge with any left-over fruit and vegetables that are available; the warthogs get porridge with milk and honey; and the bantams get dried kernels. Now why would anyone prefer a meal other than his own?

According to the pecking order, the horses must be fed and locked up in their camp before the dogs are fed, otherwise the horses will trot right over, chase the dogs off and steal the porridge from their plates — and even the meat and gravy, if they're in a mean mood. The pigs must be fed before the bantams, or the pigs will steal the bantams' kernels — even though they prefer porridge to kernels. The pigs, dogs, Egyptian geese and warthogs must all be fed at the same time, but if there is only Filemoni and me to do the serving it's impossible to carry all the plates in one trip. And if we don't get the feeding routine into the right sequence, the dogs will dig a hole under the wire of the camp to get at the pigs' porridge, the pigs (escaping through the same hole) will eat the geese's porridge, the geese will eat the warthogs' porridge, the squirrels and birds will eat the porridge in any untended plate, and the poor little warthogs, being the lowest in the present pecking order, will be left without dinner.

The Ordeals
of Summer

O ctober is the prelude to the season of heat, humidity, humility and madness. As the heat builds up and the humidity grows, trillions of insects arrive, bacteria and parasites thrive, snakes sneak into the house, elephants become evil-tempered, and everything else combines forces to make life uncomfortable.

One can learn to cope with snakes, to avoid elephants, to repel insects, and to endure other discomforts, but the persistent, oppressive heat will get you if you're not clued up on some essential summer-survival strategies.

If you're subjected to unrelenting high temperatures for weeks and months on end, your body starts losing its natural heat-resisting capacity and your system goes haywire.

Our first summer in the Park caught us unprepared. Unacquainted with heat-survival tactics, we were vulnerable and defenceless. As the daytime temperatures soared to 38°C and above, our bodies became sluggish and apathetic and refused to function at a normal level. At night we tossed about on sheets and pillows that were drenched with our own perspiration, and in the mornings we woke up feeling groggy and irritable from lack of sleep.

By the end of January we felt defeated by the heat. But the worst was yet to come. February and March are the hottest months of the summer. By that time, the upper crust of the earth's surface is baked to the extent that even a rain shower will no longer cool it. In fact, after a shower the earth steams like a sauna. The night temperatures no longer show any appreciable fall and the sultry nights bring little respite from the sweltering, oppressive days.

Often during that first summer I lay awake at night, listening to our daughters whimpering in their sleep, and I'd get up and go to their bedroom to fan them with a towel. Their sighs of relief made it worth the effort, as I stood there fanning myself into exhaustion.

At the end of our first summer in the Park, I was convinced that we wouldn't be able to survive another.

But by the next summer we had become a little wiser and started practising some sensible heat-resisting strategies, such as sleeping under damp towels, drinking litres and litres of cold water throughout the day and taking cold showers at regular intervals — with our clothes on. (For a while your wet clothes keep you marvellously cool.) We also learned to keep hot air and direct sunlight out of the house by closing every door and window, and even the curtains, early each morning. At night we'd open everything except the gauze screens to let the cooler night air circulate freely through the house. By repeating this performance conscientiously every day of the long hot summer, the interior of the house remains some degrees cooler than the day temperatures outside.

Yet, despite all our efforts to keep our house cool inside, the air becomes so hot and humid during the last two or three months of summer that the sultry air somehow finds its way into the house. And once the sultry air starts building up inside the house, it seems to get stuck there and prevents the cooler air from entering at night.

During our second summer in the Park Kobus built us a bed out of Lebombo ironwood logs on the patio outside our bedroom. Every year at the height of the summer (from January to March), when the nights get too hot to sleep inside, we bathe ourselves in mosquito repellent and, carrying the bare minimum of bedding outside, spend our nights under the stars. We have also installed beds on the screened veranda for the girls.

In the early evenings Kobus hoses down the paving under and around our ironwood bed several times in order to reduce the heat retained by the concrete and stone. The evaporation also serves to cool the air around the bed.

There is a fuchsia tree growing outside our bedroom, its branches spreading far over the fish-pond, the patio and the garden. When we lie on our ironwood bed at night, we can see stars hanging amongst the leaves of the fuchsia tree, caught in the intricate tracery of its branches. A whole family of paradise flycatchers uses the tree in summer for nesting, and on moonlit nights we see their long tail feathers hanging over the sides of the nests above us.

Numerous other birds also roost in the tree at night. Unfortunately they all wake up before sunrise and promptly greet the day with a noisy dawn chorus. They also perform their ablutions at that time of the morning. To avoid being on the receiving end, we have to grab our bedding and flee indoors. The tree is also home to a whole community of caterpillars who, for unknown reasons, plunge from the tree on to our bed at night. And sometimes nectar drips down from the tree's crimson flowers.

One summer, when the nectar and caterpillars were particularly irritating, Kobus spread and tied a tarpaulin across the branches directly above the bed. The caterpillars, however, were not to be put off and acquired a new trick in order to share our bed with us. They would drop on to the tarpaulin, creep up to the edge and, leaning over to check the bed's position, would dive down at an oblique angle. The caterpillars won: the next summer we didn't bother to put the tarpaulin up.

Despite the irksome activities of the tree's inhabitants, sleeping outside is still better than sleeping in the stuffy house. Snakes worry me, though. We woke up one morning to find that a large spitting cobra had spent the night in a sandy hollow at the edge of the patio beside the fish-pond — within spitting distance of the bed, if you'll excuse the pun. On another occasion I was awakened in the middle of the night by a cold, creeping pressure moving over my legs. I leapt from the bed like one possessed, informing Kobus that there was a snake on the bed. He evacuated the bed as rapidly as I had. But it was only a bat.

Another of our summer ordeals is the frogs. They arrive in the spring to take up residence in the fish-pond and they stay there until the end of summer. It's not the frogs themselves that we mind, it's their nightly choir practice. It's so loud that normal conversation is impossible and Kobus and I end up yelling at each other just to communicate.

Whether we sleep inside or outside, the effect is the same. The pond stretches right up to the edge of the patio and along one side of it, ending almost inside our bedroom, and the frogs' voices resonate throughout the room. The only way to cut down the noise would be to sleep inside with the sliding doors closed, but then the heat would be suffocating.

The frog choir consists of members of various species who croak in different voices. There are basses, baritones, tenors, altos, contraltos, mezzo-sopranos, and so forth. They perform a score which appears to be prearranged: there is a double rhythm section (the one slow, the other lively) which drones and quavers a complex backing to a monotonous melody. The melody consists of an unremitting repetition of crescendos and diminuendos. The occasional soloist, trilling high or booming low, is just enough to break the tedium, but not enough to quell the irksome monotony of the score. It's hard to fall asleep with frogs croaking tutti fortissimo in your ears.

Eventually you may fall asleep, teeth gritted and fists clenched, but you won't sleep for long. At a given moment, the frogs all shut up and the sudden silence jerks you awake. For a while the respite is heavenly and you can feel your teeth and fists unclenching. Even the dogs sigh with relief. But then you suddenly remember that the frogs are only taking a breather and that the lull won't last long. And you tense up, waiting for the choir to burst into song again. Before long, they do just that. The repeat performance opens with a couple of basso-profundo croaks — which I think is the conductor saying, 'All together now: very loudly!'. And, presto! The appalling opera is in full cry again.

We have often tried to repatriate the choir. Armed with a torch, a fishing net and a bucket of water, we pounce on the choristers. Catching each and every one of them and scooping them all into the bucket, we trek down to the river and dump the lot in the water.

But frogs don't quit easily. They are depressingly stubborn. Within two or three hours they are all back and, despite their exhausting journey up the steep river bank, they take up where they left off before we interrupted their performance.

As time passed, we became wiser and changed our tactics. Nowadays we no longer dump the frogs into the river in front of the house. To ensure that they can't possibly find their way back, we load them into Kobus's pick-up and drive them some kilometres downriver before evicting them. For several nights thereafter we sleep in blissful peace. Until a new choir moves in. (Or perhaps it's the old choir which has wilfully found its way back after all?) The choristers arrive singly or in small groups, and start practising individually for the Great Ensemble Performance. As soon as the ensemble appears to be plenary, we embark on the deportation process again.

There are days when the mercury rises to 40°C, and sometimes as high as 45°C. At times like that, you become lethargic and your friendliness quotient is accordingly reduced. Even the dogs become irritable.

In 1986, Kobus built a large swimming pool under the shady trees in the front garden. It was the best thing that had ever happened to us at Mahlangeni. To fall sizzling into a whole pool full of cool water is an experience straight out of heaven. It's like breaking a fever, like quenching a big thirst, and like coming alive again after having been baked in a warm oven for too long. The longer you stay in the water, the better — the water eventually cools you right down to the bone. After a successful cooling-down session in the pool, your body temperature remains under control for quite a while afterwards, and you can go on with your work feeling quite human and friendly again.

In the evenings we dive into the pool just before going to bed, and then we don't dry ourselves off before lying down. It really works. If you've stayed in the water long enough to cool right down to the marrow of your bones and then get on to the bed — wet — your reduced body temperature allows you to get a really good night's rest. Provided the frogs have been evicted, of course.

Kobus erected a small wall, some forty centimetres high, around the swimming pool in order to keep the frogs out. Initially

231

the wall also kept the Egyptian goslings out, but once they got bigger, they tried to lay claim to the pool. This resulted in some hefty arguments between us and the geese. Many a time, on a hot afternoon, as I was floating calmly by myself in the pool, a goose would plummet from the sky and land in the water next to me with a loud splash, startling me almost out of my wits.

The main bone of contention, however, was the fact that the geese didn't always leave the pool as they found it, and we'd have to clean up after them. Eventually, after some serious shouting, we managed to convince the geese that we, too, are territorial beings and that the pool belongs to us. It's not that we're being selfish. They have the fish-pond to swim in, as well as the river.

The swimming pool has contributed a great deal to our quality of life at Mahlangeni. Floating about lazily in the cool water on a hot summer's night, listening to the sounds of the bush and watching the stars flickering above is — to quote Kobus — the sort of experience that changes your whole outlook on life. Before we had the pool, tempers often became so heated in the summer that we wanted to throw each other to the lions. But now that we have the pool, we feel a lot better about life and our summer tempers have cooled considerably.

Autumn and Winter

E arly in May, as the days and nights become cooler, frogs stop croaking, snakes go away, bugs and insects disappear, and elephants become friendlier. The mad days of summer are over, and a mood of serene beauty and tranquillity settles over the land.

The savannahs turn blond, the mopani woodlands display their autumn finery of golds and bronzes, and the sky becomes a deeper, softer blue. At twilight, the river sparkles ruby-red in the lazy afterglow of the sun, and the lingering, smoky blue dusks add a mystical mood to the magic hour.

And so, goodwill is revived and dignity restored as summer mellows into the halcyon days of autumn, and you find yourself wishing that this season of graceful living could last for ever.

During June the nights suddenly become so cold that you have to sleep under blankets. The early mornings are chilly and you have to wear something with long sleeves until the sun gets warmer later in the day. The days are mild (with an average maximum temperature of 26°C) and the crisp air is so invigorating that you find yourself bouncing with energy and chuckling with the joy of life. You forget about wishing that autumn had stayed for ever.

As the seasonal pans and creeks dry up, game herds gather in large numbers at perennial rivers and dams. By mid-winter, the river banks in front of our house become a popular rendezvous for many species of game, including the larger herbivores such as elephant, buffalo and giraffe. A pack of wild dogs puts in an occasional appearance, and we hear lions roaring in the neighbourhood almost every night.

As the deciduous trees and shrubs shed their leaves and the grasses are grazed short, the bewildering tangle of the summer vegetation disappears and one can see far and wide into the bush. We love to go camping, walking and riding at this time of year. The winter landscapes of pale savannahs and bare woodlands under an azure sky have a stark and classic beauty.

Although winter is usually the most pleasant of the seasons in the Park, there are times when nature makes a cruel mistake and turns winter into a period of ugliness and anguish.

When normal rainfalls occur in the late summer, there is sufficient grazing to last the animals throughout the winter. But when the rainfall has been scant, August will herald the appearance of bare patches in the veld, and by September the grass cover may disappear completely in places. The change in the condition of the animals becomes apparent and — with it — the struggle to stay alive until the return of the rains.

At least water is never a scarcity. Besides the five major rivers which cross the Park, there are sufficient boreholes with windmills and reservoirs throughout the Park to supply drinking water for the animals. The watering places — which are fed by the reservoirs — are regularly inspected and maintained by the game rangers and their field staff.

From 1985 to 1989 our summer rainfalls had been below average. Apart from a tremendous downpour in February 1988, we were experiencing increasingly dry periods, and in the late summer of 1989 the rains failed to come. The subsequent winter brought one of the most serious droughts that we had ever seen in the Park. By July virtually all the grass had disappeared, and dust devils skipped across the barren savannahs.

Even on the river banks, the grasses and shrubs were grazed right down to ground level, and the evergreen riverine trees were stripped of leaves as high as the animals could reach.

Then the August and September winds arrived, dancing through the withering woodlands and across the bleak plains and causing the last of the dry, brittle patches of grass to disintegrate. The drought dragged on, and the earth panted for moisture, and day by day the condition of the herbivores deteriorated.

One evening near the end of August, we noticed two bushbuck standing outside our fence, gazing hungrily at our verdant garden. (Our lawns stay green throughout the year as we pump water from the river to irrigate them.) The bushbuck looked so hungry that we opened the front gate to let them in. They spent the whole night grazing on the lawns. From that day on, we left the front gate open in the evenings so that they could come in. At first only the two bushbuck came, then three, and eventually there were six who grazed in our garden every night. We closed the gate once they were all inside to prevent marauding lions from following them in at night. Our dogs have been trained not to harass antelope and other animals and they left the bushbuck in peace. Early in the mornings we opened the gate again, allowing the bushbuck out.

One afternoon we noticed a family of starving warthogs standing outside the fence, gazing longingly at the garden. A while later they were joined by a small herd of scrawny impala. We hoped that the warthogs and impala would follow the bushbuck in through the gate but, sadly, they didn't. They were too scared of the smell of humans and dogs in our garden. The bushbuck, of course, had spent most of their lives grazing on the river bank right in front of the house and, being used to our smell, had become quite tame. On the following evening the warthogs and impala turned up again, and eventually one plucky impala ewe ventured in after the bushbuck, but the others wouldn't follow. Since there was nothing we could do to lure them inside, I resorted to feeding them from our vegetable garden. Every evening I would harvest two or three baskets of lettuce, spinach, chard, carrots, tomatoes, cauliflower, broccoli and cabbage, and drop it outside the fence for the warthogs and impalas.

In the morning the vegetables would be gone, and the spoor along the bank would indicate that the impalas and warthogs had returned in the night to feed.

Fortunately our vegetable garden is large and we always plant enough vegetables to see us through the winter, as well as enough to freeze for the hot summer months when nothing will grow. I knew I was feeding our precious summer provisions to the hungry animals, but it didn't matter. We could buy tinned vegetables in the summer.

As the drought dragged on, the condition of our hippos deteriorated rapidly. We could hardly bear to look at their gaunt shapes as they left the river in the early evenings to set out in search of food. They had always grazed on the river banks at night. Now the banks were depleted of grass and foliage, and the hippos had to trek many kilometres inland every night in search of fodder.

By the end of that fatal September, two of our hippos had died of hunger. One morning I went to the vegetable garden, harvested all of our remaining cabbages and piled them into a wheelbarrow. I wheeled them down to the bank and across the shore and dumped them at the waterside. I knew that this was a pretty futile attempt to save the hippos from starvation. The amount of fodder required by a hippo is so enormous that all of our cabbages would only be sufficient to keep perhaps two or three of them alive for a day or so longer, and there were more than twenty hippos to consider.

I didn't see them eating the cabbages, but by late afternoon I noticed that they had disappeared. It gave me little consolation, however, as another hippo died that same evening.

Kobus and I were sitting outside at sundown when we saw the hippo shuffling across the shore towards the bank. He dragged his feet like someone who is infinitely weary. Then he just stopped and collapsed in his tracks.

We sat very still and didn't talk. I knew that Kobus was as distressed as I was by the sorrowful sight that we had witnessed.

The magic hour had lost its charm. The riverine landscape was bleak and barren, and the river only a narrow stretch of muddy water. Life seemed so sad and cheerless to me then, that I could think of nothing but sorrowful things. Our neighbouring baboons didn't turn up on the far bank in the evenings any more. They had left in search of greener pastures which didn't exist.

Our vegetable garden was almost empty. I wouldn't be able to feed the starving impalas and warthogs much longer. Our lawns weren't green any more — the pump on the river bank could no longer reach the receding water level. Our borehole supplied only enough water for our personal and household needs. The bushbuck had eaten all my flowers and most of our shrubs, as well as all my newly planted papaw trees. Soon there would be nothing left in the garden for them to eat. I knew that flocks of vultures would arrive the next morning to feast on the dead hippo.

There was really nothing but sadness all about us.

The dusty, windblown sun hung lopsidedly above the dwindling river, hovered a while behind the silhouettes of dying trees, and then slipped away.

In the gloom of the fading light, we sat waiting for the darkness to blot out the pitiful landscape and consign it to oblivion.

What are we doing here... and why? I wondered. What is there to keep us in this godforsaken land where the rain will never fall again?

It seemed senseless to try to conserve nature's creatures if nature herself had a death wish.

I wanted to go and live some place else, anywhere, as long as it was a wilderness area where it rained all the time.

Kobus sat silently beside me, gazing towards the south-eastern horizon. I was about to share my lachrymose thoughts with him, when he lifted his hand and, pointing to the south-east said, 'Look... lightning.'

I turned and looked. Presently, a distant flash zigzagged above the horizon. It looked like a long-forgotten miracle. We stared long and hard at the south-eastern sky, willing another flash to appear.

A pearl-spotted owl called out, and its sweet melody seemed to linger a while in the quiet evening. From the barren woodlands to the south of the river, the stirring cry of a jackal rose. And then the lightning flashed again.

From somewhere, the whooping howl of a lone hyena soared into the night and drifted over the bush in rising and falling echoes. A soft breeze stirred through the garden, and soon the south-eastern sky was lit continuously by the distant lightning.

We knew then that the rain would come again. Perhaps not that night, or even the following day. But soon.

The Rains

The following evening flashes of lightning played continuously across the whole of the southern sky. Later that night, as the distant thunder rolled over the bush, we could smell the rain. It came the following morning — on the seventh of October. But it fell too hard, stopped too suddenly and disappeared into the parched earth so rapidly that the vegetation hardly had a chance to realise that it had rained. Only six millimetres had fallen.

Yet, it was a promise.

Surely the time had come for nature to mend her ways.

And so she did — on Sunday, the twenty-second of October.

To our dismay, we weren't home on that important day. To make matters worse, we couldn't even get home — because of the rain.

We had travelled to Johannesburg to spend the weekend with my parents. When we left the city early on the Sunday morning it was raining on the highveld, and we hoped that the rain would follow us home.

As we reached the escarpment later in the day we saw that the lowveld ahead of us was blanketed in dark, dense clouds. Shortly after we'd made the descent into the lowveld, we drove into thick sheets of rain. When we reached the Phalaborwa gate to the Kruger Park at four o'clock that afternoon, it was still pouring. Stopping at the gate, Kobus asked the gate official how much rain had fallen and was informed that upwards of eighty millimetres had already been recorded.

Our spirits were so high that we couldn't contain ourselves. We laughed and chatted excitedly as we drove along the track to Mahlangeni, telling one another how the bleak landscape would soon turn into a lush paradise, how beautifully the spring flowers would bloom, and how fat the animals would get. As we passed herds of scrawny animals along the way, we urged them to hang in there: soon — perhaps within a week — there would be an abundance of new, succulent shoots for them to eat.

The girls urged their father to drive a little faster. As soon as we got home, they wanted us all to go for a walk in the rain and to splash and play in the muddy pools.

Driving, however, wasn't that easy. The track was incredibly muddy and, to make matters worse, our city car (a recently acquired sedan) didn't have four-wheel drive. We slithered along and Kobus had to drive very carefully to avoid skidding right off the track.

Perhaps, if we hadn't been so heady with excitement and so eager to get home, we wouldn't have chanced our luck on the treacherous road. We should also have known that the numerous creeks between Phalaborwa and Mahlangeni would be in spate, but in our optimistic state of mind we assured ourselves that the floods wouldn't be too strong yet, and that if we hurried we would be able to get through.

Barely three kilometres beyond the gate, we arrived at the first creek. It was, of course, in spate, but not too badly, and we managed to get across. A kilometre further along we encountered a second creek in spate. This time we stopped and waded into the flow to estimate the depth of the water before driving through. Sandra detected a washaway on the upstream side of the crossing, and Kobus duly stuck to the downstream side. We repeated the performance at the third creek, and were quite worried by the time we reached the fourth.

We had been on the road some twenty minutes already, and had travelled barely six kilometres. Our worst fears were confirmed when Sandra and I discovered a deep and wide washaway in the fourth creek. The car wouldn't be able to get through. We had no choice but to turn back, and we were terribly disappointed. But our spirits lifted again when Kobus told us that he would drive to ranger Dirk Swart's house, near the gate, and ask him for the loan of a four-wheel-drive vehicle. Once again, we slid from creek to creek, stopping at each one and feeling our way through the water with sticks to check for new washaways before driving through.

When we finally arrived at Dirk's house, we were muddy and soaking wet.

Dirk helped us load our luggage into the back of the pick-up and lent us a tarpaulin to keep our suitcases dry. Leaving our car at Dirk's house, we set off again.

The four-wheel-drive vehicle made the going much easier. We crossed the first three creeks again, and even the fourth one with the deep washaway presented little trouble. Another two creeks were soon crossed and we were in a confident mood. But after some eighteen kilometres, our confidence suddenly turned to apprehension. We had reached the marshy plains near the Nhlarweni creek, and to the west of the track a wide stream of water was rushing towards the creek ahead. When we reached the bank of the creek a short while later, we gaped in astonishment at the sight in front of us. The creek was flooding its banks and had turned into a wide river. We stopped on the bank, all got out, and started wading into the water with sticks. Soon we were almost knee-deep in the water and the current was so strong that we had to lean into it to keep our balance. Kobus ordered us back to the truck and went into the creek by himself. He returned a few minutes later. The flow was too deep and he wasn't prepared to take the risk of driving across.

Once again, we turned back. At seven that evening — three hours after we had first arrived at the gate — we stopped in front of Dirk's house again. We, as well as our luggage, were soaked. The water had streamed in under the tarpaulin and our suitcases were awash in the back of the pick-up.

Dirk and his wife Hennie kindly offered us accommodation for the night, but we knew that they already had other guests and we didn't want to impose on them. We decided that we would spend the night at the children's school hostel. It would be empty on a Sunday night as the Park children only return on Monday mornings.

The hostel, however, was locked up, and the superintendent nowhere to be found.

Then we remembered the personnel office near the gate. The building has two bedrooms which may be used by Park staff in times of need. We drove there, but when we saw the door open, the lights on inside, and the veranda stacked with luggage, we knew that other people had already taken refuge there.

We sat in the car and wondered what we should do. We knew only a few people in town, none of them well enough to arrive unannounced on their doorstep on a Sunday evening seeking accommodation and dry clothes — we were shivering by this time. Eventually we thought of the Du Plessis family, teachers at the local high school. Once, after a school athletics meeting, they had invited us over for tea. Could we impose on them? Somehow, it didn't seem right. Five soaking people arriving at your door, hungry and looking for beds, could place quite a strain on your hospitality.

We arrived at a decision. We would ask school friends of the girls to put them up for the night — then only two people would arrive at the Du Plessis household.

We drove into town and to the houses of Sandra's and Karin's friends. Both families were very kind about putting up our daughters for the night. Hettie asked if she could stay with us instead — the eldest Du Plessis daughter, Riks, was a good friend of hers. At eight o'clock the three of us stood at their door and knocked hesitantly. Coretha du Plessis opened the door and exclaimed, 'Good heavens, you poor people! You're soaked! Come right in!'

We explained our predicament to her, and she warmed our hearts with her prompt invitation to spend the night.

I hate arriving anywhere unexpectedly and invading other people's privacy, especially when they have to go to any trouble. But the warm welcome and hospitality of the Du Plessis family turned the evening into a very pleasant one. We were given dry clothes and warm food, and we soon felt a lot better.

Later that night the rain stopped, and the new dawn was bathed in sunshine. We readied ourselves to tackle the drive home, and fetched Sandra and Karin from their friends' houses. It was a school day but, since all their clothes were soaking wet in the suitcases, we decided that the girls should come home with us. We would take them to the hostel the following morning. Hettie, who was in her final year at school, decided that she didn't want to miss a day as the exams were drawing close. Riks kindly lent Hettie some clothes, and we dropped her off at school before driving home. I would pack her a suitcase and take it to her the next day.

The creeks had ebbed somewhat, and after two hours of difficult but uneventful driving in Dirk's four-wheel-drive truck, we arrived home at last. Although the river was also in spate, the causeway wasn't submerged. After the prolonged drought, its level had been so low that it would take quite a lot of water before the river would submerge the causeway again.

It was good to be home at last. The damp landscape sparkled in the sun and the sweet fragrance of the wet earth was everywhere. Sandra and Karin spent the rest of the day exploring the neighbourhood and splashing about in muddy pools.

Hettie, unfortunately, had a frightening experience that afternoon at the hostel.

After school, she decided to go for a walk in the bush around the hostel to see how the rains had affected the surroundings. She hadn't planned to walk far, but although it began drizzling lightly again, she was enjoying her stroll so much that she unknowingly wandered further and further from the hostel. She walked north-eastwards into the bush, wading barefoot through muddy pools and following the spoor of small animals on the wet ground.

Hettie is my absent-minded child. She often gets so lost in her dreams that she forgets where she is. When she finally realised that she was out of sight of the hostel, she turned around quickly and started making her way back. But she misjudged her direction and began walking south-east instead of south-west. There are no distinct landmarks in the homogeneous mopani woodlands of that area, and once you lose your sense of direction, you're in trouble.

After walking for some distance and not finding the hostel, Hettie became worried. She decided to wait for a while for the sun to appear from behind the clouds so that she could calculate her directions more accurately. The sky was so overcast that she had to wait almost ten minutes before the sun finally tinged the edge of a cloud. Realising that she had been heading south-east instead of south-west, she adjusted her course and set out.

After a while she looked up at the sky to check the sun's position once more, but the sun had completely disappeared behind the thick clouds again. Not wanting to lose more time, she continued determinedly in what she hoped was a south-westerly direction.

Presently she saw a large flock of vultures perching in a stand of leadwood trees ahead of her. Aware that vultures indicate the presence of predators, she altered course, making a wide, downwind detour of the leadwood trees while straining her senses for danger signals. She walked a fair distance before she felt confident that she had circumvented the danger area. Then she tried to correct her course again, but became confused. The sun stubbornly remained hidden behind the clouds. She strode doggedly on, trying to ignore the elephant and buffalo spoor crossing her path.

Little did she know that she had not turned enough to the west and was in fact striding out in a southerly direction. In hindsight, this was probably a blessing because she arrived — after more than an hour's walk, at the main tourist road between Phalaborwa and Letaba. Close to tears with relief, she sat down right there beside the road.

After about ten minutes, a car approached from the direction of Letaba, and she stood up so that the driver would see her.

He did, and promptly pulled up alongside her. The driver was a young man, and he looked very surprised at finding her there.

'Hi!' he said. 'Are you in trouble? Where's your car?'

'I don't have one,' said Hettie. 'Could you perhaps give me a lift?'

'Sure! Of course,' said the young man. 'Get in.'

She got in, and as they pulled back on to the road the young man said, 'But... if you don't mind my asking, why are you here... alone in the bush?'

Feeling embarrassed about admitting it, but having no other choice, Hettie told him she'd gone for a walk and got lost.

'You did?' he exclaimed. 'Phew! That's bad. There are wild animals out here — did you know that?'

'The reason I got lost,' she explained, 'was because it was raining and I couldn't see the sun.'

'Yeah, that's really bad,' he sympathised. 'But you shouldn't walk out here, you know. This place teems with wild animals. There are lions and leopards, and everything. Honestly, it's extremely dangerous.'

'I don't normally get lost,' said Hettie.

They passed an elephant bull grazing at the side of the road.

'There,' said the young man. 'See what I mean, huh?'

She nodded.

'So, where'd you walk from?' he asked. 'How far?'

'From the hostel,' she answered. 'I don't know how far.'

Looking puzzled, he asked, 'What hostel? Where?'

'It's just inside the boundary of the Park,' she explained. 'About two kilometres to the north of the gate.'

He turned in surprise and looked at her, saying, 'You don't actually live here... in the Park? Do you?'

She said, 'I do. But, honestly, this is the first time I have ever got lost.'

The young man asked her a thousand and one questions about her life in the Park, and finally said: 'You know, I've just spent four terrific days in the Park, and I've seen just about everything — lions, cheetahs, wild dogs, elephants, the lot! But this is the best of all: a lovely, lost young girl in the bush next to the road! You've made my vacation!'

Some eight kilometres from the point where he'd picked her up, they reached the turn-off which leads to the hostel. Hettie sheepishly asked the young man to off-load her a little distance from the hostel. She didn't want her friends to see her arriving in a tourist's car and find out how stupidly she had got lost in the bush. He did as she asked, but only after thanking her for what he described as 'the most memorable part' of his visit.

As she entered the hostel grounds, acting as nonchalantly as she could, the supper bell rang. The children who were still outside saw her coming in through the gates and concluded that she'd just returned from a quick stroll before supper.

And so no one at the hostel, except her sisters, ever found out how 'disgracefully' she'd lost her way in the bush on that rainy afternoon. (Game rangers' children are, of course, above that sort of thing.)

Soon after those first rains had fallen, trillions of seeds germinated under the moist earth and decked the landscape in soft, green carpets of new shoots. Tiny succulent leaves began to bud on the previously barren trees, and then masses of wild flowers sprang up everywhere, opening their blooms to splash the grassy carpets with a profusion of colours.

The bush was finally alive and well again and bustling with new life and growth.

Within only two weeks, a wasteland had turned into paradise.

Bush Concert

There is a lot of prose and poetry that describes nature as serene, peaceful, quiet, tranquil, and so forth. Bach even composed a partita called *The Harmony of Nature*.

I'll agree that there is harmony in nature (although I don't quite know exactly whàt that means) but I'm not so sure about the peace and tranquillity.

Mahlangeni is probably as close to nature as you can get. But life here isn't always peaceful, and it's certainly never quiet. The birds, for instance, never shut up, except at night. And the hippos grunt and bellow day and night. The baboons who sleep in the jackalberry trees across the river kick up a tremendous din in the mornings and evenings. And if they have differences to settle, they argue and scream late into the night. Fritzie and Fiela snore their heads off each night, the frogs croak fortissimo, the leopard growls, hyenas howl, owls screech, and jackals wail. And, sometimes, lions roar so close to us that the house trembles.

Some nights, the local breeding herd of elephants turns up to graze in the reedbeds along the river, and the reverberating, rumbling sounds of their contact calls roll right into our bedroom. Baby elephants can be very difficult and will shriek to high heaven if they don't get their way. The exasperated mothers, aunts and grannies groan and grumble — until the mother of the offending infant cannot take it any longer and screeches a strident warning. If that doesn't make the impossible imp shut up, she raises her voice to a stunning, full-throated trumpet. The volume of a full-blast trumpet resounds to the heavens and can probably be heard in a neighbouring galaxy. This jangles the baboons' nerves and they start wailing and screaming.

Our dogs are tolerant of most animals, but baboons irritate them beyond endurance, and when the baboons kick up a shrieking shindy, there is nothing — not even Kobus's shouting — that will deter the dogs from barking their lungs out. There is a hyena somewhere around here who starts howling as soon as the dogs start barking. I don't know why. He just does. The louder the dogs bark, the louder he howls. The cacophonous concert annoys the hippos and they complain vociferously. If the concert were harmonious — which it isn't — their booming bellows might detract from the harmony.

It's not easy to fall asleep when the bush concert is turned to full volume.

And in the early dawn, when we feel as if we have only just nodded off, the two Egyptian geese arrive and startle us awake with their raucous trumpeting.

That's nature for you.

Never a moment of peace.